I Want to Be Famous

I Want to Be Famous

When Everybody and Nobody Is a Celebrity

Bobby Finger *and* **Lindsey Weber**

CROWN
NEW YORK

CROWN
An imprint of the Crown Publishing Group
A division of Penguin Random House LLC
1745 Broadway
New York, NY 10019
crownpublishing.com
penguinrandomhouse.com

Library of Congress Cataloging-in-Publication Data
Names: Finger, Bobby author | Weber, Lindsey, 1986– author. Title: I want to be famous : when everybody and nobody is a celebrity / Robert Finger and Lindsey Weber. Description: First edition. | New York : Crown, [2026] | Includes bibliographical references. Identifiers: LCCN 2026007084 | ISBN 9798217088324 hardcover | ISBN 9798217088331 ebook. Subjects: LCSH: Fame. Classification: LCC BJ1470.5 .F56 2026
LC record available at https://lccn.loc.gov/2026007084

Hardcover ISBN 979-8-217-08832-4
Ebook ISBN 979-8-217-08833-1

Editor: Aubrey Martinson
Production editor: Sohayla Farman
Text designer: Andrea Lau
Production: Jessica Heim
Copy editor: Rachelle Mandik
Proofreaders: Janet Renard, Shasta Clinch, Julie Ehlers, and Eldes Tran
Publicists: Mary Moates and Josie McRoberts
Marketer: Allyson Coy

Manufactured in the United States of America

1st Printing

First Edition

The authorized representative in the EU for product safety and compliance is Penguin Random House Ireland, Morrison Chambers, 32 Nassau Street, Dublin D02 YH68, Ireland, https://eu-contact.penguin.ie.

For the Wholigans

Fame is prison

—LADY GAGA

Contents

I Want to Be
Famous

Chapter 1

A Grand Theory of Whos and Thems

Meghan Markle, Evelyn Nesbit & Chappell Roan

At the end of October 2016, a journalist for the British tabloid *Express* named Camilla Tominey published the first report that Prince Harry, Duke of Sussex, was "secretly dating a stunning US actress, model and human rights campaigner." One could almost hear the sound of every reader cocking their head at once. *Who?* Exactly. It was Meghan Markle. If you knew her at all, it was likely due to her long-running stint as paralegal-turned-lawyer Rachel Zane in the USA Network legal drama *Suits*. And if you didn't watch *Suits,* then you probably didn't know her at all. (Harry certainly didn't! According to his memoir, *Spare,* he googled her after they first met, and quickly found a few sex scenes. "[I] witnessed her and a [*Suits*] castmate mauling each other in some sort of office or conference room . . . It would take electric shock therapy to get those images out of my head.") The two had been set up on a blind date in London earlier that year, and for their third (!) date Harry convinced Meghan to join him on a trip to Botswana. Soon enough, everyone had the story: Prince Harry was officially dating an American *Who*. But she wouldn't be one for much longer. The reveal of their relationship made Markle, who spent some fifteen years chugging along in Hollywood, a *Them* overnight.

When people ask us for a quick explanation of our podcast *Who? Weekly*'s ethos, we'll likely launch into some form of that classic "grocery-store checkout" story. While the scenario is a little dated, it tends to get the job done. (Although we may need to think of a new scenario for Gen-Z.) Picture it: You're at the grocery store. You head to the checkout. You see a display of tabloid magazines. On the covers of some, you see famous faces you recognize: Those are *Thems*. On others, you might see faces presented to you *as famous* and think to yourself, *Who are these people?* Those are *Whos*. (There are also *Nahs*, slang for, well, ourselves—those of us who don't fall into either category. If you're reading this, you're probably a *Nah*. Don't be offended.) It's a simple, straightforward binary; celebrities fall into just two buckets: *Whos* and *Thems*.

That it takes only a brief moment of relevance to create a celebrity is predicated on the idea that everyone will, at some point in their lives, be famous for fifteen minutes. It's a foreboding proposition often attributed to Andy Warhol—but it wasn't anything he ever said. What Warhol *did* say, however, perhaps better reflects the current celebrity landscape: While being photographed in 1966, Warhol reportedly remarked matter-of-factly that "everyone wants to be famous." To which his photographer, Nat Finkelstein, responded, "Yeah, for about fifteen minutes, Andy." Over half a century later, his assertion feels almost like an underestimation. In the past, a Who's fame would have begun fizzling out at fifteen minutes. These days, Who-lebrity has a longer tail, and can easily be extended for fifteen years.

Celebrity has long been discussed as a hierarchy upon which fame level ascends the first few letters of the alphabet. Traditionally this took the form of a ladder with four rungs—the entirety of fame spanning from D- to A-list. At the top are the people "everyone" knows, the bona fide superstars with whom the public is on a first-name basis. *Madonna. Oprah. Taylor. Denzel.* Further down are the ones desperately trying to climb a little higher. (The aspiration to become more famous is implied, for if two rungs were good enough, why not just use a stepladder?) It's in the middle where things have always gotten murky, as the transitions from B to C can be altered by a change in the cultural wind—a hit song in June may not be remembered the following April, just as a long-hustling character actor may finally book a big, scene-stealing role in the latter half of their career. But letters, like grades, imply judgment, and over time "D-list" evolved into a kind of pejorative label few celebrities—besides Kathy Griffin, who claimed it as the title of her long-running Bravo reality show *My Life on the D-List*—would ever embrace. This implicit value judgment is the ladder's most fatal flaw, and has rendered it a largely unhelpful tool in our splintered celebrity landscape, so in our frustration we took it upon ourselves to design another.

If A-listers are calling the paparazzi, and people whose names we'd never seen before can fill stadiums, it's truly impossible to tell the difference between a B- or C-list celebrity anymore. The monoculture has faded fast. Sure, we're all quite familiar with Cher, or any other of the remaining big Gen-X or Boomer Hollywood stars, but there is a lack of younger talent filling those spots and claiming those A-list slots. Not a lack of *talented people,* more so a lack of stars who have received enough coverage to be known by the masses.

The list of access points for stars to get "enough coverage" to make a leap into the A list has been shrinking for years. Because how would you go about getting the most eyes on whatever it is you have going on: Win the Super Bowl? Star in a summer blockbuster? Get splashed on the front page of the *New York Post*? Win an Oscar for Best Actress? Well, both the Super Bowl and the Oscars have plummeted in viewership since the advent of streaming, and movie theaters are still hoping to bounce back post-Covid. And ending up on the front page of the *Post*—while a terrifying idea—isn't guaranteed to grab as many eyes (or clicks) as it once did. We aren't all looking in the same direction anymore. Why would we all continue to watch the same TV show or movie when there are endless TV shows and movies to stream? Why would we all listen to the same music when there are tens of millions of songs on hand to stream? Monocultural events used to be plentiful, even sought out and looked forward to. Now an epidemic of choice has splintered our attention spans.

We've always been obsessed with the utter shamelessness that's intrinsic to celebrity. It just so happens that the stars most engaged with the idea of celebrity (*Stars really do be just like us!*) are the ones keeping things interesting. We've deemed certain types of behavior "Who-y"—calling the paparazzi on yourself, showing up at "the opening of an envelope" (or perhaps, less metaphorically, a brand-new Sephora)—but they're the necessity of being famous in the modern age. Naturally, that means a celebrity can make a jump from Who to Them. (Just as Thems can transition into Whos . . . and back again!) While some "grad-Who-ations" are more debatable, it can be quite obvious when someone makes the leap.

TAKE THE CASE of Meghan Markle: former *Suits* star, current Duchess of Sussex, and at one time responsible for giving Great Britain's royal family the shake-up of their lifetimes. The media coverage of her romance with Harry was absolutely absurd, overwhelming, and altogether breathless.

> EXCLUSIVE: My name is Meg—but you must call me 'Your Royal Highness!' Enchanting birthday party video shows royal bride-to-be playing Queen for a day . . . and, yes, she's wearing a CROWN! (*Daily Mail,* March 2018)

> **Meghan Markle's royal wedding overshadows her 'Suits' nuptials. (*Page Six,* April 2018)**

> Princess Diana 'will be there at Prince Harry's royal wedding—as a ghost', say psychics. (*The Mirror,* March 2018)

> **Meghan Markle allegedly asked her father to stop speaking to her sister. (*Page Six,* August 2018)**

> Meghan Markle Isn't Speaking to Her Dad. He's Asked the Queen to Intervene. (*The New York Times,* December 2018)

All in all, it's one of the most immediate Who-to-Them ascensions of the twenty-first century.

In July 2015, before meeting Harry, Markle wrote an essay for *Elle* magazine headlined "I'm More Than an 'Other,'" in which she described herself as "an actress, a writer, the Editor-in-Chief of . . . lifestyle brand *The Tig*, a pretty good cook and a firm believer in handwritten notes." (It's true that Meghan has truly impeccable handwriting; she did freelance calligraphy work, and wrote the invitations for singer Robin Thicke and actor Paula Patton's ill-fated wedding.) *The Tig* was actually more of a blog (a good blog, all things considered!) where Markle would regularly post recipes, entertaining tips and tricks, travelogues—everything you'd expect from internet writing in the early aughts. "What began as a passion project (my little engine that could) evolved into an amazing community of inspiration, support, fun and frivolity," she wrote in her final missive—posted in April 2017. Before that, with perhaps the beginnings of an exciting new romance and, deeper down, perhaps an awareness that her newfound superstardom was already taking hold, Markle's blog featured such aspirational content as "Mushroom Pasta with Creamy Truffle Sauce" (posted on February 28, 2017, a month after a report in *People* confirmed that the couple spent their "first holiday together" in Norway to see the Northern Lights) and "Awards Season Entertaining Tips" (posted on January 25, 2017, a few months before Harry would fly to Toronto to spend Easter holiday weekend with Meghan and skip the traditional service at St. George's).

But despite her commitment to being EIC of *The Tig*, Markle was now standing directly under the spotlight on the world's stage. Updating a blog went against the very essence of her newfound Themdom (whether or not she *knew* she was a Them, she knew things had certainly shifted). Why bother wasting precious time on a small vanity website when she was organically getting attention from what felt like every news outlet in the world—and now, incredibly, press she didn't need, or even want! *Thems don't blog!* (OK, save for the advent of Substack, but that didn't hit until 2021 or so. A current reality, sure, but not something we support. We'll say it again: *Thems don't blog!*)

Thus, in 2017, leading up to the publishing of a "tell-all" cover story in *Vanity Fair* and an official "sit-down" with the BBC, Markle shut down *The Tig*. "After close to three beautiful years on this adventure with you, it's time to say goodbye to The Tig," she wrote on the site. "Keep finding those Tig moments of discovery, keep laughing and taking risks, and keep being 'the change you wish to see in the world.' Above all, don't ever forget your worth—as I've told you time and time again: you, my sweet friend, you are enough. Thank you for everything." Even more glaring: a source was telling *People* that the blog's shuttering had nothing to do with Prince Harry—a claim no one was likely to believe. "The Tig has been a labor of love for Meghan," said the source, "but it's a full-time job. She wants to focus [on] this season of *Suits*, which [is] just starting filming and spending more time in the field on her philanthropy." *Sure!* Perhaps the nod to "philanthropy" was another way of saying that doing charity work was about to become Markle's full-time job as a member of the royal family.

If you had asked us if we thought a relatively random actor from an American legal dramedy on the same cable network that aired *WWE Smackdown* would go from an American Who to a Royal Worldwide Them and then *back to America* as an American Them (having denounced royalty!), we probably would've asked you which rom-com plot you were referring to. (*Red, White & Royal Blue* meets *Notting Hill* meets . . . *The Princess Diaries*?) The combination of Markle's existing Whodom and the ripped-from-the-pages-of-a-fairy-tale narrative that had a California girl getting married to a literal prince in the hallowed halls of St. George's Chapel at Windsor Castle was almost too much for us to believe, let alone for the tabloids to handle. "If Markle and Prince Harry are indeed headed to the altar, she will become the first American to marry into the royal family since Wallis Simpson famously wed King Edward VIII, forcing his abdication from the throne, almost 81 years ago," wrote journalist Sam Kashner in that 2017 *Vanity Fair* cover story, "Meghan Markle, Mad About Harry!"

Interest in Markle arguably had two peaks in those first few years of her global fame; one represented the height of her public adoration: her wedding. She and Harry wed on May 19, 2018, at Windsor Castle. Though smaller and more sparsely attended than Harry's older brother William's wedding some seven years prior—a mere 600 guests, compared to William and Kate's 1,900—the event was still broadcast live around the world, and even if you didn't care about the central couple, it was worth watching for the stargazing alone. How exciting it was to see Thems like George Clooney, Oprah Winfrey, Serena Williams, Sir Elton John, and the Beckhams entering the castle alongside a bunch of Whos who could only be recognized by fans of *Suits*. It was arguably the television event of the year, but how quickly things changed.

As a couple, they'd last twenty-nine months as full royalty, calling it quits with an unceremonious 2020 Instagram post: "After many months of reflection and internal discussions, we have chosen to make a transition this year in starting to carve out a progressive new role within this institution. We intend to step back as 'senior' members of the Royal Family and work to become financially independent, while continuing to fully support Her Majesty The Queen."

After stepping down as working members of the royal family, the couple moved to the United States. The following year, they sat down for an interview with former wedding guest Oprah Winfrey, during which Markle revealed the bitter truth about the hatred and racism she endured from her royal in-laws, painting them as monsters with a delicate brush. (Her sister-in-law Kate Middleton, she revealed, once made her cry!) In what was arguably the most upsetting moment from the interview, Markle told Winfrey that, while pregnant, she was told by an unnamed member of the royal family that there were "concerns and conversations about how dark [Meghan and Harry's son Archie's] skin might be when he's born." Markle later divulged her "clear and real and frightening" thoughts about suicide, which Harry said were not addressed by their family. "It was not a conversation to be had," he told Winfrey. Finally, Oprah asked Meghan a question that echoed around the world: "Were you silent, or were you silenced?" "The latter," the duchess answered. The interview, conducted on a beautiful patio in Santa Barbara, California, complete with furnishings from a line by former *Brady Bunch* star Christopher Knight, was, among other things, a harrowing exploration of how a sudden rise in fame can have grim repercussions on one's mental health and relationships. Like Diana before her, going from Who to Them had disastrous consequences for Markle.

Harry and Meghan briefly lived in Tyler Perry's spare Beverly Hills mansion—an ideal respite for two Thems—and signed "a deal in the neighborhood of $100 million" with Netflix, *The New York Times* reported. (Eventually they would buy a $14.7 million home in Montecito, where Winfrey and Ellen DeGeneres were among their neighbors.) Markle didn't need to blog about place settings and flower sprinkles when the demand for her image (and her newfound narrative) meant that she could now sell a TV show about those exact things. In March 2025, Markle's *With Love, Meghan* premiered on Netflix. *With Love* was *The Tig* on steroids: It's as if she'd taken the blog's ethos, aesthetic, and purpose from Who to Them (much like what happened to Markle herself). The series was quickly critically maligned (a mix of the show being somewhat boring and inauthentic but also perhaps due to Markle's existence as a divisive figure), and just as quickly renewed for a second season. Markle and Netflix also teamed up to sell some of the pantry items she was most known for at that point: jam, wine, and, naturally, *flower sprinkles*.

The story of Markle's ascension from Who to Them really does have *everything*: a fairy-tale romance, shocking scandal, political intrigue, lawsuits (at one point, Markle sued the *Mail on Sunday* and its parent company, Associated Newspapers, for publishing private letters she'd written to her father), and even some good old-fashioned whistleblowing. While Markle's situation checked all the boxes for shooting a relatively unknown person into the global consciousness, sometimes it only takes one of those categories to go from Who to Them. Monica Lewinsky, Milli Vanilli, O. J. Simpson, James Frey, Caitlyn Jenner, Tonya Harding, Heidi Fleiss . . . all Thems born of pure scandal—from memoir fabrication to Olympic disgrace to running a Hollywood prostitution ring. It might be a bit of an oversimplification at this point, but the Kardashian family didn't become household names until Kim's sex tape blew up and landed them a long-running reality show on E!. And what about the cast of *Vanderpump Rules,* who somehow elevated the cheating plot line of a reality TV show into a mainstream sex scandal, dubbed "Scandoval," propelling its victim, Ariana Madix, into a slew of advertising deals (Bic, SoFi, Lay's, Bloomingdale's, Duracell, Uber One); a run on *Dancing with the Stars;* a gig as host of *Love Island;* and a brief stint in *Chicago* on Broadway? Mind you, Scandoval was merely the standard repetition of plot lines that had already occurred on *Vanderpump Rules*. How this particular betrayal lodged itself into the public psyche, we'll perhaps never know.

WE'LL SEE IF Madix's Themdom stands the Warholian test of time, but the Who-to-Them trajectory via scandal is not just a modern phenomenon (even if we've given it modern nomenclature). Take Evelyn Nesbit, an ambitious chorus girl whose 1906 star turn came when her husband, railroad heir Harry Thaw, murdered her lover, a wealthy architect named Stanford White. (White helped design Madison Square Garden, Tiffany's, and the Washington Square Arch in New York.) Nesbit's celebrity emerged only during the trial—leading her to be cast as the original "Gibson Girl" and her tragedy to generate more newspaper sales than her talent ever could. The first trial ended with a hung jury; a second trial ended with Thaw being found insane. (And a bribe for Nesbit to testify in Thaw's favor that really didn't pan out for anyone.) As for Nesbit, her time as a Them was brief in the early 1900s sense: She landed vaudeville and film gigs after the trial but never achieved anything bigger than that moment. She worked as a burlesque dancer in the 1930s, battled addiction to alcohol and morphine, published a memoir (her second!) in 1934 called *Prodigal Days,* and finally moved to California, where she taught sculpture. She was eventually hired as a "technical adviser" on the 1955 movie *The Girl in the Red Velvet Swing,* a fictionalized account of her life. (It starred a young Joan Collins.) In her 1967 obituary Nesbit is quoted as having said,

"Stanny White was killed, but my fate was worse. I lived." Had life as a once-Them, now-Who been a fate worse than death?

While some called Nesbit's case the trial of the century, others might argue that title goes to the Them-making legal saga focused on newspaper heiress Patty Hearst. "The trial, said one lawyer-spectator, had all the elements of theater: a script, actors, wardrobe, props," reported *Time,* when the twenty-one-year-old stood trial for her part in the April 1974 Symbionese Liberation Army robbery of a Hibernia Bank branch in San Francisco. Hearst claimed that she'd been kidnapped and tortured, and that she'd agreed to join the group lest she be killed. Her lawyer, F. Lee Bailey, argued she'd been swept up in "coercive persuasion and brainwashing," which didn't convince the jury. Hearst's seven-year prison sentence was commuted by President Carter after two years, and she was eventually pardoned by President Clinton. What remained, however, were the echoes of the trial—shooting its "star" into forever fame: "a kind of peculiarly American legal Super Bowl," wrote *Time.* Hearst's story would remain a phenomenon, despite Hearst herself mostly fading into the backdrop of Hollywood (a 1981 memoir, roles in John Waters films, and a slew of awards at the Westminster Kennel Club Dog Show). Unlike Nesbit, it was Hearst's nepo lineage that would elevate the event to its "trial of the century" status and secure her Them status long after the 1974 proceedings.

Others are more forgotten by time. Barbara Lee Payton was discovered (perhaps in the truest sense) in a club on the Sunset Strip in the 1940s by a Paramount producer named Andrew Lyles. One night he and Joan Crawford spotted Payton from across the room, prompting Crawford (not one for compliments) to utter, "If her acting is as good as her looks, she is going to be big in this town!" Soon Payton was a model, then an actor, all while maintaining the nickname given to her by a journalist, the "new queen of clubs," as she partied as thoroughly as she worked her way up the Hollywood ladder. She was at one point Bob Hope's mistress—and allegedly had flings with the likes of Gregory Peck, Howard Hughes, Errol Flynn, Marlon Brando, and Gary Cooper. (If it all reminds you of millennial star Lindsay Lohan and her infamous "Sex List," you're not alone.) Payton was as famous as it gets in the late 1940s and early '50s, but it was a quick rise and an even quicker fall: By the '60s, heroin and alcohol addiction found her "living in a falling-down, red brick apartment building located right on the edge of the Hollywood Freeway," wrote John O'Dowd in *Kiss Tomorrow Goodbye: The Barbara Payton Story*. Hollywood film historian Tony DeMartino told O'Dowd: "Even though the place was unbelievably filthy, Barbara was very nice and happily obliged my request for an autograph." Today only the DeMartinos of the world remember Payton—her legacy is that of a tragic figure, recalled in history books and in the archives of *Vanity Fair*.

PUBLICIZED TRIALS, WHISTLEBLOWING, and viral sensations are all categories of notoriety that *could* elevate you from Who to Them in a snap. But the speed at which you go from a nobody to somebody who might be splashed across the front page of a newspaper doesn't necessarily lead to a long-lasting residence in the world of Thems. In fact, it might work against you. Take Rebecca Black, the star of the much-maligned (and later ironically embraced) music video "Friday"—sung endearingly off-key but nonetheless a wretched earworm that is still floating around in the mass millennial subconscious. The video could've propelled her from a Nah to a Them overnight upon its release in 2011, but instead she flew straight into Who territory. While "Friday" made her the talk of the web for longer than most, it didn't lead to lasting fame. People soon moved on. But being a Who can be as lucrative as you make it. Black grew up and admirably did end up achieving her childhood dream of becoming a real (working) pop star. Her singing has improved greatly, but she still has to sing "Friday" Every. Single. Time. she performs, which can't be great for her psyche.

How else do you make the leap? You could release a smash album, like Charli XCX's *Brat*. It can simply be a hit single, like Cardi B's 2017 "song of summer" banger, "Bodak Yellow," or Sabrina Carpenter's addition to the genre, 2024's "Espresso." Maybe the breakout work of Timothée Chalamet in *Call Me by Your Name*. Or the Disney Channel crossover of Zendaya when she starred in the first season of *Euphoria;* Quinta Brunson's creation of (and starring role in) must-see TV show *Abbott Elementary;* or nepo model Gigi Hadid on the Victoria's Secret Fashion Show runway (or just on every billboard in New York City). Though awards used to play a much bigger role in cementing celebrity status when more people actually tuned in live to watch them, they can still act as springboards to Themdom. Adrien Brody shot to fame after winning the Oscar for *The Pianist* (though, let's be painfully honest, assaulting presenter Halle Berry with a kiss before accepting the award had plenty to do with the press attention), and Brandi Carlile became ubiquitous in the music industry after taking home three Grammys in 2019. When it comes to theater, the act of grad-Who-ation is a little trickier. Broadway stardom is a niche space in which success doesn't necessarily equate to broad notoriety (thanks primarily to the audience's financial and geographical barriers to entry), but the Tony Awards can sometimes be crucial stepping-stones toward Themdom, in that winners will often catch the attention of Hollywood. Viola Davis's two Tony wins, in 2001 for *King Hedley II* and in 2010 for *Fences,* begat prestigious, high-profile film roles, notably her Oscar-nominated performance in 2008's *Doubt* and her Oscar-winning performance in 2016's *Fences.* Coupled with her network TV stardom in the Shonda Rhimes–produced *How to Get Away with Murder,* Davis has become one the most adored performers of her generation.

But actors don't have all the fun; other industries can crown Thems too. The success of Sally Rooney's *Normal People* (both the book and the subsequent TV adaptation, which also happened to turn Irish hunk Paul Mescal into a Them) made Rooney a literary Them. Though classical music isn't exactly blowing up the Billboard Hot 100, cellist Yo-Yo Ma is absolutely the Themmiest classical musician. (The man tours so much that he's essentially a one-man Rolling Stones.) As the most famous film composer across multiple generations, John Williams is arguably as well-known as the themes he scored for *Raiders of the Lost Ark, Jaws, Star Wars, Harry Potter,* and *Jurassic Park.* He didn't win the 2025 Super Bowl, but do a relationship with Taylor Swift and a chart-topping podcast have Kansas City Chiefs tight end Travis Kelce achieving Themdom? (Certainly.) It often takes a television show to bring a chef into the Them-osphere—much like it did for Anthony Bourdain, Gordon Ramsay, and Ina Garten—but cookbooks and "viral" recipes can keep you there. When Samin Nosrat published her seminal cookbook *Salt Fat Acid Heat* in 2017, she wasn't famous outside of culinary circles. But the book's wild success led to a prominent role as a food writer and recipe developer at *The New York Times*, as well as a Netflix series, both of which connected her work directly to her face. By the time her second book, *Good Things*, was released in 2025, Nosrat wasn't just a name on a cookbook or recipe byline, she had become a *celebrity chef*.

The joy of assigning Who and Them is that it's an art, not a science. A key to the binary is realizing that it's all relative; someone who might be a Them to *you* might not be a Them to *us*, and our splintered celebrity landscape makes these gaps even bigger. Generationally, there's always been a split: It's normal for parents to be unfamiliar with who their kids are into, be it JoJo Siwa or the latest Twitch streamer. (Meanwhile, ask pretty much *anyone* under the age of twenty-five if they're familiar with the work of Bea Arthur. They won't be.) There are also niche genre divisions. If you're into surfing, you're gonna know a whole lot more surfers than Kelly Slater—thus, many of them will be Thems to you. Or if you're into podcasts, you might think Ira Glass is simply the most famous guy in the world. (OK, maybe that's a stretch, but you'd definitely be able to pick him out of a lineup. But most people couldn't.) Part of the fun of the binary is that it can be objective or subjective, depending on the context. If everything were as simple as black and white, the two of us wouldn't have much to discuss.

The Who–Them divide used to be primarily economic, and it still can be. Thems book starring roles in big films, sell out worldwide stadium tours, and the like. But with social media and a diminishing concern about the integrity of certain varieties of advertising (or just the amount of advertising one might be taking on), a Who can also make as much money as a Them without even close to the same amount of social capital. Historically, Thems avoid overexposure, while Whos don't tend to worry about that. (And if you don't have to hustle, why bother! It's not classy to let them see you sweat.) Culture has shifted to be more forgiving toward the shameless capitalist money grab of celebrity. The attitude often seems to be *Hey, if there's money to be made, can't blame them for making it!*

If Whos can make money like Thems, gain the same access to big awards shows and film festivals and red carpets as Thems—even date Thems if they so please—why even bother becoming a Them at all? For one, sometimes a celebrity of any level can't control how high they rise. If you're working in the entertainment sphere and something you do pops off beyond your estimation, isn't that ultimately a good thing? (Your managers, agents, record label, or studio execs certainly think so.) But there's a prestige that Thems claim that can beguile a Who: a prestige that leads to more critically acclaimed projects, in which artistry is the number-one goal, not merely profit. Which leads to another thing not often spoken of, because it's simply difficult to look beyond the present moment: *legacy*. Thems have the hope of a legacy in their field, while Whos might not. For so many big stars, part of the dream is being universally remembered for making some sort of impact.

Ironically, it's the constant striving for Themdom (or just "celebrity" at large) that makes a Who that much more compelling; to be a Who is to have more freedom than a Them. Whos can take risks, while Thems are encouraged not to: Remember Ava Max launching her 2020 album *Heaven & Hell* by performing "live" in Roblox? The pop singer beamed into the game from her bedroom, singing "Sweet but Psycho" for a virtual arena of manic, boxy avatars bouncing up and down in virtual reality's most chaotic space. (The performance ends hilariously with a mega-sized Ava Max avatar, complete with her signature uneven blond "Max cut," flying in on a floating island and then leaping into a hole filled with virtual lava.) And Whos like Ava are often ahead of their time: In 2024, Lady Gaga beamed into Fortnite and performed at the "Fortnite Festival" to promote *Chromatica,* an album that was, at the time of the "festival," already four years old. (The performance marked the poetic closing of a loop that opened back in 2019 when she tweeted, "What's fortnight [*sic*]?") Whos also have the privilege of being famous and yet can exist in the world in a bit more peace. They'll get recognized while out and about; maybe someone will come up and ask for a photo or offer to buy them a drink, but nothing like the mobs that often surround Thems. Especially in our age of cellphone cameras, the public is ruthless when it comes to snapping a keepsake to share on their various social channels. And as far as privacy goes, Whos might exist in the best position on the spectrum that goes from NO ONES CARES to EVERYONE CARES. If only a few people *truly* care, your personal business might be tracked on a niche subreddit or tweeted by a hardcore stan account—it might even get picked up by a tabloid or two! But for the most part, you're able to exist in the world without the world watching. When Whos want attention, they're usually able to grab it. When they don't, it only takes a bit of maneuvering to stay out of the spotlight.

We celebrate Whos not only because they keep us entertained but also because we truly believe that the liminal space occupied by celebrities before reaching Themdom is a better and more interesting place to be. Whos may be relegated to living permanently in the dreaded "Khia asylum"—what Stan Twitter calls home to pop stars who can't help but flop, despite their best efforts, named quite rudely after rapper Khia (justice for "My Neck, My Back [Lick It]"!)—but it might not be as bad a home as it seems.

MUCH LIKE THE TABLOIDS, we crave Whos who crave *us*. Thems will always have that mysterious allure—especially as they fight to maintain privacy, leaving us all the more curious—while the gloriously thirsty Whos provide us the access to their lives that make way for coverage. And what we love about Whos is the implicit understanding that this is how the game works. Has the fame ladder grown taller as the Whos multiply and the Thems dwindle? Or has it shrunk down to two simple rungs: "I know who this person is" and "I do not know who this person is"? For a Who's purposes, it doesn't really matter if the average person knows who they are. A Who's job is a kind of alchemy: convincing the average person that they should.

Being thrust into Themdom can even throw someone off the fame thing altogether. Singer Chappell Roan's music exploded in early 2024 after a Coachella performance went viral, which included the premiere of her song "Good Luck, Babe!" Musicians presumably pursue their career with the hope that their music reaches people far and wide, but Roan quite immediately fought back against the long-held assumption that, by becoming famous, she forfeited the right to privacy. She told *The Face,* "No one understands that it truly falls all on you," adding: "I feel like fame is just abusive. The vibe of this—stalking, talking shit online, [people who] won't leave you alone, yelling at you in public—is the vibe of an abusive ex-husband. That's what it feels like. I didn't know it would feel this bad." She became the first huge pop star of our modern era to actively push back against fans instead of taking the typical, canned reaction of breathless gratitude.

"Would you go up to a random lady and say, 'Can I take a photo with you?' and she's like 'No, what the fuck?' and then you get mad at this random lady?" Roan said on a TikTok post, after accusing fans of stalking her family and yelling at her in the street when she wouldn't pose for photos. Celebrity had come for Roan hard and fast: "This is a lady you don't know and she doesn't know you at all. Would you assume that she's a good person [or] assume she's a bad person?" Unfortunately for Roan, being famous now comes with a lot of parasocial baggage. The more fans feel like they really *know* their favorite artist, the more money they'll spend on supporting them—buying tickets to their shows, buying limited-edition drops of their merchandise, buying the sponsored products they're paid to push, and so on. But Roan wasn't having it: "It's weird how people think that you know a person just because you see them online and you listen to the art they make," she said, sending a confusing message to a fandom raised on overly gracious pop stars. Lady Gaga wouldn't *dare* disrespect an adoring, if overbearing, fan like that! Or maybe she would if she'd met Chappell Roan back in 2008: On her 2025 album, *Mayhem,* in the song "Perfect Celebrity," she sings: "*You make me money, I'll make you laugh . . . You love to hate me.*" She's describing the experience of Themdom, but the perfect celebrity might just be a Who.

Chapter 2

The 2010s Killed the Cover Star

Theda Bara, Frank Sinatra & Beyoncé

There's a famous story about the first moviegoers that goes something like this: In 1895, a crowd of Parisians went to a theater to see something brand-new. Instead of an onstage, live performance, they watched the projection of images—*moving* images—on a two-dimensional screen. A larger-than-life-size train sped toward them, smoke billowing out of its engine. The audience gasped! They screamed! Some even fainted (perhaps a distant relative or two of Marion Cotillard) and shouted things like "*Mon dieu!*" This new medium of motion pictures was mistaken for magic, and audiences couldn't believe that this image of reality was merely a projection.

It's quite the yarn, but unfortunately it's not entirely true. A more believable version is that the first public screening of the Lumière brothers' *L'arrivée d'un train à La Ciotat* (Arrival of a Train at La Ciotat) happened in 1896—at a theater in La Ciotat, a town on France's southern coast. (The Marion Cotillard assumption stands.) Despite being one of cinema's foundational tales, told ad nauseam by cinephiles *to* cinephiles, as if they're the first ones to have ever heard the story, there's no evidencc that an audience ever erupted into panic and chaos over the sight of a projected steam engine. German film historian

Martin Loiperdinger lamented the story's refusal to die in his paper "Lumière's *Arrival of the Train:* Cinema's Founding Myth," writing, "Such a tale of more or less drastically amplified panic assumes naïve viewers who had the wool pulled over their eyes and therefore succumbed to a filmic delusion of reality." Contrary to popular belief, even the first moviegoers knew what they saw on screen wasn't real life. To discover the truth about the famous people entertaining them, they were already conditioned to go somewhere else: the press.

Since their beginnings in the early twentieth century, movie studios have known that they could not be kept afloat by their creative output alone. To turn the act of cinema-going into a ritual, rather than a novelty, Hollywood needed audiences to care about the people who starred in their movies as much as they cared about the movies themselves. Celebrity journalism began when actors were, quite literally, silent. Major stars like Mary Pickford and Douglas Fairbanks were glamorous yet mute, at least onscreen, so the studios needed magazines like *The Motion Picture Story Magazine* and *Photoplay* to give the actors a voice. *Motion Picture* was founded by J. Stuart Blackton, a studio head, while *Photoplay* was backed by the Motion Picture Patents Company in exchange for publicizing their releases. The magazines were effectively industry propaganda disguised as editorial content about fashion and beauty in a direct appeal to the presumed primary moviegoing audience at the time: women. The film industry later assumed that, thanks to the mass enlistment of men during World War II, more women had time to see movies. So they made more movies *for* them. These were precursors to what we now know as "chick flicks"; back then, they were called something *much* more elegant: "woman's films." "Despite the fact that statistical analyses of audiences during the 1940s suggest that this was not ultimately the case, the anticipation of a female audience resulted in a situation wherein female stars and films addressed to women became more central to the industry," writes author Mary Ann Doane in her book *The Desire to Desire: The Woman's Film of the 1940s.* If you've seen 1940's *Rebecca,* 1945's *Mildred Pierce,* or 1944's *Gaslight*—well, you've seen a "woman's film." These movies were less about a wedding planner accidentally falling in love with her client and more, respectively, about domestic life, family, and a woman whose husband slowly manipulates her into believing she is going insane.

The press followed suit. In a study on fan magazines of the time, Stephen Sharot explains the strategic positioning of women in early movie advertisements, as leading men were lower on the marketing hierarchy than "female stars." "References to a female star and 'her leading man' were ubiquitous in fan magazines: Tone was the 'leading man for Crawford in Sadie McKee', Loretta Young 'returns to the screen as the heroine of The Unguarded Hour with Franchot Tone as her leading man' and Douglas is Gloria Swanson's 'new leading man,'" Sharot writes. "Full-page photos of the female stars in their new films sometimes included small insert photos of their leading men."

IN HER POPULAR internet-column-turned-book *Scandals of Classic Hollywood,* Anne Helen Petersen attests that practically every showmance, beard, and PR stunt chronicled in modern gossip rags like *TMZ* and *Us* had not only been done to death for the better part of a century but had been done better, and to a more extreme, exciting effect, in the past. Before Madonna and Michael Jackson, there was Judy Garland and Mickey Rooney; before Pamela Anderson and Liam Neeson, there was Rock Hudson and Doris Day. We've been fooled again and again, but we'll keep eating that showmance slop.

Take the story of Theda Bara, an actor often referred to as the film industry's very first sex symbol. Born Theodosia Goodman in Cincinnati, Ohio, she shot to fame in part by cultivating a "man-eating," vampiric image that relied heavily on sultry approximations (read: appropriations) of Eastern culture, and in part because she released nearly *two dozen* films in the first five years of her career. In 1915, while promoting *A Fool There Was,* in which Bara plays a psychic vampire who destroys the life of a decent, hardworking family man with her exotic, despicable femininity, the studio held one of the very first press conferences, at a Chicago hotel, to introduce their new star to the world. The air, writes author and historian Michael Mayo, was "thick with incense." He adds:

> Theodosia was decked out in furs and veils and played Theda to the hilt. After it was over, [publicity agents Johnny Goldfrap and Al Selig] told one reporter, a young unknown Louella Parsons, to hang around. She was on hand to see Theodosia rip off the costume, throw open the drapes and gasp "Gimme air," just as the boys had planned.

Two years later, during a promotional push for the long-lost 1917 version of *Cleopatra*, publicity agents decided to tell reporters that Bara's name was an anagram for "Arab Death"—which it was, though not *intentionally*—and that she was "the reincarnation of a daughter of Seti, high priest of the pharaohs," which is, at best, a pretty tough thing to prove either way. Petersen writes that Bara was pushed to become "the sort of figure the fan magazines craved." Nearly a century before the concept of a "stan army" was born and exemplified by popular social-media accounts like @PopCrave, actors (and the publicists behind them) bending to fans' desires was an established and effective strategy. Louella Parsons, the "young unknown" reporter who detailed Bara's first big stunt, went on to become one of the most prolific and influential celebrity gossip writers of all time.

For decades, *Motion Picture* and *Photoplay* were the primary sources for celebrity news and gossip, walking the tricky line between pleasing audiences and pleasing the studios by appearing to reveal secrets that wouldn't damage anyone's reputation. Said Joan Crawford in 1973, "In the old days the Hollywood press had real power, yet they could be so—well, discreet is a nice word . . . I mean, they had to know something about what went on between me and Clark [Gable] . . . but they kept quiet . . . There was such a thing as a gentleman of the press." The relationship between these magazines and the studios that funded them was symbiotic, to say the least. "Fan magazine writers often spent their time working as studio publicists or press agents," writes film historian Anthony Slide in his book *Inside the Hollywood*

Fan Magazine, "alternating careers, with little regard for the dividing line between the one and the other." Much like a freelance writer might take an assignment for *Vanity Fair* while also doing a bit of copywriting on the side. This has always been the nature of journalism.

But something changed in the middle of the century. World War II fundamentally altered the media landscape by making audiences wary of propaganda and hungry for authenticity, and pioneers of what came to be known as New Journalism like Lillian Ross and Helen Lawrenson began profiling celebrities in the pages of more highbrow magazines like *The New Yorker* and *Esquire*. These writers were far less interested in pleasing studio heads and publicists than they were in revealing truths about their subjects. Suddenly celebrity journalism had split into two distinct categories; "character analysis of feet and ankles" by Hugo H. Smythe in *Photoplay* was junk food, but a salacious, literary profile of Marlon Brando in *The New Yorker* that caused the star to threaten its writer, Truman Capote, with murder? That was the main course.

"By Their Feet Ye Shall Know Them" reads the headline to Smythe's cheeky (or, more accurately, footy) feature. "Do you blame Gloria Swanson for showing her pedal extremities so often in her pictures? . . . The tootsies of Corinne Griffith, garbed in pumps equipped with sensible heels . . . are here presented for your careful inspection . . . How the feet and ankles of our beloved Mary Pickford look when she takes a morning stroll." *Slow down, Smythe!* Long before Wikifeet proudly tracked the size and details of famous feet, *Photoplay* was setting the stage for *Us Weekly* features like "Umbrella Holders: Handlers? Ha! Stars Provide Shelter from Storms" and "Celebs Earning Their Keep! Soaking Up the Sun or Dancing in the Streets, These Stars Make Their Jobs Look like a Breeze." Meanwhile, Capote's Brando profile is a feat of the very opposite, revealing detail in depth and scope: Brando's issues with fame, directors, even monks. ("It's like the other day on the set," he said. "We were working in a temple, and one of the monks came over and asked me for an autographed picture. Now, what would a monk want with my autograph? A picture of me?") Capote spares no detail in his descriptive language, a word count unheard-of in a magazine meant for a quick skim, or to merely promote a project: "with what chameleon ease Brando acquired the character's cruel and gaudy colors, how superbly, like a guileful salamander, he slithered into the part, how his own persona evaporated."

Journalism started to read more like novels. Was it because the readers wanted it that way? Or was it just the writers, each worked up to publish the next great literary feat? "It is hard to explain what an American dream the idea of writing a novel was in the 1940s, the 1950s, and right into the early 1960s," wrote Tom Wolfe in *New York* magazine. "The Novel was no mere literary form. It was a psychological phenomenon." And so the celebrity profile followed suit. This shift to New Journalism was a way for writers to prove they had what it took while also making $2 per word to go long on whatever celebrity feature they'd been assigned.

One of the most famous and influential pieces in the history of magazines, as well as a prime example of New Journalism, is Gay Talese's "Frank Sinatra Has a Cold." First published in the April 1966 issue of *Esquire,* it's filled with color and detail, humor and insight, and written in the kind of expressive prose more expected from literary fiction than the pages of a men's magazine. The piece is such a compelling, thorough portrait of a profoundly frustrated and unhappy Sinatra at his near peak that you may not notice until finishing its 15,000 words that Talese never speaks to him, not even once. Sinatra refused to be interviewed for the piece, but that didn't prevent Talese from finding the story through secondary sources and his ornate observations. ("It was obvious from the way Sinatra looked at these people in the poolroom that they were not his style, but he leaned back against a high stool that was against the wall, holding his drink in his right hand, and said nothing, just watched Durocher slam the billiard balls back and forth.") Somehow the apex of the celebrity profile—the white whale that magazine writers have been chasing ever since—had been written without access to the celebrity being profiled.

The late '70s saw the fall of *Motion Picture,* which had changed names and then folded in 1977, and *Photoplay,* which published its final issue three years later. And then it was the '80s! Time to party!

Video killed the radio star, and all that! That self-serious New Journalism stuff wasn't over, exactly, but it was far from the norm. At the time of its collapse, *Photoplay* had only six staff members, all of whom were shuffled over to a magazine that was in its ascendant phase: *Us* (later known as *Us Weekly*). The film fan magazine, a staple of Hollywood since its inception, had officially been subsumed by something more broadly appealing: a general-interest entertainment magazine featuring puffy celebrity profiles and gossip surrounded by fashion and beauty content. Its first issue, published three years after the first edition of *People,* featured a rugged, distracted-looking Paul Newman on the cover, flanked by headlines including "Helen Reddy and Husband: Ten Years of Making Up" and "Our Five Biggest Diet Myths."

For the next several decades, the Themmy celebrity profile reliably fell into two distinct buckets: the harmless, brazenly promotional blurbs found in magazines like *Us* and *People,* and more revealing, long-form reporting in magazines like *Esquire, The New Yorker,* and, of course, Tina Brown's *Vanity Fair*. During Brown's reign as editor in chief, the publication published too many iconic cover stories to count, including plenty that revealed the private suffering of Princess Diana (written by Brown herself), and a profile of Demi Moore whose cover image—of a naked Moore with hands covering her very pregnant body—quickly became one of the most memorable and parodied celebrity portraits of a generation. The accompanying piece, penned by Nancy Collins, was as revealing as its lead image, with Moore candidly discussing her reputation while munching on a meal of steamed vegetables. Writes Collins, "She doesn't seem angry about the Industry dish accusing her of becoming an instant prima donna, just a tad defensive. 'From my perspective I've got a very professional reputation,' [Moore] shrugs. 'I'm strong and opinionated, but I'm not difficult in the sense that *Is my motor home big enough?* It doesn't bother me . . . It's a lot more interesting to write about me being a bitch than being a nice woman.'"

In discussing her thoughts on more tawdry gossip in the context of highbrow celebrity journalism, Moore suggests a symbiotic relationship between the two: Both feed off of each other in such a way that pleased the talent and studios as much as the publishers. If audiences wanted more from a celebrity than their creative output, they had two roads down which to travel—and with any luck, they'd travel down both. For nearly a century of Hollywood history, publicists were the walls preventing the public from accessing their clients without permission. But in the late 2000s, that wall came crumbling down.

THERE IS PERHAPS no better way to exemplify how the celebrity profile changed in the new millennium than through the coverage of the century's two biggest artists: Taylor Swift and Beyoncé Knowles-Carter.

It was a feud to end all feuds (even though it didn't), spanning five years of a rapidly evolving era of social media. On September 13, 2009, the same year Twitter's user base began to skyrocket, Taylor Swift's "You Belong with Me" won the MTV Video Music Award for Best Female Video, an upset given the fact that Beyoncé:

A) was more famous at the time, and
B) had a nominated video whose accompanying song was a genuine cultural phenomenon.

"Single Ladies (Put a Ring on It)" topped the Billboard Hot 100 chart for four weeks; its buzzy, discordant beat was inescapable for months, whether at the grocery store or a house party. While Taylor was accepting the award, Kanye West ran onstage, snatched the microphone, and said, "Yo, Taylor, I'm really happy for you, and I'mma let you finish, but Beyoncé had one of the best videos of all time! *One of the best videos of all time!*" Footage of the incident quickly went viral. As this was years before television networks realized the importance of clipping their own broadcasts for online consumption, the video was posted and deleted due to copyright claims again and again and again—but not before millions of people were able to share and watch (and rewatch) what would go down as one of the most consequential awards-show moments (of all time).

Within hours of grabbing Taylor's mic and coming to Beyoncé's perhaps unwanted defense, West published a new entry on his old-school blog (*KanyeUniverseCity*) in which he wrote, caps lock his own, "I'M SOOOOO SORRY TO TAYLOR SWIFT AND HER FANS AND HER MOM. I SPOKE TO HER MOTHER RIGHT AFTER AND SHE SAID THE SAME THING MY MOTHER WOULD'VE SAID. SHE IS VERY TALENTED! I LIKE THE LYRICS ABOUT BEING A CHEER-LEADER AND SHE'S IN THE BLEACHERS!" Sorry for *what,* Kanye? He went on to reaffirm his position that Beyoncé's video for "Single Ladies" was superior. The apology clearly didn't stick. Only a few months later, West apologized once more, this time on Twitter, writing, "I'm sorry Taylor."

Over the next few years, when traditional media would ask each of the stars about the state of their "feud," they'd keep things buttoned up. In a 2015 cover story for *Vanity Fair,* Swift told writer Josh Duboff, "I like [West] as a person. And that's a really good, nice first step, a nice place for us to be." (Later she said of West's then-wife, Kim Kardashian, "I love Kim.") It was newsworthy in that Swift confirmed a friendship the public could only speculate about, and yet pure puffery in that the confirmation was diplomatic to the point of near meaninglessness. The piece, titled "Taylor Swift: Apple Crusader, #GirlSquad Captain, and the Most Influential 25-Year-Old in America," was a turning point for the glossy, high-status celebrity magazine profile. This piece was meant not only to promote its celebrity or the journalistic bona fides of its publisher but also to straighten up what social media had destabilized. In 2015, audiences still sought out the truth from publications that committed their stories to print. The last word was still expected to be written in ink.

But that *wasn't* the last word for Taylor or Kanye, was it? In 2016, West debuted a new song titled "Famous." Its lyrics called out his supposedly snuffed feud with Swift in explicit terms. "*I feel like me and Taylor might still have sex / Why? I made that bitch famous.*" While not the best of Kanye's lyricism, the song was quickly a Twitter trending topic, and when West began receiving backlash for his songwriting, he staunchly came to his own defense without the help of any middleman, tweeting, "I called Taylor and had a hour-long convo with her about the line and she thought it was funny and gave her blessings." In no mood to wait for printing presses or TV producers, Swift's publicist, Trina "Tree" Paine, published a statement on Swift's Twitter account, which had over 60 million followers at the time: "Kanye did not call for approval, but to ask Taylor to release his single 'Famous' on her Twitter account. She declined and cautioned him about releasing a song with such a strong misogynistic message. Taylor was never made aware of the actual lyric 'I made that bitch famous.'" Yes, a publicist was involved, but an external publication was not. Swift's and West's Twitter accounts effectively *became* the AP wire.

Later that year, Kim Kardashian was profiled by writer Caity Weaver in *GQ*. In the story, she referenced "video proof" of Swift approving West's lyrics and claimed that Swift's attorneys told her to "destroy the footage." Three paragraphs of the piece chronicle Weaver's attempts to confirm the existence of the footage through representatives for West and Swift, but readers were left with more questions than answers. ("Let's stipulate here that Kim Kardashian West is not the kind of person who forgets that the tape-recorder light is blinking," Weaver writes. "But just because a rant is carefully chosen for its audience doesn't mean it isn't genuine.") Cut to July 17, 2017, when Kardashian acknowledged National Snake Day (a real thing!) with a tweet filled with snake emojis and pointed fans to her other social-media accounts, where she confirmed the rumored tape's existence by simply . . . *posting it*. Within the hour, Swift had released a statement on her Twitter account: a screenshot of a paragraph written in the Notes app alongside the caption, "That moment when Kanye West secretly records your phone call, then Kim posts it on the internet." Her rebuttal read, in part:

> He promised to play the song for me, but he never did. While I wanted to be supportive of Kanye on the phone call, you cannot "approve" a song you haven't heard. Being falsely painted as a liar when I was never given the full story or played any part of the song is character assassination. I would very much like to be excluded

from this narrative, one that I have never asked to be a part of, since 2009.

Part of that final sentence, "I would very much like to be excluded from this narrative," quickly became a meme, with Swift quoting the line herself in the music video for the lead single of her next album, *Reputation,* which she teased with imagery of—*what else?*—a snake. By the time *Reputation* was released, it had eaten its tail and then some.

THIS FEUD MARKED a turning point in the behavior of our most famous celebrities. Social-media accounts were no longer novelties or mere brand extensions; they were channels of communication unlike anything the world had ever seen: platforms to be honed, monetized, and in some cases weaponized. A social-media account is a place to promote your latest TV show, movie, album, or, if you're Danielle Jonas, a sponsored partnership with the National Pork Board. ("I cooked up one of @kevinjonas' favorite meals, Garlic & Rosemary Roasted Pork Tenderloin!") It could even be a place to make yourself seem more relatable by commenting something mildly funny on a photo posted by another famous person, a behavior that spawned the wildly popular Instagram account Comments by Celebs. And more seriously, a social-media account was a celebrity's first line of defense if they had something to clarify, confirm, deny, or apologize for. The celebrity profile wasn't rendered worthless by any means, but it did suddenly become a less urgent and powerful tool in the standard PR arsenal.

Like so much of the internet, social media began as a solution to a problem that didn't actually exist. No one *needed* to know what everyone else was doing or thinking or watching or complaining about at any given moment, but—once you signed up for Facebook, Twitter, and later Instagram—wasn't it fun to know anyway? And once you got used to a constant stream of knowing, wasn't it hard to go back to a time when the lives of others (friends and celebrities alike) were more of a mystery? Lindsey's rewatching *Gilmore Girls* . . . yet again, Bobby's crying to Sufjan Stevens, #JustGayMillennialThings. And Rihanna is on the beach! Years of conditioning have made us forget that those three scenarios should not exist on the same news feed, let alone the same plane of consciousness. One could even argue that the mundane details of a friend's life are as irrelevant as those of a celebrity, but there's no winning that argument anymore. Less than a decade after the founding of Facebook, celebrities were regularly amassing more followers on their personal social-media accounts than major magazines could claim in circulation or websites could claim in monthly visitors. The power to break stories about themselves was in their hands alone, and, more important, so was the power to cultivate their image consistently, without the need for an interview or even a promotional peg.

Though the internet affected the speed and volume with which we saw celebrity images, they still required a middleman before reaching the moment of publication. A photo is just data on a drive or a negative on a film roll until someone decides to share it with the world. If Solange had beaten up Jay-Z on an elevator while Beyoncé calmly watched them without a security camera there to film it, *did the fight happen at all?* If Britney Spears had shaved her head away from any cameras, *would she have actually been bald?* The answer to both of those questions is obviously *yes,* but the response, had no images been made public, would have changed the course of modern celebrity history.

You can imagine the power celebrities must have felt when they saw their follower counts increase in the early 2010s. Celebs suddenly had the ability to speak to their fans directly, as Swift did amid Kanye's "Famous" drama. Social media made that happen. Not only were there no editors, publicists, or paparazzi, there was a much bigger audience than there once was. How freeing it must have felt to finally be in control of your public image—and also, how totally fucking dangerous.

Though celebrities now had a host of new avenues to connect with fans, the celebrity profile didn't just keel over and die. It merely evolved, in part because of a changing media landscape and, more grimly, a decline in the overall profitability of the journalism industry. Because younger generations weren't subscribing to magazines like *Vanity Fair, Rolling Stone, Essence,* and *GQ* at the same level they used to, those outlets weren't sending reporters to Los Angeles to spend a week with a celebrity as often as they used to. Profiles such as Swift's from 2013 ("Taylor Swift's Telltale Heart" in *Vanity Fair*) and 2016 ("Taylor Swift: The Rolling Stone Interview" in *Rolling Stone*) were written after a day spent with the artist—a light lunch, followed by a long conversation on a terrace, perhaps, and capped off with an event of some kind at night. But her next big cover story, published by *Rolling Stone* in 2019, was something else entirely. It was the stripped-down, acoustic version of an overproduced piece of stadium rock. Writer Brian Hiatt teases in the piece's intro that Swift will discuss "the past three years of her life, in depth, for the first time." He describes the conversation as "often not a light one," and Swift herself as having "built up more armor in the past few years." But the resulting piece isn't one with Talese-esque hallmarks of literary detail and secondary sources (or Capote-esque reveals and truths), it is, simply, a transcribed Q&A—no doubt inspired by a growing trend that began a couple years prior, when David Marchese's "In Conversation" series of long-form Q&As for *New York* became widely discussed and praised pieces of celebrity journalism. It's hard not to see Hiatt's interview with Swift as a compromise of sorts: By agreeing to a serious interview structure with a friendly publication, Swift could more deftly control the tenor of the resulting piece; and by conducting the interview in a single sitting (without throwing a lunch bill and Uber receipts on top), *Rolling Stone* was able to save a few bucks.

But wait, you might be thinking, *I still read plenty of traditional profiles as well as Q&As! They're published all the time, by the exact magazines you've mentioned!* Sure, but have you noticed that after reading them you feel like you didn't learn anything at all? And doesn't it seem like the more titillating headlines of decades past—from the aforementioned "Frank Sinatra Has a Cold" to the classic *Vanity Fair* profile of Julia Roberts from 2007, "Mommy's Being Famous Right Now"—have been replaced with vague, lazy non-sentiments like a 2025 piece in *The New York Times* titled "How Reese Witherspoon

Figured Out Who She Really Is." Writer Ian Hurley bemoaned the state of the celebrity profile in 2018, writing in *The Pacific Standard,* "Nowadays, there's an inescapable feeling of narrative control that comes with the profiles of our biggest stars . . . It is a product of a more reputation-driven age that even stories that are supposed to seem revealing are often nothing more than an exercise in performance." A celebrity has no reason to risk ruining their career—or the success of their latest project—with a genuinely revealing profile, and the editor in chief of a magazine with falling advertising revenue has myriad reasons to accept a publicist's strict rules for an interview. When the famously press-averse Beyoncé surprised fans with an *Essence* cover Q&A in 2024, fresh off the final dates of her record-breaking *Renaissance World Tour,* she didn't reveal any news about her very famous family or rumored next album. She had only one thing on her mind, or more accurately, her scalp: Cécred, her new haircare line. How thrilling it must have been for the writer, Brooklyn White, to interview one of the most famous and influential artists in the world. And how surprising it must have been when the interview was largely about shampoo. And if that weren't enough to exemplify the state of the profile in 2024, its total lack of detail about Beyoncé's appearance—what she wore, how she did her hair, the way she smiled—suggests the interview wasn't in person or even over Zoom; it seems like Beyoncé had only made time for a phone call.

5 Headlines That Prove Celebrity Profiles Are More Vague Than Ever

- "Chris Evans Is Having Second Thoughts" (*GQ*, 2023)
- **"Greta Lee Is Getting Used to This" (*The Cut*, 2024)**
- "Robert Downey Jr. Doesn't See Things the Way You Do" (*Esquire*, 2024)
- **"Keke Palmer Is in Control" (*Glamour*, 2022)**
- "Madison Beer, Her Way" (*Paper*, 2026)

It's difficult to begrudge Beyoncé, or any celebrity, for an unwillingness to be open books, but it's quite easy to feel judgmental over the things they are open about. In that sense, the celebrity profile is a manifestation of a famous person's worst fears and biggest aspirations, a chance to prove their worth to their adoring fans with as much authenticity as they can muster while simultaneously navigating the tricky obstacles that come with fame. Though Beyoncé is often mocked for her lack of openness with regard to the press, she's obviously made the calculation that it's a preferable subject of ridicule to whatever may arise from being more transparent with her fans. There's a video from February 2001 that seems to go viral online every four to six weeks, at least on *Who? Weekly*'s admittedly chaotic algorithm. In it, Beyoncé, Kelly Rowland, and Michelle Williams are being interviewed by an ITN reporter on the red carpet of the Brit Awards:

"What do you think the government should be doing about the foot-and-mouth epidemic?" the reporter asks the three members of Destiny's Child.

Beyoncé, the group's supreme leader, answers first, not missing a beat. Her face remains steely and assured as she says, "We don't know anything about that. All we know is, we just got here."

The reporter pushes. "It's a deadly virus that's decimating the nation's livestock."

"Oh," Beyoncé says, now smiling as though she's just witnessed a magic trick. "The thing about the four-legged animals! Didn't that kill, like, forty million animals or something? That's crazy." She shrugs.

Beyoncé spent the aughts figuring out her place in Themdom, appearing in movies like *Austin Powers in Goldmember* (an international hit); *Dreamgirls* (an Oscar nominee, but not for her performance); *The Fighting Temptations* (a flop with an incredible soundtrack); and *Obsessed* (an entertaining camp disaster) while simultaneously releasing chart-topping, critically acclaimed solo albums. During this time, she'd find herself on the receiving end of several awkward interviews, from a stilted segment on *Late Night with David Letterman* in 2006 to her widely lampooned appearance on Tyra Banks's daytime talk show,

Tyra, during which she was asked a series of questions centered on alternate spellings of her name (such as "*Brie-oncé: What's your favorite type of cheese?*"). To bring this full circle she released a song that spawned what many called the greatest music video of all time at the end of the decade and cemented her place as a Them. Gone were the days of awkward press; she was instantly, suddenly untouchable—stratospheric. "Single Ladies" won three Grammys, was named Video of the Year at the VMAs and the BET Awards, and went eleven times platinum in the United States. Her next album, 2011's *4,* was yet another success (it's also the favorite of both of this book's authors), but it marked a turning point in her approach to the press. Her final cable-TV interview ever—as in, *ever*—was with Piers Morgan, a conservative British journalist, that same year. Her pregnancy was announced not by releasing a statement but by caressing her baby bump at the end of a VMAs performance. (She even countered allegations that it was fake with a YouTube video of herself rubbing her exposed baby bump while exclaiming, "Oooh baby!") Her longtime publicist, Yvette Noel-Schure, seemed to have strategized that rarefying Beyoncé, making her more inaccessible and reliant on her own social and digital channels, would help the team better control the way she was perceived.

In a 2022 interview with *Forbes,* Noel-Schure defined herself thusly: "I'm a protector. I'm a protector of narratives." It's a refreshingly blunt way of describing the role of a publicist in our modern era, and one that lays bare how much the role has transformed since *Photoplay* writers were moonlighting as film publicists. Back then, publicists were narrative *creators,* more akin to storytellers than reputational bodyguards, and Noel-Schure is nothing if not tremendous at her job. Beyoncé began retreating from traditional forms of publicity in early 2013, when she gave two of her final traditional interviews ever. For *GQ,* she ate sushi with writer Amy Wallace at her Manhattan office, fielding questions about her childhood, inspirations, and upcoming album, which was still veiled in mystery at the time. Her unwillingness to open up *too* much is most evidenced by the multitude of quotes

Wallace includes from *Life Is But a Dream,* the HBO documentary that was released a month after the *GQ* piece. A profile published by *Vogue* the following month, also tied to the release of *Life Is But a Dream,* shows a similar dependence on the documentary as a primary source, and its most telling secondary interview is with Michael Lombardo, HBO's president of programming. "I think there's a decision by artists to have an honest conversation with their fans and not wait for paparazzi or weekly periodicals to define who they are," Lombardo tells writer Jason Gay. "There's such a voracious appetite to deconstruct certain personalities. And I think it's terrifying to an artist." Just ten months later, *Beyoncé* was released without warning—complete with an accompanying video for each song, defining the visual album as we know it—and became a global sensation. Her follow-up, 2016's *Lemonade,* was released with a similar strategy, and since then, her approach to publicity has mirrored her approach to album releases: She does things entirely on her own terms.

When she appeared on the cover of *Vogue*'s 2015 September issue, she gave them no interview. *The New York Times*' snarky coverage of the piece was published with the headline "Beyoncé Is Seen but Not Heard." It was Frank Sinatra all over again.

Three years later, she appeared again in the 2018 September issue of *Vogue,* and this time the accompanying article was a transcribed, stream-of-consciousness monologue told to writer Clover Hope. Beyoncé had been heard once again—but only on her terms. There were no questions or answers, only statements she chose (presumably, well in advance) to have published. Her cover stories for *Harper's Bazaar* in 2021 and *GQ* in 2024 were, again, softball Q&As tied to product launches—her clothing line Ivy Park and whiskey brand SirDavis, respectively. Beyoncé doesn't need to spend much time promoting her artistry, but these interviews aren't *really* about her music; everyone's heard her music, and plenty of people adore it. Her clothing and whiskey brands, the ones with names the average consumer may not immediately associate with Beyoncé Knowles-Carter, require a bit more help. And if you're *Harper's Bazaar,* you agree to whatever terms

Queen Bey has demanded to get her image on your cover with the illusion of something potentially revealing inside.

WHILE PROMOTING THE 2025 film *Sinners,* for which he would later win the Academy Award for Best Actor, Michael B. Jordan shared a piece of advice given to him by Denzel Washington, a veteran of the screen, the stage, and the Hollywood promotional machine. In a profile published on *Vulture* by writer Zak Cheney-Rice, Jordan says Washington once told him, "Why would [audiences] pay to see you on a weekend if they see you all week for free?" It's an ideology that celebrities who became Thems long before the internet—the ones who tried to stay out of the press when they weren't promoting a new project—took for granted, and one that has also served Jordan well in the Them stage of his career. (Later in the piece, Cheney-Rice describes the star as "both knowing when to talk and, perhaps more important, when not to.") It's a rarity for someone of his generation, but it's also a privilege afforded to those, like Jordan, who have already put in years of prior promotional work.

You've probably noticed that this chapter focused primarily on two of the biggest celebrities alive, inarguable Thems who have found more success, adoration, and money than most artists could ever dream of. Beyoncé and Swift are in the unique position of being able to avoid promotional labor because their work needs little to no promotion. But what about everyone else? The young, largely unknown upstarts who depend on publicity to further their careers? Those, dear reader, are the Whos. For as long as their jobs exist, celebrity journalists will need celebrities to talk to. Plenty of Thems are still willing to play the game, but every time one isn't, a Who will always be there to sub in.

Chapter 3

Gossip: A Reckoning

The *Daily Mail,* Perez Hilton & @PopCrave

In 2003, the *National Enquirer* paid a woman $20,000 for her story about an alleged affair with Arnold Schwarzenegger. Only two days after the Kindergarten Cop himself announced his candidacy for California governor, the magazine's parent company, American Media, Inc. (AMI), signed a contract with Gigi Goyette that stipulated that any information she had about Schwarzenegger would be given exclusively to them.

Strangely, the *Enquirer* had already published a cover story only two years earlier on Schwarzenegger's infidelities, describing an alleged seven-year sexual relationship with Goyette during his marriage to Maria Shriver. ("Arnold's Dirty Secrets—Why He Can't Run for Governor" was the headline that stopped the star's first go at governor dead in its tracks.) Now they were paying Goyette (and her in-the-know friend, Judy Mora, who got $1,000 in cash) for stories they would never publish.

At the very same time that Goyette was telling her story to the tabloid, Schwarzenegger was negotiating a consultation deal with David Pecker, then-CEO of AMI, the now defunct magazine publisher acquired by McClatchy Media Company (MMC) in 2024. Pecker wanted

Schwarzenegger to be the executive editor of two of their publications—*Muscle & Fitness* and *Flex*—initially founded by Joe Weider, the "Father of Bodybuilding" who had first brought Schwarzenegger to the United States from Austria in 1968. (Before Pecker got his hands on Weider's mags, Weider paid Schwarzenegger's living expenses in exchange for several interviews in his magazines.) After Pecker and Schwarzenegger's deal closed in 2003, Pecker's *Enquirer* was suddenly devoid of the usual Arnold coverage: "The edict came down: No more Arnold stories," said one senior AMI staffer, as reported in *Los Angeles Magazine*. He was crowned "A New American Patriot" by another Pecker-owned tabloid, *The Star*. This time, he was elected governor. And Pecker attended his coronation—uh, *inauguration*—on November 17, 2003.

Speaking to the *Los Angeles Times* in 2005, the now-governor's communications director, Rob Stutzman, denied any connection between AMI's mag deal with Schwarzenegger and the company's legal dealings with Goyette and Mora: "That's what they do. Obviously, part of their business is the tabloid business."

What is "the tabloid business"? Does the best scoop win? Or is it all just Pecker's brand of "catch and kill" journalism, securing a scoop only to bury it? That same reciprocal arrangement is what helped Schwarzenegger finally quell the stories about his alleged affair with Goyette as well as accusations of assault against multiple women, just long enough to get him elected governor. (And years later, the same technique would be used to help push Trump toward the presidency: yet another Pecker-driven plot for influence.)

The *Enquirer* doesn't have the influence it once did—perhaps evidenced by Pecker's storied difficulty in finding a buyer for it. But maybe you didn't realize that after a series of mergers and acquisitions, MMC gobbled up many of the celebrity publications we used to see at every grocery checkout aisle. They've since shuttered *InTouch, Closer,* and *Life & Style,* leaving *Star* and our beloved namesake *Us Weekly* as two of the few that remain on newsstands today. So while these mags may each have their own masthead full of reporters, it wouldn't be odd for them to overlap in exclusives, to share sources, or to be handed the same decree from management.

Let's say there's an A-lister gearing up to announce a big tour, a big movie, a big memoir, a big *whatever:* Give MMC a story, and they'll gladly slap you across all the titles over the next few months. There's rarely an exclusive in the world of tabloid media without some sort of handshake deal behind the scenes.

Celebrities have been working with tabloids for as long as the two have existed. From these decade-long "catch and kill" agreements to simply phoning the paparazzi and letting them know exactly where they'll be so they can roll up and get the shot, the idea that the rich and famous simply cannot avoid being front-page scandals is a popular misconception. While there are certainly restaurants where paparazzi might hang out waiting for a celeb to enter (Craig's, the Corner Store, and Nobu Malibu, to name a few), there are just not enough freelance paps these days to scour the streets of L.A. and NYC. With celebs posting photos of themselves directly to social media, why would a tabloid pay for a photo they could simply source *for free*?

The only mainstream tabloid currently publishing out of the clutches of AMI is *People* magazine—owned and operated by People Inc., who often fall within the "lifestyle" side of celeb journalism. (They also run pubs like *Entertainment Weekly, Food & Wine, Southern Living,* and *Travel + Leisure.*) When *People* isn't scaring its readers with terrifying headlines ripped from local crime blotters ("Pregnant 22-Year-Old Shot at Sports Bar. Her Unborn Baby Died, and 'Reckless Behavior' with a Gun May Be to Blame"), they're aggregating TikToks and Reddit threads ("Widow Demands Her Kids Get a Share of Late Husband's Ashes Despite His Dying Wish Stating Otherwise") without providing much, if any, supplemental reporting, or taking a celeb pic and adding an affiliate link ("Brittany Mahomes Just Proved a Black One-Piece Swimsuit Is Always in Style—Shop Inspired Looks from $21"). *People* used to be shorthand for *famous* people! Now it's *all people;* a story about Jennifer Aniston receives as much weight as a story about a regular woman named Jennifer, the subject of a 2025 story headlined "Woman Tells Husband His Cooking Is 'Trash.' Now He's Thinking of Ending Their Marriage." Much like with the rest of the media, the internet fully democratized *People* magazine.

■ ■ ■

"ALL LITERATURE IS GOSSIP," Truman Capote told *Playboy* magazine in 1976 after spreading the stories of his powerful confidants, "the swans": Gloria Vanderbilt, Babe Paley, Slim Keith, Lee Radziwill, Mona Williams. "What in God's green earth is *Anna Karenina* or *War and Peace* or *Madame Bovary*, if not gossip? Or Jane Austen? Or Proust?" Well, that might depend on how much you love gossip. We mean *good* gossip—gossip told with lurid details, embellishments, and a delicious flourish. That's the category of gossip Capote was attempting to defend. Because if all literature is gossip, why can't all gossip be literature? "Gossip is the absolute exchange of human communication," said Capote. "It can be two ladies at the back fence or Tolstoy writing *War and Peace*."

He was defending his own work, but also the work of the columnists who came before and would come after him—all intent on treating gossip as worthwhile storytelling, or even creditable journalism. In 1924, Walter Winchell began reporting Broadway gossip at Bernarr Macfadden's *New York Evening Graphic* (a tabloid people nicknamed the "porno-graphic") before a gig at the *New York Daily Mirror* had him syndicated to thousands of papers across the globe; Sheilah Graham wrote the gossip column "Hollywood Today" for over thirty-five years, beginning in the 1930s (and happened to be F. Scott Fitzgerald's final lover); in 1938, Dorothy Kilgallen launched a daily gossip column called "The Voice of Broadway" that once angered Frank Sinatra into calling her the "chinless wonder"; "Suzy" (the pen name of Aileen Mehle) anonymously chronicled high society at the *Miami Daily News* starting in the 1950s; and columnist Rona Barrett, "the Czarina of Hollywood," would walk up to stars at press junkets in the 1950s and '60s and ask: "How good a fuck are you?" as an attempt to get anything besides canned answers from media-trained stars.

At their peak, these gossipmongers were celebrities in their own right, often because they could only suss out gossip by insinuating themselves among the famous people they wished to cover—a delicate dance! Tips and sources and quotes were only accessible to those who went out and got them. If it meant you became the story, so be it. Thus, the relationship between gossip columnists Louella Parsons and Hedda Hopper (itself the subject of George Eells's 1971 dual biography, *Hedda and Louella*) was at first a symbiotic friendship and then a brutal rivalry. Parsons's bluntness could change the trajectory of a star's career with a single headline. In the 1920s she was the first to report on silent film actor Fatty Arbuckle's murder charge—coverage that ruined his reputation despite a later acquittal. A decade later, a considerably more trivial bit of gossip nearly stopped Katharine Hepburn's rising star dead in its tracks. "Photographers have agreed not to take a single pic of her because she's been so rude," Parsons wrote, effectively forcing Hepburn to reframe herself as a charmer by acquiring the film rights to *The Philadelphia Story* (thanks to a little help from her pal Howard Hughes's pile of cash). Hopper, on the other hand, was originally an actor, and would regularly tip Parsons off in exchange for a mention: "They liked each other a lot. If anything happened on a set—if a star and leading man were having an affair—Hedda would give Louella a call," said Dorothy Manners, Parsons's assistant of thirty years. But once Hopper launched her own gossip column, "Hedda Hopper's Hollywood," in 1938, the two began fighting each other for scoops. "Louella Parsons is a reporter trying to be a ham; Hedda Hopper is a ham trying to be a reporter!" Hopper once said of her rival, who worked until she physically could no longer do so in 1965, at age eighty-four. She was replaced by Manners, but the column never recovered.

"L.A. is now a town with no gossip column. No one wants to let these demons loose again," said Liz Smith of the duo. Smith was perhaps the last true gossip columnist of that era of influence, the kind who could command an almost million-dollar salary for her nationally syndicated column that ran (in various outlets throughout her career) for more than thirty years. Smith's style was of "an insider, not a tattle," noted writer Ben Widdicombe in *Vanity Fair*. She befriended celebrities and actually managed to keep them as friends, a practice unheard-of by modern-day gossip writers. (Or just impossible to imitate, unless you're of the "famous friend" ilk, someone like Vas J. Morgan, who ended his career as a gossip blogger after befriending a slew of celebs.) Smith died at the age of ninety-four in 2017, having seen many years of the internet gossip reporting that came after her and having been appalled by it. "I don't pay attention to any of them. I never know whether the stories are true," she said of *Gawker, TMZ,* and "celebrity websites and blogs" in an interview with *The New York Times.* "She was confounded by 21st-century celebrity culture, which values round-the-clock social-media transparency over the removed mystique of past Hollywood stars," wrote Widdicombe.

WHILE SMITH RAILED against the modern tabloid era, the Vanessa to her Ariel (a reference for Disney adults and children alike) is likely a gossip blogger who appeared in the mid-2000s: Perez Hilton. For as hated as he was (by journalists and celebrities alike), Mario Armando Lavandeira Jr. changed the tabloid landscape with his self-titled blog, *Perez Hilton.* ("Perez" for his Latin roots, "Hilton" as in Paris Hilton, who was at that time an easy and lucrative target.) He wasn't the only one doing it—there was also Trent Vanegas's *Pink Is the New Blog,* Michael K's *DListed,* and Elaine Lui's *LaineyGossip*—but Hilton's nasty brand of commentary was uniquely addictive. It fought back against the neutered state of both tabloid and magazine journalism, with Hilton's memorable Microsoft Paint decorating celeb photos. (Sometimes with jokey Mad Libs–esque quotes, sometimes squiggles and dots alluding to cum or cocaine. Sometimes both.)

Hilton was more than problematic, even in his own day: He regularly outed closeted actors, made jokes about celebs' weight, and spread gossip about the lives of underage stars. (He even prematurely reported Fidel Castro's death in 2007.) "I'm more trustworthy than *Page Six,*" Hilton once bragged to *Radar* in 2006. And while the First Amendment protected the blogger from a slew of defamation lawsuits (the lengthy "Legal issues and controversies" section of his Wikipedia page speaks for itself), no one was visiting *Perez Hilton* for accuracy.

Reading the site felt like hearing a juicy, whispered story from a friend—the *OK, don't repeat this, but . . .* type of gossip, the *I've heard this from a few people, and . . .* type of gossip, the type of gossip that was a dash of hearsay, a bit of conjecture, and 100 percent entertainment. Just how your favorite group text might be today, Hilton wasn't bogged down by a set of journalistic ethics.

Until, at least, the culture caught up with him. In 2010, Hilton posted a video to YouTube called "I'm Going to Be Doing Things Differently" in response to bullying accusations, and only a couple years later he appeared on *Oprah's Lifeclass* in a segment called "How Perez Hilton Changed the Negative Energy in His Life," telling Oprah, "I don't want to be that person anymore . . . I want to use my platform for good." His pseudo-redemption tour continued through the aughts, but Hilton couldn't quite figure out how to use these modern, post-WordPress platforms in a way that stuck with the gen pop: He was banned from TikTok in 2020 after criticizing influencer Charli D'Amelio for dancing in a bikini. The celebrity kingmaker had finally been officially exiled from the royal court. ("I am feeling numb, and I don't want to seem overly dramatic, but I feel like my world is crumbling," he said in a video response to the ban. "This feels like a death to me.")

Hilton came and went, but the internet had discovered how fun gossip could be without the tabloids. Online culture pulled celebrity blinds from message boards to the mainstream. *Crazy Days and Nights*, a no-frills, text-heavy site run by "Enty Lawyer" (since outed as a lawyer named John Nelson), regularly ran unvetted, anonymous bits of gossip written in entertaining code language. *Gawker* launched its own controversial celeb feature in 2006, the "Gawker Stalker": a Google map that pinpointed submitted celebrity sightings throughout NYC. It had a catchy title and a greater purpose: *Gawker*'s mandate was to break down the decades-old pay-for-play systems of tabloid media. (And stir up a little controversy along the way? Sure, why not.) You couldn't actually stalk celebs with the Gawker Stalker because *it wasn't posted in real time*—but its threatening name had the feature shut down within the year. "We completely acknowledge that there are very many creepy people out there, but the truth is, if there is someone really intending to do a celebrity harm, there are much better ways to go about doing that than looking at the Gawker Stalker," *Gawker* editor Jessica Coen said to the Associated Press. "If you're using the map to do that, you are a really bad stalker." Not to mention, these posts were gossip minutiae that would barely be of interest to even a properly vetted tabloid magazine: "Spotted outside the Carroll St. stop on the F line, Saturday 10/15: Paul Giamatti, looking like he was waiting for someone, pushing an empty baby stroller. He was looking comfortably disheveled, as one would expect, but his hair (or what's left of it) had grown a little longer perhaps than it should."

The Gawker Stalker project didn't last long beyond *Gawker* co–editor in chief Emily Gould's appearance on *The Larry King Show,* where guest host Jimmy Kimmel held little back. *Gawker* was already seen as a "nasty," bottom-feeding blog: "You're throwing rocks at people," the creator of *The Man Show* snarled at Gould on live TV, with the majority of the viewers already firmly seated on his side. To which Gould replied: "Aren't they kind of protected by piles of money from those rocks?" After the takedown, Gould wrote in *The New York Times* more decisively of the mission statement: "Our posts are written by ordinary people with no obligation to tone down their insults in order to maintain access to a celebrity, as gossip reporters must."

IF INNOCUOUS CELEBRITY sightings being posted online doesn't seem as scandalous as it did to Kimmel in 2007, that's because you're familiar with the tactics of the Gawker Stalker's descendant, Deuxmoi. Long after Kimmel and his celebrity pals had mostly given up rallying for privacy, thanks to the ubiquity of selfies and Twitter (now known as X, but we don't acknowledge that), an anonymous poster going by Deuxmoi debuted her *Gossip Girl*–voiced knockoff. *Deuxmoi* had existed as a blog for a few years at this point, but in 2020, the account started an Instagram-based tip line, full of celeb sightings that ranged from dull ("Saw biden in DC," a tipster once submitted. "Likely place for him to be," she replied) to damning, like teasing an upcoming bombshell about Armie Hammer (and we all remember what that one was, right?).

"I've always stayed true to what I said from day one, which is that this information is not proven to be based in fact," she told *The New York Times* in 2020. "I don't do any additional research. I'm not a reporter . . . I feel like my content is as truthful as the person who's sending it in." She attempted to legitimize this lack of sourcing to *Vanity Fair* in 2021, telling them, "I don't want to be Perez Hilton, I don't want to be Ted Casablanca, I don't want to be whoever, Jared whatever-the-hell-his-last-name-is . . . That's not what this account is. The account is just about sharing stories. Sharing information." (Jared "whatever-the-hell-his-last-name-is" is, in fact, referring to Jared Eng, the proprietor of JustJared and JustJaredJr and one of our favorite sources of gossip about young stars we've never heard of.)

How far we'd come from Gould having to justify the Gawker Stalker's existence! Deuxmoi explained that her platform has quite literally nothing to do with journalism. (A FAQ section at one point read, "Believe what you want, or don't believe any of what is posted. This was started for F-U-N. Also, this is my private account so I can reveal or not reveal whatever the FUCK I want.") She wouldn't be beholden to any sort of ethical standards placed upon publications. Deuxmoi even had her own rules for publicists, ones that differed from those of her predecessors. She wasn't in the business of completely rejecting their input (much like *Gawker* and others had been, as part of their mission statements), but sometimes accidentally playing alongside them: "I don't work with any publicists unless they conceal their identity to me and are feeding me information," she told *Distractify*.

Unlike Perez Hilton or *Gawker*—or even us, for that matter—Deuxmoi isn't in the business of commentary; she prefers to let the blind items speak for themselves. In that way, she's able to shield herself from most of the kinds of criticism endured by her predecessors. (Can you really take responsibility if you're anonymous?) Maybe that's because she knows that without any sort of fact-checking, she's likely to post things that are straight-up false. And that's OK with her; it's almost part of the process—adding to her overall brand authenticity, if not factuality: "I'm not afraid to say, this was a fake tip or this was wrong information, because it happens." Much like the blind items of

Crazy Days and Nights or the gossiping regulars on the essential and hyperactive message board *Lipstick Alley*, this is where entertainment blurs with reported celebrity news.

5 Funny Blind Items That Made Us Go "Huh? Who?"

- "Which superstar's daughter annoyingly talks French to people who don't necessarily know French, repeating the same phrases whenever she doesn't want to really answer a question?" (*Village Voice*, 2010)
- "This A-list mostly movie actress who is a multiple Oscar winner/nominee, literally has two, maybe three friends. If all of them are busy, our actress will literally just sit in her home and not do anything. Apparently she just sits there and waits for someone to text or call her. She doesn't read or watch television or doom scroll, she just sits there. Not Jessica Chastain." (*Crazy Days and Nights*, 2022)
- "PSST! I can't name names now, but can you guess which Hollywood lesbian is known for her humor, but finds nothing funny about snoopy workmen in the home she shares with her lover? Absolutely no men are allowed in the house—only female repair crews." (*National Examiner*, 1999)
- "Years ago, this A+ diva was a regular at a certain NYC hotel. She would often forget where she lived and/or how to get home so she would just stay overnight. The rub? She lived a few blocks away." (*Gawker*, 2022)
- "This lovable funny boy with a squeaky clean image has a scandal brewing." (*Deuxmoi*, 2021)

At some point, however, all this unverified gossip leaves you seeking a little . . . *verification*? Even if *People* and the like have lost their edge—and surely their timeliness—what they haven't lost is their sourcing: In a market crowded with he said/she said, a proper scoop has become more valuable than ever. The actual journalism these mags do now stands out in a landscape of liars and unsourced rumors. When Deuxmoi claims something based on an Instagram DM or a text message, the real ones know it's worth waiting for confirmation from an actual outlet with even a soupçon of journalistic integrity. Because even if these publications were engaging in occasional tit-for-tat coverage directly with publicists, at least they *had* the contact info of said publicists?

SOMEHOW, THE BEST-OF-BOTH-WORLDS publication has to be the dreaded Rupert Murdoch–run British *Daily Mail*—a tabloid practically as old as dirt that has morphed into the sensationalist gossip "literature" Capote craved, mixed with deeply sourced reporting. The *Daily Mail* has come a long way since its beginnings as a history-altering addition to the news landscape. First published by brothers Harold and Alfred Harmsworth in 1896, the "Busy Man's Journal" was cheaper and immediately easier to read than its competition. And about 130 years later, the publication that is sometimes derisively called the "Daily Fail" or "Daily Wail" is just as known for its xenophobia as it is for its incredibly entertaining headlines.

Who? Weekly listeners already know that we may be named in honor of the stateside rag *Us Weekly*, but you're more likely to hear us reading *Mail* headlines. It wasn't in Harmsworth's 1896 mandate, but no one loves a run-on more than the modern online version of the *Mail*: "PICTURE EXCLUSIVE: Kevin Costner's first wife Cindy Silva, 66, seen grabbing groceries almost THREE DECADES after her marriage to the actor came crashing down." Does a woman getting groceries have anything to do with her wedding to an actor over thirty years ago? Absolutely not, but the *Mail* is going to squish those two items together in its signature style. How about the utter *literature* of "Mischa Barton shares sweet hug with her boyfriend Gian Marco Flamini . . . as they pick up a Range Rover from a tow yard"—have you ever read anything quite as vivid?

Tabloids have always had to be as expressive with language and imagery as possible. Why else would you be compelled to grab a copy while waiting in the grocery checkout aisle? And now more than ever, when the fame landscape is so fractured, not every cover can be of Jennifer Aniston, Brad Pitt, or George Clooney. In her paper "SHOCKING SECRETS REVEALED! The Language of Tabloid Headlines," Dr. Deborah Schaffer notes that how much one can exaggerate without actually lying is a game tabloids often play, and no matter the subject, descriptive language is king: "It should be immediately apparent that the foremost device identifiable in tabloid headlines is the use of content rich vocabulary—words that get the attention of the reader either through reference to a particularly interesting topic (e.g., 'romance,' 'divorce,' 'sex,' 'scandal,' etc.) or through evoking powerful, often emotional connotations (e.g., 'weird,' 'sizzling,' 'stripped,' etc.)."

It helps that with its conservative bent, the *Mail*'s natural stance is to be faux scandalized by pretty much everything celebs might do. In the *Mail,* you might "display" your underwear through a sheer black bodysuit; "show off" your washboard abs in a racy bralette; "ditch" your bra and wear black knickers; or "stun" in a "VERY dramatic" sheer gown and thong—and those are just four headlines about singer Rita Ora. Her relevance in the *Mail* is unparalleled: If your news diet involved reading their "Showbiz" section every day, you might consider her the Most Famous Woman in the World.

The *Mail* has also managed to push the limits of speculative journalism while battling the stringency of the U.K.'s libel laws. (Libel is published defamation, while slander involves defamatory statements in other forms, like speech.) That's where headline modifiers like "alleged," "seemingly," and "amid" come into play: "Hilary Duff touches down in London ahead of her nostalgic concert amid Ashley Tisdale's 'toxic mom group' drama" or "Damson Idris and Lori Harvey seemingly rekindle romance with very public appearance at Golden Globes." Even phrases like "fueling rumors" push a narrative while not quite confirming or denying anything at all: "Orlando Bloom fuels Katy Perry split rumors as he's set to attend Jeff Bezos wedding 'as a single man.'" Tiptoeing around direct accusations is popular; in the

United States, free speech laws are prioritized, while the U.K. prioritizes one's right to not be defamed.

And if the *Mail* claims their intentions are to report the "truth," not to defame, it doesn't even matter. Libel laws in the U.K. make it so there's no need for the defendant to have any intention to defame to get sued for defamation. In 2007, actor Keira Knightley won £3,000 in a libel case against the *Mail* after they published a story about a teenager who had died of anorexia alongside a picture of Knightley in a bikini. In 2009, actor Kate Winslet sued the *Mail* after they published a story with the headline "Should Kate Winslet Win an Oscar for the World's Most Irritating Actress?" But Winslet wasn't asking the tabloid to prove she was irritating (although that would've made for an incredible court case), she was accusing them of lying. Writer Liz Jones expressed doubt about a quote that the once "down-to-earth" actor gave to *Elle:* "I don't go to the gym because I don't have time, but I do Pilates workout DVDs for 20 minutes or more every day at home." To which Jones countered, "She might say it is down to 20 minutes of gentle Pilates a day but, trust me, it ain't. I've done that amount of Pilates for years and I do not have anything approaching Ms. Winslet's enviable muscle tone." Winslet won the dispute: The court ruled in her favor and the *Mail* bought her £25,000 worth of Pilates DVDs.

MORE RECENTLY, A dispute between two popular WAGs (that's "wives and girlfriends" of professional athletes) demonstrated how those libel laws easily extend to social media. Former Manchester United footballer Wayne Rooney's wife, Coleen, accused Leicester City striker Jamie Vardy's wife, Rebekah, of leaking stories about her to the press—via seemingly private Instagram stories, no less. But it's *how* she proved the leak that got more press than the stories being leaked themselves. Earning herself the title "Wagatha Christie," Rooney purposely posted fake stories on Instagram that only Vardy could have seen. There was a fictitious basement flood and an ideation of a plan to revive her TV career—both stories appeared soon after, word-for-word, in *The Sun* newspaper. Eventually, in October 2019, Rooney posted that she'd blocked all accounts from seeing her stories, apart from the one she'd suspected was doing the leaking, revealing: "It's. . . . . Rebekah Vardy's account."

In return, Vardy sued for defamation. A High Court judge ruled that the post outing Vardy for leaking stories to *The Sun* was "substantially true" and that while the information in the posts was "trivial," information generally "does not need to be confidential or important to meet the sting of the libel." Perhaps what lost Vardy her libel claim had more to do with the series of unfortunate incidents that befell her own evidence in the case. There were broken laptops, deleted encrypted WhatsApp messages, and a phone that had been "accidentally" dropped into the North Sea before it could be used for evidence. "[It was] most unfortunate, because it was only a short time after the court ordered that the phone should be specifically searched," a lawyer for Rooney said.

Meanwhile, over in the United States, a judge threw out a 2014 defamation lawsuit against Fox News Channel after commentator Michelle Fields said on live TV that Lindsay Lohan and her mother, Dina, did cocaine together. (To be clear, her exact words were "Lindsay Lohan's mom is doing cocaine with her.") Fields had named Lohan and her mother in a segment that aired two days after actor Philip Seymour Hoffman died of a heroin overdose. About two weeks later, a different Fox News host apologized to the Lohans on-air for making comments they "cannot verify," but once the case appeared in court it was quickly dismissed by a judge who declared: "Truth is a defense." The judge also defined Dina Lohan as a "public figure" (perhaps the most important aspect of the ruling) and asserted that the comment wasn't made maliciously. It didn't help the Lohans' case that in 2012 Lindsay's father, Michael, recorded a phone call in which you hear Lindsay say: "Dad, [Mom's] on cocaine. She's like touching her neck and shit."

In fact, our free-speech laws protect gossip so thoroughly that Americans can't even be punished by U.K. libel laws. When author

Rachel Ehrenfeld's book *Funding Evil* alleged that a Saudi businessman financed terrorism, she was sued for libel in the U.K. and lost because she didn't appear in court. (Sometimes called "libel tourism," such cases arise when a plaintiff chooses to sue from a country with weaker free speech protection.) But instead of enforcing the U.K.'s decision, the New York legislature passed a bill called the Libel Terrorism Protection Act (or "Rachel's Law"), which prevents U.S. courts from enforcing foreign libel judgments that don't meet U.S. standards of free speech. And the federal SPEECH Act took Rachel's Law even further, extending similar protections nationwide.

HEADLINES ONCE CAUGHT our eyes on crowded magazine racks, an attempt to sell us a copy so we could read more. Once our eyes shifted to our screens, online publications had to replicate the model. Thus, "clickbait"—a name given to the phenomenon of crafting headlines juicy enough to obtain a misguided click-through—became the norm. Looking back, everyone will point to *BuzzFeed* as the originators of the form, as they even developed a specific headline style adjacent to the tabloid standard, but with a little twist: "Tyra Banks Is Embarrassed by Old Throwback Photos Just Like the Rest of Us" or "13 TV Stars from the '90s You Probably Had a Crush On." Both lure the reader in with the promise of something more *personalized*. Clickbait also became an easy target for old media to have a jab at. It helps that even the name was catchy: In 2014, Jon Stewart said to *New York* magazine: "I scroll around, but when I look at the internet, I feel the same as when I'm walking through Coney Island. It's like carnival barkers, and they all sit out there and go, 'Come on in here and see a three-legged man!' So you walk in and it's a guy with a crutch."

But clickbait had a short run, thanks to new search-based algorithms. Tech giants like Google (who held the keys to the clickbait, in a way, with search engines) made it so these lowbrow headlines were not as easily served to their targets. Online publications raced to adapt. In a 2014 blog post called "Why BuzzFeed Doesn't Do Clickbait,"

BuzzFeed News editor in chief Ben Smith wrote that *BuzzFeed* wasn't even *doing* clickbait anymore because clickbait had "stopped working around 2009."

If the *Daily Mail* represents the best of the sensationalist-yet-sourced old world, the best of the new world has to be the Twitter-based micronews aggregator @PopCrave. Their ubiquity has a lot to do with speed, an increasing cultural appetite for snippets (versus actually having to read entire articles), and the wry, winking humor that only comes with freedom from the traditional newsroom attitude toward the news. The account was founded as @PopCultureShady in 2015 by a Miami-based journalism school dropout named Will Cosme. The handle was updated to @PopCrave in 2016 and steadily gained followers as it tweeted culture news: "Your Go-To Source for Pop Culture News, Chart Updates, Music Releases & More!" read *Pop Crave*'s initial bio. "There's no 'off' button for *Pop Crave*," Cosme said in 2020. The account didn't break news; it aggregated as fast as it could—specifically with little commentary or journalistic follow-up. Unlike *Us Weekly* or *People*, *Pop Crave* didn't have to reach out to anyone's publicist for comment. Why would it?

Pop Crave no doubt stemmed from Twitter's stan account economy—superfans mostly post on Twitter and mimic tabloid headlines but often ironically use the language of tabloids in the coverage of their subjects. "Rachel Zegler Source" (@ZeglerSource) captions a video: "Rachel spills the tea on playing Fiona, Juliet and Evita for British *Vogue*," while Joseph Quinn HQ (@joequinnHQ) posts photos: "New look at Joseph Quinn as Johnny Storm in 'THE FANTASTIC FOUR: FIRST STEPS.'" There's a Kiernan Shipka–focused account called "@shipkafiles"; "Margaret Qualley Daily" (@QualleyDaily); and perhaps the most straightforward of them all: "Joel Kinnaman News" (@jkinnamannews). These accounts don't have to follow any sort of journalistic standards, but you often see them trying to uphold veracity in their posts by citing their sources and even fighting against misinformation in their replies.

Pop Crave took the stan "reporting" to the next level: Their focus wasn't as niche as a specific star (although Cosme admittedly has favorable biases toward Frank Ocean and Tinashe), but instead applied this approach to culture as a whole. *Pop Crave* gives the same platform to everything it covers—from a new photo taken of a pop star ("Lola Young stuns in new photo") to New York City politics ("Andrew Cuomo concedes New York City Democratic mayoral primary to Zohran Mamdani"). And it's up to the algorithm to decide where that coverage goes. A popular refrain on Twitter is someone tweeting that they can't believe they found out [INSERT IMPORTANT NEWS HERE] from *Pop Crave*. And *Pop Crave* relishes that responsibility: being fast and being first, with the intention of perhaps being the first place you'll see news you might not expect. In 2024, *Fast Company* reported that *Pop Crave* broke news on the assassination attempt on President Trump on September 15 at 2:41 P.M.—"well before it was shared by the accounts of the Associated Press (2:45 P.M.), CNN (3:10 P.M.), NBC News (3:13 P.M.), and *The New York Times* (3:21 P.M.)."

Just as old-school tabloids like the *National Enquirer* and the *New York Post* each had their own language (the *Enquirer*: "CHARLIE SHEEN'S AIDS COVER-UP"; "LISA MARIE AND EX-HUBBY IN SECRET HIDEAWAY"; "IT'S NOT BRAD'S BABY"; *New York Post:* "TOMKAT KAPUT! Katie goes Holmes alone"; "HUMA CUTS OFF WEINER: Splitsville after Post sext shock"), the new guard also loves to play with old-school headline traditions, mixing them with modern-day internet-speak. *Pop Crave* in particular ushered in its own signature with the word "stun." Just as pop star Sabrina Carpenter might "stun at Dior's Men['s] fashion show in Paris," so might an actual celestial object: "Strawberry Moon stuns in the UK." Then there's "Malia and Sasha Obama stun with Destin Conrad at his album listening party" and "Chappell Roan stuns in elevator & car." ("Elevator & car" is not the name of a magazine; Roan was simply just riding in an elevator and then a car.) "In the *Pop Crave* journalistic universe, 'stuns' is the queering of the mundane, turning the simple act of being into the hallowed act of becoming eminently newsworthy," wrote Tobias Hess at *Paper*. To stun on *Pop Crave* is merely to *exist*! (But to be newsworthy enough for a *Pop Crave* tweet.) Unlike publications that came before it, *Pop Crave* has no clickthrough fantasies—if there's a business model, it's not hoping to serve banner ads or integrated sponsored video. It's run on attention and sharing; therefore, the only goal is to put the story (be that a video or a photo or just information) right up front.

Pop Crave is in the business of putting it all out there; they're the answer to the clickbait era, or at least what happens when the media realizes that the old headlines aren't working anymore. Back to the supermarket checkout counters we'll go, or at least to a new word for attention-grabbing: "thumbstopping"—getting someone to quite literally stop their thumb along an endless scroll through their social feeds.

"'i can't believe i found out from popcrave😂😂😂' yes you can. you learn most things from popcrave. it's the future now," tweeted @ali_sivi (aka *Who? Weekly* favorite "Bald Ann Dowd") in August 2024, pointing out that even the notion that finding out important news from *Pop Crave* might be strange or surprising is, in fact, not strange or surprising at this point. No longer was "finding out from *Pop Crave*" an insane twenty-first-century experience. It was just the way we experience the news.

Chapter 4

When Thems Act Like Whos (and Vice Versa!)

John F. Kennedy Jr., Tyra Banks & Nicki Minaj

Do you remember the iconic "flying compact" moment from the 1995 MTV Video Music Awards? Even if you didn't watch it live over three decades ago, perhaps you saw a clip of it while thumbing through a TikTok account centered on '90s nostalgia, or maybe recounted by Hal Sparks on an episode of VH1's *I Love the '90s*—the series that was, alongside *I Love the '80s* and *I Love the '70s,* effectively a graduate-level cultural history class for elder millennials. Ahead of the VMAs, Kurt Loder and Madonna sit atop a raised platform for a pre-show interview. Mid-broadcast, the two are interrupted by an EFO (easily-identified flying object) thrown at them from the street below. The camera lingers on Madonna, mid-answer to a question about whether her album *Bedtime Stories* "reflects a new smoochiness in [her] life," as her eyes follow a makeup compact succumbing to gravity right in front of her face, narrowly avoiding impact. As the camera rolls—this was live TV, back when people actually watched live TV—Madonna and Loder look over the side of the platform to face the street, quickly figuring out what's going on. "Hi, Courtney," Loder says with a nervous disdain, seeing Courtney Love in the street below. It's hard to tell whether he's frighteningly amused or just plain frightened. "That's Courtney, everybody's favorite."

Madonna keeps her cool. Despite nearly being bonked in the head by the compact of a woman she clearly despises, Madonna calmly asks that Love not be invited up to join them. ("No," she says deadpan. "Don't.") But Love's thirst for the camera proves irresistible to Loder, who rightfully sees the potential not just for good TV but for fantastic, generation-defining TV. He tells Love to come on up. (A great reason why we need more live TV!) In a devastating summation of the incident, Madonna says into the mic (as if directly addressing not Loder but the audience at home), "Courtney Love is in dire need of attention right now."

After running up the curved staircase, Love asks if she's interrupting—*of course she is!*—giving Madonna, Loder, and the cameras a wholly unconvincing display of regret. She's hunched over in a near-genuflection, seeking forgiveness as much as she's seeking a camera. The year is 1995; Love had only recently ascended to Themdom, thanks in part to the tragic, highly publicized death of her husband, Kurt Cobain, and the surprise success of her band Hole's album *Live Through This* just a week after. But she was still up on that platform behaving like a Who. After all, she wasn't the one being interviewed by Kurt Loder, and her own VMA nomination (for Alternative Video, which she lost to Weezer) wasn't as exciting as Madonna's (who did win Best Female Video of the Year for "Take a Bow"). But despite being lower in the MTV hierarchy that night, Love found a way to enter the focused glow of a spotlight occupied by someone significantly Themmier. She behaved shamelessly. She behaved surprisingly. She noticed a camera that wasn't pointed at her and, using the limited tools in her purse arsenal, literally ascended to Madonna's level and improvised a hostile takeover. Because, to a Who, attention is an end whose means are *always* justified. Whereas to a Them, attention isn't something to crave, as it's what they've already got. Usually. But sometimes even the most famous Thems find themselves in the same "dire need" that afflicted Love all those years ago.

Before social media, celebrities in that state of dire need were beholden to their hardworking publicists and the sight lines of other people's cameras for that dopamine rush of recognition. These days they don't have to interrupt a live TV broadcast to scratch that particular itch; they just need to grab their phone and post a picture . . . or make a call to their favorite paparazzi photographer. Whatever the method, photos are sure to be seen by millions on their social-media feeds in a matter of minutes.

BUT SOME CELEBRITIES are going to get photographed whether they like it or not, and it's important to recognize the difference between a paparazzi photo and a paparazzi *walk,* better known as a "pap walk." (Not to be confused with pap *smear,* which is something celebrities might not want to share with the public.) A pap photo can result anytime a celebrity leaves their home, regardless of how desperate they are to be seen. A pap *walk* is an inside job, a coordinated outing that the celebrity and paparazzo find mutually beneficial. When Rihanna and her partner, A$AP Rocky, go out to dinner, they will be spotted, whether at a trendy hotspot or humble food truck. When they frolic on the beaches of her home country of Barbados, locals snap pics and sell them to *TMZ*. Both of those examples result in pap photos, but neither exemplifies a pap walk. It's Themmy for a paparazzo to find you. It's Who-y to give one your calendar.

One of the greatest, funniest pap walks of our time occurred during one of our darkest eras: the first year of the Covid-19 pandemic. In the spring of 2020, Shawn Mendes and Camilla Cabello were one of pop music's most powerful couples. Their songs "Senorita" and "Havana," respectively, each peaked at number one on the Billboard Hot 100 and still seem to be played on loop at every CVS in North America. But despite the ubiquity of their two biggest hits, the couple always rang a little hollow. One of the most successful young men in pop dating one of the most successful young women in pop should have been a formula for rabid public obsession—Justin Timberlake and Britney

Spears for a new generation, minus the matching denim—but they never quite clicked. It felt too calculated, too obvious, showcasing a romance that was convincing in song, but not in real life. In 2020, they were objectively Thems, but thanks to the lockdowns, their need for attention resulted in behavior that could only be described as Who-y.

For what felt like months, we were blessed with bizarre, near-daily paparazzi photos of the couple taking a morning walk in their Miami neighborhood. The pair were always on the same strip of residential street, wearing the same kinds of mismatched, raggy clothes that so many nonessential workers spent their days and nights lazing around in throughout Covid's early period. As photos, the images border on relatable. There they were, going on their little daily walks, absorbing as much vitamin D as possible, social distancing from everyone outside their domestic bubble, trying to find a routine to keep their sanity . . . OK, maybe they *weren't* calling the paparazzi! Maybe paps were just showing up because they knew Mendes and Cabello's routine! It was such a bizarre time for everyone that, had they just been still images, we probably would have given them the benefit of the doubt and would not be discussing them here. But then we saw the video.

Once the couple's stroll was a *moving* image, the question of whether they'd called the paparazzi themselves was, in our estimation, answered definitively. Picture it: the "Stitches" crooner and the "Shameless" songstress moving so slowly that Dame Judi Dench would have asked them to speed up. It's actually difficult to walk slowly when your body is capable of quickness (Mendes is six-three; his legs are quite long!), and the videos of Shawn and Camilla shuffling down their sidewalk looked physically painful. At the very least, they looked utterly absurd. The reveal was a hilarious punch line to a long-simmering joke. As our world was turning upside down, laughing at these slow-walking celebrities felt pretty nice. The people who seemed to have everything we all so desperately wanted at the time—endless deliveries of whatever they could possibly need and big homes in which to spread out, especially. But they were unsatisfied and emotionally starving, *just like us!* Mendes refused to admit they walked at a sedated snail's pace so the paparazzi could grab a good shot, saying that the viral video merely captured a moment when they were "pretty overwhelmed by the world [and] . . . were just like, 'Let's just walk slow and kind of just meditate,'" but it's hard to see their shuffle as anything but an example of two very famous musicians who are unable to perform thanks to a global pandemic and therefore in, to use Madonna's words, "dire need of attention."

But thirst—a desire to be perceived by the public—is not inherently Who-y; what's Who-y is the visible effort that goes into satiating that thirst. Plenty of Thems are capable of seeking attention without appearing thirsty. When Beyoncé posts a random photo dump on her Instagram grid, the photos are usually so well composed and styled (and presumably taken by a professional photographer) that you reject the urge to think of her as being "in dire need of attention," as likely as that may be. She's just reminding us that she is, in fact, one of the most famous people in the world. When Taylor Swift pops by Via Carota for the third time in a single week with her latest best friend, the paparazzi images are littered with the dropped jaws of bystanders. Even if she called upon her own photogs (or the paps in Tree's contacts list) to show up, how Who-y can a photo be when it features normal people gawking in obvious states of starstruck disbelief? There are plenty of reasons a celeb might want control of their paparazzi photos—vanity being above all else—so why not call (and, likely, *pay*) for them yourself?

Another common form of Who-y behavior begins with a primal urge for what anyone living under capitalism experiences: money. Well, not just money: *more* money. When we see people in our everyday lives take an extra job to pay for an increase in rent or for a growing family, we're impressed by their tenacity while simultaneously resentful we have to live in a world where wages haven't kept up with inflation. But when we see celebrities take on an extra job, on the other hand, we find them greedy and distasteful. Sure, he has two kids, but after selling his tequila company for a billion dollars, does George Clooney really *need* another Nespresso paycheck? Does Jennifer Lopez's bank account, already bursting at the seams, need even more commas in its balance? *Don't you people have enough?*

■ ■ ■

IT'S EASY TO ask ourselves those questions. That is, until a celebrity creates a product we're willing to consume, at which point the cynicism goes right out the window (along with the money we've spent on the product). Sometimes a very famous person wants to make a little extra dough by starting a particular type of side hustle one would more reasonably expect from a less famous person. In this way it's not *quite* spon—especially if they decide to slap their name on the product, which they often do. These business ventures typically consist of home goods (Drew Barrymore's air fryers for Target), beauty products (FLOWER Beauty by Drew Barrymore), and alcohol brands (Barrymore Wines), but our personal favorite reflects our own industry: the launch of an all-new media outlet.

For the better part of a century, one of the Themmiest surnames in this country has been Kennedy. The lineage descending from Joseph P. Kennedy Sr., father of John, Ted, Bobby, Eunice, and so on, is the closest thing this country has to long-standing royalty. And in the mid-1990s, the closest thing we had to a prince, the media darling John F. Kennedy Jr., launched a magazine of his own called *George,* despite not being named George and having no experience working at magazines. Well before the term was applied to his much younger relatives, including Arnold's son Patrick Schwarzenegger; Twitter favorite Jack Schlossberg; and Chris Pratt's wife, Katherine Schwarzenegger-Pratt, we had an all-timer nepo-baby moment: the high-profile announcement of a business that existed solely because its creator, JFK Jr., was the preternaturally sexy and beloved son of President John F. Kennedy and Jacqueline Kennedy Onassis.

George was ridiculed by seemingly everyone in the press, which is acceptable because poking fun at nepo babies is almost always punching up. (Unless, of course, you are a nepo-baby *journalist,* like the son of journalist Carl Bernstein and writer/director Nora Ephron, Jacob Bernstein, in whose case it's more of a lateral swing.) Six months ahead of its inaugural issue, *The New York Times* introduced the magazine to readers, writing with a smirk, "Its editor and publisher have no publishing experience. Its parent company puts out fashion, automobile and decorating magazines but knows nothing about political magazines, which is what *George* will be, or sort of be. If all this sounds like a less than surefire formula for success, hold on." It was media-on-media violence, and we loved it. And why *wouldn't* they poke fun at such a silly idea? The whole endeavor was a head-scratcher.

George's first cover reveal represents a time when Thems who decided to expand their personal brands—or even acknowledge the existence of personal brands at all—were genuinely newsworthy. At the press conference during which the magazine was announced, John John is standing behind a podium in a slim-fitting double-breasted black suit, hair coiffed like the politician everyone imagined he'd eventually be. (Horny members of *any* political party would vote for him.) He's smiling proudly at the cameras, extending his right hand to point at a poster-sized print of the cover. *Look at this incredible thing,* he seems to be thinking. *Isn't this amazing? I did this. This is all me. My daddy was JFK, by the way. Yes, like the airport.* Your eyes, which were initially focused on the handsome, famous man doing the gesturing, now slowly pan to the object at which he's gesturing: a photo of Cindy Crawford styled as what can only be described as the result of an *America's Next Top Model* challenge where Tyra makes the contestants dress up like sexy presidents. Her wig is cropped and gray, and she's wearing a ruffled colonial jabot under her military coat. Her navel is exposed. It's a good photo! She's even smizing! Cindy Crawford has never looked less than stunning. But as a magazine's declaration of intent, it's comically baffling.

In 2019, *The Hollywood Reporter* published a very entertaining oral history of *George*. It's one of the rare long features that isn't tied to any particular news item or anniversary, and instead to the simple fact of the magazine being a thing that happened. (It's a funny thing to remember, *whenever* you happen to remember it!) In it, Joe Armstrong, adviser and friend of Jacqueline Kennedy Onassis, and Rosemarie Terenzio, JFK Jr.'s executive assistant, explain how the magazine got its name. Armstrong recalls a week he spent with Jackie on Martha's Vineyard while John John was on vacation in Vietnam with his girlfriend Daryl Hannah. You might suspect that Kennedy called and told his mother, "Mummy, tell Joe that I was going through the tunnels in Vietnam and it hit me today that the magazine ought to be named *George*." But Terenzio claims that the name actually came from Lou Adler, a music producer who happened to be Hannah's brother-in-law. Kennedy thanked Adler for his input, recalls Terenzio, "by putting him on the masthead." Back then, we didn't have a term for a nepo baby who decided to launch a magazine without any experience in journalism and have his Themmy girlfriend's brother-in-law name it. Today, we'd call it utterly Who-y.

Martha Stewart launching a magazine is Themmy. Oprah launching a magazine is Themmy. Even for Chip and Joanna Gaines, the Texan couple who shot to fame in the 2010s thanks to their HGTV show that popularized something called shiplap, launching a magazine is Themmy. These are all celebrities for whom a media enterprise made clear, discernible business sense as an extension of their existing brand. An action as Themmy as launching a magazine becomes Who-y when it has no clear tie to the celebrity's existing brand. Jackie O, with her career as a book editor, could have launched a magazine and it would have been Themmy. Even Carolyn Bessette, with her status as a fashion icon and muse, could have launched a magazine in a way that would have been seen as Themmy.

This is all to say that there is something deeply humanizing about an incredibly famous person who does something random and totally out of their wheelhouse in order to achieve some kind of monetary or reputational gain. Had JFK Jr. announced his candidacy for, oh, *mayor of New York City* at a 1995 press conference in lieu of pointing at a photo of Cindy Crawford in Revolutionary War drag, the country would have likely accepted it as something inevitable: the child of a famous politician following in the footsteps of his famous parents. Much like when Jack Schlossberg, JFK Jr.'s nephew, announced his run for Congress. Lack of experience be damned! At least he had finally stepped up and made a decision to do something the public could understand. Thems are Thems in part because they are so well defined, at least professionally. We are familiar with, and in many cases monetarily support, their skills and their abilities, so when they surprise us by stepping out of their proverbial lane, we recoil in disgust or simply laugh. Actors should act, singers should sing, and the children of famous politicians should date them, run for office, or both.

To best explain what makes a business Who-y, it's important to mention one that absolutely is not. One of the most famous celebrity-run business ventures is Newman's Own, the nonprofit American food brand begun by Paul Newman in 1982. Here was one of the most famous actors of a generation using his image and his name (they're both in the logo) to do something objectively good—Newman pledged to donate all after-tax profits to charity. When you buy a bottle of Newman's Own Caesar dressing, part of you has a sinking suspicion that you've somehow contributed to the gas tank of his grandchildren's private jets. What kept the venture from dinging his reputation and fame level in those final decades of his life was its pro-social admirability. After the brand was launched, Newman went on to receive two Oscars, one Emmy, one Tony nomination, two Grammy nominations, and one role in which he voiced a blue racing car for Pixar, which suggests that all that salad dressing did nothing to tarnish the love showered upon him by fans and critics alike. But not every career swerve taken by a Them goes down as easily or as inspirationally as Newman's benevolent entrepreneurial venture. Sometimes celebrities do good, and sometimes they just do Goop.

Gwyneth Paltrow founded Goop in 2008, nine years after winning an Oscar for *Shakespeare in Love* (a movie in which she is legitimately radiant) and four months after starring in *Iron Man,* a movie she barely remembers making. (When reminded by *Vanity Fair* that she had been in seven Marvel films, Paltrow responded, "That can't be right. I can't have been in seven. Is that true?" Reader, it was.) Like Paul Newman, Paltrow put herself in her brand's name. Unlike him, she split the moniker apart and added two spooky vowels because a friend and branding executive named Peter Arnell told her that "all big internet companies had two o's." (Look what happened to Yahoo!) The company's first iteration was an almost painfully basic newsletter in which Paltrow shared recipes she enjoyed cooking for her family—like banana nut muffins and turkey ragù—and hotels she recommended for people visiting London, like Blake's and the Berkeley. From the jump, *Goop* was decidedly not relatable. Paltrow's version of lifestyle content was shamelessly aspirational, and though she didn't acknowledge her privilege explicitly (that kind of transparency was still a decade or more away from being the norm), she asserted it with every keystroke. As it was founded amid the glory days of blogging, *Goop* received its fair share of criticism from snarky publications like *LaineyGossip, Salon, Gawker,* and *Jezebel.* Nevertheless, and despite a growing chorus of internet commenters who couldn't stop complaining about such a brazen and unrelatable ode to rich people spending money, *Goop* persisted. The brand was, in a sense, *Martha Stewart Living* for the digital age: an instruction manual for living with wealth. But unlike Paltrow, Stewart *became* a Them by doing this kind of aspirational lifestyle content. Paltrow already was one, and the shocking left turn at the peak of her career was a risk. That the risk paid off made it an anomaly.

5 Unrelatable Things *Goop* Has Recommended to Its Readers

- A candle that smells like Gwyneth Paltrow's vagina ($75)
- An Hermès mahjongg set ($46,000)
- Sennheiser Orpheus earphones ($55,000)
- A Ouija board designed by Edie Parker ($1,995)
- A La Grande toothpaste squeezer that "lets no paste go to waste" ($340)

Nearly twenty years later, Goop is still around. Thanks in part to Paltrow's pseudo-retirement from acting, it has become a primary element of her legacy. When seeing her in our Instagram feeds or on the cover of a magazine, one no longer assumes it's because she's promoting a film or television show; we assume she's promoting the Goop lifestyle. Take a video she posted in the summer of 2024 from a villa in Italy. It opens with her topless (just boxers and a long braid) at a beautiful stove, cooking what she describes as "a Tuscan inspired high protein #boyfriendbreakfast skillet with sausage from the local butcher, white beans, spinach, cherry tomatoes and of course eggs." There's no call to action directing her fans to a recipe or blog post on Goop's website—she's not selling the Le Creuset cast-iron pan the dish is cooked in or the comfy white shorts she later wears while stirring sausage, but it oozes the vibes that Goop can potentially help its readers imitate. The Oscar winner's most lucrative skill was once acting. But now it's being an object of envy. (Or, more kindly, aspiration.) By persisting through those early years of criticism, Paltrow was able to turn Who-y behavior into something so Themmy, it inspired other Thems to try lifestyle entrepreneurship for themselves. But the work of her imitators rarely transcends Who-y behavior, meaning the endeavors either shut down fairly quickly, like Blake Lively's disastrous Preserve.us, or persist without making much cultural impact, like Dua Lipa's *Service95:* a newsletter that has enough devoted readers to warrant a full-time staff of writers and editors but has never once come close to causing as much of a stir as Goop's jade eggs. Even Kourtney Kardashian's Poosh, the similarly double-o'd lifestyle website (its name so close to Goop, reads as a *Saturday Night Live* parody), was a mere cultural blip in comparison to other, larger Kardashian ventures.

IT'S IMPORTANT TO remember that a Them's side hustle is not necessarily Who-y. Beauty brands like Rihanna's Fenty and Hailey Bieber's Rhode Cosmetics were instant successes, bringing both their founders to entirely new echelons of wealth that were arguably impossible via their original income streams of music and modeling stardom, respectively. Celebrity alcohol brands are so prevalent at this point that people like George Clooney, Ryan Reynolds, and Beyoncé can launch them without risking Themmy degradation. (Not to mention, if and when they flop, no one really notices.) The market is so saturated with those kinds of celebrity-endorsed products that to release one is almost an expectation of Thems these days. The Who-y investments are the ones that have no precedent, coming out of left field and leaving their fans in a near daze wondering why, exactly, someone whose movies or music they loved is now suddenly selling, among other things, *sponges*. As in, the ones you scrub pots with. In your kitchen. You know, the thing in your sink that you probably should have thrown away when it started getting stinky two weeks ago. Hold that thought.

In 2014, after nearly two decades in show business, Eva Mendes stopped acting. There was no formal announcement, no long magazine profile, no press release or oddly written Notes app screenshot posted to her Instagram grid. She just stopped appearing on screens, big and small. But after she'd spent the better part of two decades with constant acting work, it didn't take long for fans to notice her absence. Nearly a decade later, a reporter from *Variety* asked her straight: *Why'd you quit?* "I got tired fighting for the good roles," she said, adding that her focus turned to parenting after she and Themmy boyfriend Ryan Gosling had children. "I don't really miss it."

But Mendes wasn't talking to *Variety* to explain her absence from Hollywood. She was promoting something. Not a movie or a television show or a memoir, but sponges. *Her* brand of kitchen-sink sponges—made by Skura, a company she co-owns. Mendes spoke to *Variety* amid a mini press tour, also appearing on NBC's *Today,* which projected the chyron "EVA MENDES ON HOLLYWOOD, FAMILY & PASSION PROJECT." (The "passion project" being a sponge company.) She stole scenes from Will Smith in *Hitch,* she showcased her dramatic talents in *We Own the Night,* and she even flexed some European art-house sensibility in the Cannes hit *Holy Motors,* but as it turns out what she *really* wanted to do now was to help people clean their kitchens. Or so she was saying. *Variety*'s interview with Mendes ends in mid-thought, with a quote from Mendes about how the pandemic turned her into a clean freak.

> "Like so many people, I was cleaning like a freak and overly doing it," Mendes recalled. "I ordered a bunch of sponges, but Skura stood out to me. The fact that it has the fade to change technology

and it's made out of polyurethane and not cellulose and it doesn't hold onto bacteria."

That's the story's ending quote, *its kicker*! Like, *We'll leave you here, with this to take with you and to think about when you think about Hollywood star Eva Mendes.* It's as if reporter Marc Malkin had been so confused to hear Mendes say the words "polyurethane," "cellulose," and "bacteria" that he ejected from the cockpit without bothering to land the plane. That's what happens when a Them behaves in a Who-y way; it leaves us discombobulated, unnerved. Had she announced a return to acting—maybe a stint on Broadway or a role in an indie film—we would have been elated. (She's getting back to her roots! How chic! How understated!) Instead, we're just sitting here laughing at a morning television interview during which the star of *Hitch* tells a reporter how much she hates when her kitchen sponges get stinky. You may decry relatability, but there's a line there and she crossed it, into camp.

Some Thems engage in embarrassing extracurricular behavior that would never in a million years be labeled Who-y. The most effective antidote to perceived Whoiness is well-received creative output. Stars like Ben Affleck and Jennifer Lopez have proven themselves as generational Thems for whom the rules of celebrity simply do not apply. It's not that they break the rules, it's that the ones they create for themselves are more powerful than the status quo. If a Them is a Who at heart—someone who loves being as public of a person as possible, who will accept any offered brand deal, who will speak candidly each time a microphone is in front of them—their Them status will never be in question as long as they're making work that the public adores. And one of our Whoiest Thems is the person for whom the word "multihyphenate" feels like an understatement: Tyra Banks.

Just a few years after bursting onto the modeling scene in 1988, Banks decided that one job wasn't enough. She started acting in 1993, in an appearance on *The Fresh Prince of Bel-Air,* which she followed up with a role in John Singleton's acclaimed film *Higher Learning.* In 2003 she created and hosted the reality competition series *America's Next*

Top Model, a long-running project that did more to further her own career than those of its contestants, none of whom ever lived up to the show's titular promise. Later, she launched a daytime talk show, predating other Themmy non-journalists like Drew Barrymore and Jennifer Hudson's entries in the format by nearly two decades. Off-camera, she pursued an interest in writing, and published her first YA novel, the utterly bizarre dystopian sci-fi fantasy *Modelland,* in 2010. Two years later, she was among the first high-profile celebrity attendees of Harvard's Executive Education Program, which she cited upon announcing her beauty brand, Tyra Beauty, in 2014. "Do you know how good it feels to tell the world why I attended Harvard Business School?" she asked *People* at the time. After Tyra Beauty shuttered in 2017 amid claims it was nothing but a predatory multi-level marketing scheme, she returned to Harvard to "[ponder] the massive undertaking" of launching a Modelland theme park in Santa Monica. When Covid put a stop to that particular kind of in-person group experience, and unwilling to let her multiple stints at Harvard Business School go to waste, she pivoted once more. SMiZE Cream, the first iteration of her ice-cream brand, named for her most iconic invented word ("smize" means to smile with your eyes), was launched just a year into the pandemic as a direct-to-consumer product, with packs of four pints shipped for a whopping $89.95. (That's roughly $22.50 per pint.) The venture was both unpredictable and inscrutable, with its central selling point being that it included a "SMiZE surprise" in every pint that few understood until dishing out the cash to try it for themselves. When she changed the name from SMiZE Cream to SMiZE & DREAM in 2023, Banks claimed it was to highlight the company's focus on "building dreams," though many suspected the actual rationale was because potential customers assumed SMiZE Cream was yet another beauty product.

The story of SMiZE & DREAM could fill an entire book, but the way it exemplifies Thems behaving Whoily can be summarized in just two sentences: (1) She opened brick-and-mortar stores in just four locations (Washington, D.C.; Santa Monica, California; Dubai, UAE; and Sydney, Australia) without ever giving a comprehensible explanation as to why she chose them; devoted her social-media presence to promoting the brand in a nonstop stream of bizarre videos detailing her creative process; launched something called Hot Ice Cream in the winter of 2025 despite the fact that "hot ice cream" doesn't make any sense; and was sued for $2.8 million by a former landlord for allegedly breaking the terms of a ten-year lease for a SMiZE & DREAM location in Washington, D.C. (2) Despite all of those peculiar, arguably desperate developments unbefitting of someone at her level of fame, *People* magazine was there chronicling the business with exclusive reporting from the jump. Even when launching one of the most inexplicable celebrity businesses of the century, Tyra Banks is a Them audiences care about.

In the summer of 2025, another of our Whoiest Thems, Katy Perry, "went to space" on a rocket owned by Amazon founder Jeff Bezos, then-fiancé of her dear friend Lauren Sanchez—alongside Oprah Winfrey's best friend Gayle King, Sanchez herself, and a pair of actual scientists. The stunt garnered a nauseating amount of coverage from respected news outlets, including the cover of *Elle*. ("For All Womankind: The Stars of Blue Origin's All-Female Flight," the cover read, equating their eleven-minute flight with 1969's moon landing.) Sanchez and her almost-astronaut friends were covered by what seemed like every living publication: the highbrow, the lowbrow, and every random website in between. But for Perry (the only true Them aboard) it was ultimately a Who-y act. Aligning herself so closely with a billionaire who represents everything wrong with culture rendered her both desperate and embarrassing. But! But!! Or (as the Katycat in us wants to argue), it's doubtful that Perry would have even agreed to the flight had it not followed the disastrous rollout of her critically maligned and commercially ignored seventh studio album, *143*. Her ascension into an atmospheric region technically defined as "space" was an act of thirst meant to garner any sort of positive press. Fresh off record-breaking tours and Grammy-winning new music, artists like Beyoncé or Taylor Swift never would have set foot in that shuttle. Not because they wouldn't dare align themselves with an evil billionaire but because their thirst had recently been satiated.

No matter our light ribbing, the Who–Them binary is ultimately not a value judgment. Though we may roll our eyes at Katy Perry subjecting herself to a dangerous fake-astronaut mission in an attempt to win back the love of her once-adoring public, not every instance of Who-y behavior is something to laugh at. As ever, context is crucial! In many instances, Who-y behavior is a result of structural inequities that render a Them's preferred, or at the very least formerly lucrative, career path untenable. For every Meryl Streep or Julia Roberts, women who have maintained a consistent level of fame and success for several decades, there are myriad celebrities whose cinematic peaks were followed by the middle-age career slump suffered by so many women in Hollywood, and further followed by periods of peculiar choices that were largely a result of the industry's deep-seated misogyny and racism. When Themmy opportunities begin to dry up—roles that bring in critical acclaim, huge paydays, and maybe even awards—actors are left with three options: retire, change careers, or pivot to Whoiness. Before mocking a celebrity for selling a random product on their Instagram, it's worth asking why they might have made the decision to do so. If the answer is pure thirst, laugh away. If it's more complicated, maybe gift them a double-tap and move on.

If *Who? Weekly* were an actual publication, like our namesake *Us Weekly*, we'd probably have a section inspired by their long-running feature "Stars—They're Just Like Us!," a weekly photo spread of very famous people doing banal things like pumping gas, taking out the trash, or tipping a barista. (Or perhaps more likely *not* tipping a barista.) Perhaps ours would be called "Thems—They're Just Like Whos!," in which we point out Thems doing Who-y things like, oh, launching a lifestyle brand (like Meghan Markle), starting a podcast (like Amy Poehler), or randomly telling their fans how much they love playing *Warhammer 40,000* (like Henry Cavill). With every passing year, it feels like celebrities are becoming more and more comfortable letting the guard down on their Themminess, so we'd have plenty of instances to publish. Let's just say it's good for our media dreams that launching magazines is no longer a lucrative possibility, because *Who* is already the name of a long-running Australian tabloid magazine—

one that does often cover its share of Whos, like Australians Robert Irwin and Ruby Rose.

Celebrities have realized that the shortening of news cycles and attention spans (thanks to an unending spigot of content) means shame is less of a virtue than ever before. For the most part, celebrities can now be thirsty—for either attention or a little extra dough—and not face extended consequences from fans and commentators. There's simply too much other stuff, both high- and lowbrow, to be concerned with. It's shame immunity that led to the 2025 Super Bowl being chock-full of poorly written and conceived ads starring Thems. Keke Palmer told us to play a Monopoly app on our phones; Greta Gerwig and Charli XCX told us to use Uber Eats; Bad Bunny told us to eat Ritz crackers. Ten years ago such a display would have been debasing for everyone involved, but these days we forget everything the day after it happens. Remember when Super Bowl ads were as big of a deal as the Super Bowl itself? It's been a while since Super Bowl ads genuinely made the rounds, and now these brands have to fight with Taylor Swift and Travis Kelce for coverage.

Beyond just sponsored content and crisis management, Who-y behavior is fundamentally grounded in a Them's dire need for attention, and the easiest way to secure it is via social media. It may be difficult to remember now, but before they became cesspools of recommended and sponsored content, Twitter and Instagram, when they were first launched in 2006 and 2010, respectively, were mere microblogging platforms meant for following people you *actually knew*. Before algorithmically delivered content fully took over the internet, these were platforms where the non-famous and famous alike would easily share a quick thought or photo with their followers. It was casual, off-the-cuff, and unrestricted by any sort of expectations. If anything, celebrities first imitated us normies on social media, relishing the opportunity to speak "directly" to their fans, especially the ones who really *got* them. It took a few years, but celebrities learned that it would become professionally dangerous to be "real" on social media when their old, offensive tweets posted and forgotten long ago resurfaced to haunt them, sometimes even coming close to derailing their careers. Chrissy Teigen, James

Gunn, and Kevin Hart have all apologized for offensive sentiments shared in years-old tweets. Before long, Thems and Whos alike abandoned these apps' original intentions (reality!) in favor of posting sponsored content and promotions for their various artistic and business ventures. But a rarefied group have kept on keeping on with those old-school, stream-of-consciousness-style posts. In many instances, the posts don't seem thirsty at all. Cher tweets as though the app is an extension of her brain, sharing oddly punctuated and capitalized messages like "Oh SHIT / GUMMY BEARS fk" or a simple, elegant address to self of "@cher hi." ("I'm dyslexic & #'s Are hard 4 me," she also tweeted.) Meanwhile, over on Instagram, Viola Davis can hardly go a day without reposting a pixelated inspirational message of unknown origin, flooding her feed with sentiments like "I have a theory that life meets you at your level of audacity" and "Courage is being yourself every day in a world that tells you to be someone else." Both of these undeniable Thems post like their lives depend on it, but not for attention, not out of *thirst*. There is a rare purity to their posts, none of which reek of ulterior, narcissistic motives. Constant posting is only Who-y when it seems hellbent on making headlines and ruffling feathers. (Not, like, inspiring the masses.) And when it comes to Thems behaving Whoily on the internet, few are doing it like Nicki Minaj.

As one of the bestselling and most influential female musical artists of all time, Minaj's legacy is solid as a rock. In the pantheon of greatest rappers of all time, even when her music underperforms, her catalog remains both relevant and pervasive—with songs like "Starships" (which is both cringe and addictive) and "Monster" (the Kanye West song on which she delivered one of the most legendary verses of the modern rap era). But instead of sitting back in her home with her family, enjoying her success in private—or even just posting Cher-like missives online like "Watching *The Sopranos* for the first time, omg"—Minaj seems to have an insatiable thirst for attention at any cost. Whether responding to anonymous haters with eye-roll emojis, bending the knee to President Trump, or starting beef with other celebrities like Cardi B, with whom she sparred back and forth on Twitter in the days following the release of the latter's sophomore album in 2025. In one of many responses to Minaj's tweets, Cardi B wrote,

> Why you keep bringing up my album?? It's not the gag that you think it is . . [.] You been in the game like 16 years . . [.] you need to compare yourself to YOUR peers that started around YOUR time. Rihanna, Taylor swift, Drake . . . those are the numbers you need to be competing wit and you can't cuz you doing lower than all of them . . . I was in high school when you came out wtf is you comparing yourself to me for???

The answer, ultimately, is because she can't truly enjoy her Themdom unless the spotlight is shining directly on her.

LET'S GO BACK to 1995, where this chapter began. Madonna was on top of the world (also physically atop the MTV VMAs pre-show platform) when she grinned and bore Courtney Love's compact-throwing—literally seated above it all, calmly and comfortably in her unquestioned Themdom. Her career would continue as it had for the previous decade, bouncing back and forth from generation-defining displays of cultural relevance like 1998's *Ray of Light* and 2005's *Confessions on a Dance Floor* to less successful ones like 2003's *American Life* and 2012's *Rebel Heart*. Though she was still a Them in 2022 (despite not having released a song that cracked *Billboard*'s Top 10 in a decade), she had a compact moment of her own, taking to social media to post a series of videos and images that were so bizarre and out of the blue that they received coverage like "Fans Alarmed by Madonna's 'Disturbing' New TikTok: 'What Happened to Her?'" and "Madonna's 'Unsettling' Pre-Grammys TikTok Video Sparks Fan Concern." In one of the videos, she lip-syncs to a song by rapper Baby Keem, mouthing along to the lyrics "*Have you ever been punched in your motherf–king face? What you say? Oh, you haven't? Alright, wait.*"

(OK!) In a series of images posted to her stories, she shared the message, "I have a confession to make. I was not circumsized [*sic*]." (OK?) *Page Six* called the confession "bizarre," and it indeed was, but more than that, it was Who-y. Why did Madonna need to remind her fans of her existence not with a caption-free selfie or an open-mouth smile that showcased her new grille? It was that dire, never-ending need for attention.

Do we need to bring back shame? Tall Australian actor Jacob Elordi, while promoting his Oscar-nominated role as perhaps our tallest Frankenstein monster, was asked by *The Wall Street Journal* what "lost art" he wished would "come back in style." "The art of shame," he quickly replies, as if it's something he's been thinking about for a while. "I wish people could experience shame a little heavier." To describe shame as an art, and not a reactionary emotion, is potent. Shame forces us to acknowledge the ways our actions can change the lives of others, placing us respectfully into a community. Without shame, politicians engage in reprehensible behavior without fear of being ousted by their constituents. Without shame, civilians say and do horrific things to others without the fear of facing any consequences. Without shame, Thems behave like Whos. The lines between the categories become blurred, making the two indistinguishable. So maybe it's time to start feeling shame again. If not for the good of the world, then at least for the good of our podcast. If Whos and Thems start acting exactly the same, well, there goes our entire concept.

Chapter 5

How Reality TV Changed the Reality of Celebrity

Elizabeth Hasselbeck, Kim Kardashian & Donald Trump

On August 23, 2000, nearly half of all American televisions that were powered on were tuned to CBS for the first-ever season finale of *Survivor,* a reality show created by Mark Burnett in which sixteen non-famous people (known as "castaways") were stranded in Borneo, Malaysia, and tasked with competing against one another until only one remained: the ultimate survivor and recipient of $1 million. Though audiences tuned in primarily to see who would be walking away with the grand prize, the episode's greatest moment afforded them the pleasure of watching one of the best monologues not just in television history but in the history of the English language. After being voted off the show earlier in the episode, no-nonsense truck driver Sue Hawk revealed which of the two remaining contestants she would be voting for. In what has come to be known as the "Snake vs. Rat Speech," Hawk said her vote would go not to Kelly, the rat, but rather to Richard, the snake. "If I were ever to pass you along in life again, and you were laying there, dying of thirst," she said to Kelly, "I would not give you a drink of water. I would just let the vultures take you, and do whatever they want with you, with no ill regrets." By the season's conclusion, America hadn't just become obsessed with watching people compete for obscene amounts of money—game shows had been commonplace on the small screen for decades—it had become obsessed with unscripted drama. *Survivor* changed television, but Hawk's speech, with its shocking pettiness and vitriol, changed celebrity. The vicious fights on *Real Housewives,* the shamelessness of *The Bachelor,* the presumption that appearing on just one season of a reality show can result in years of notoriety . . . none of it would exist without Sue Hawk voting for a snake to receive a million bucks over a rat.

These days there are myriad channels through which any cast member of a reality or competition show can maintain or even grow their fame. Unlike traditional entertainment career paths—actor, singer, musician—the reality-TV industrial complex is designed for making Whos out of Nahs. And for most who find themselves on a reality television show, aspiring to Themdom is folly; for every Cardi B (who shot to fame after appearing on VH1's *Love & Hip Hop: New York*) there are about 340 Raqi Thundas (who shot to this page of our book after appearing on VH1's *Love & Hip Hop: New York*). It's much smarter to cultivate a small niche of fans and give them as much as you possibly can across channels that have been designed to support you.

Search "What's Richard Hatch up to?" on Google and marvel at the way reality stars of yesteryear would quickly and assuredly fade into relative obscurity after their shows (or respective seasons) went off the air. During the two-hour finale of *Survivor's* first season, 51.7 million people tuned in to watch Hatch win a million dollars (as well as the generationally hideous clown car for aspiring outdoorspeople, the Pontiac Aztek). But after the talk-show circuit where Hatch discussed the thrill of the experience with popular hosts like David Letterman, Rosie O'Donnell, and Conan O'Brien, he quickly fell off the cultural map. Sure, that was in part due to his legal troubles involving domestic violence and tax evasion, but even without those hiccups Hatch had his first brush with fame while participating in a nascent system that had not yet grown accustomed to making long-term celebrities of people who win a filmed competition show. No matter *how* much skin they showed.

The first attempt at turning a *Survivor* contestant into a working entertainer came in June 2001, less than a year after the first season finale aired. As the eleventh contestant voted off the island, Colleen Haskell ended the show somewhere in the middle of its run, but she was arguably the season's most charming cast member. Young, beautiful, and down to parlay her reality-show fame into uncharted waters, she accepted a role in the studio comedy *The Animal*. The formula had worked some five years prior, when Australian *Real World: London* cast member Jacinda Barrett used the nascent but influential reality show as a springboard for what would be a prolific, if decidedly Who-y, acting and modeling career. The problems with Haskell's attempt at a similar pivot, however, were threefold: First, she would be playing the love interest of Rob Schneider, a former *SNL* star known for badly reviewed gross-out comedies; second, the movie was about a man whose internal organs are replaced with those of wild animals by a mad scientist, rendering him, well, more animalistic; third, Haskell could not act her way out of an opened paper bag inside which was a neon sign that read THIS WAY OUT. Her final line, and the film's penultimate, is as poorly delivered as it is written: "I guess there really is someone for everybody, even if you have to make them out of animal parts." (Meryl Streep herself couldn't sell that, so what do you expect from someone who was famous for coming in sixth place on a reality competition show?) Needless to say, Haskell did not act in another film after *The Animal* crashed and burned at the box office.

The show's second-season winner, Tina Wesson, did some press after her big win in the Australian outback, but the show's 30 million viewers didn't seem all that invested in her life after the victory. She quickly faded into obscurity and, unlike Hatch, doesn't even have her own dedicated Wikipedia page. An Instagram profile appearing to be hers has just over a thousand followers, and chronicles the life of a happily non-famous woman living a normal, happily off-camera life. Scrolling through its few posts, all of which were shared in 2025, you'd see a caption-free selfie in which she's smiling ear to ear and a snap of a headless rattlesnake, a streak of blood beside the lifeless nub opposite its tail, which she's captioned, succinctly, "Can't have this living by the house!" As a former *Survivor* champion, it's entirely reasonable to assume Wesson, like Mrs. Dalloway before her, decided to decapitate the reptile herself.

Enter Elisabeth Filarski. Or perhaps we should start with her exit. At the time of her appearance on *Survivor*'s second season, the Puma shoe designer was a plucky, gorgeous, twenty-three-year-old ball of charisma. She was clever, kind, and well-spoken—an instant fan favorite whose late-game elimination rattled viewers. After her season aired, she learned from Haskell's mistakes and used her notoriety to quickly begin a presenting career, judging the Miss Teen USA pageant alongside former *Big Brother 2* contestant Krista Stegall in 2001, and later hosting *The Look for Less*, a show on the now-long-dead Style Network in which she "helped viewers find designer styles at bargain prices." Those gigs were proof that *Survivor* could act as a springboard to a broader career in Hollywood (jobs that don't involve being marooned in the hot, barren center of a continent), but they represented a modest kind of success: It was an accrual of IMDb credits that would make a *Survivor* fan think, simply and sweetly, *Good for her!* What Filarski did next, however, changed the expectations of reality TV stars—and reality TV *fans*—forever.

IN 1997, ABC EXECUTIVES "needed to fill the 11 A.M. weekday time slot," so they asked journalist Barbara Walters if she "had any ideas." As Ramin Setoodeh explains in his book *Ladies Who Punch*, Walters pitched a show in which "four or five women of different backgrounds, different generations, and different opinions . . . would discuss the topics of the day, mixing humor with intelligent debate." Her idea went on to become one of the most tumultuous, storied talk shows in television history, *The View*. The original cast was Walters (naturally), affable journalist Meredith Vieira, wisecracking lawyer Star Jones, raucous comedian Joy Behar, and, for a reason unknown to everyone other than the show's producers, a doe-eyed twenty-two-year-old production assistant with no TV experience named Debbie Matenopoulos. From the jump, the show was defined by the constantly revolving door through which hosts came and went; some women were fired, some quit for good, some quit and returned later. Audiences ate it up then, and still eat it up (albeit in smaller servings) three decades later. Hiring Matenopoulos wasn't Walters's best idea—the young woman was fired after two years of ceaseless public scrutiny—but Walters vowed to atone for her misjudgment by doing something genuinely groundbreaking. In 2003 she looked to the world of reality television to find a replacement for Matenopoulos, and found one in Elisabeth Filarski . . . sort of.

You see, something monumental happened *before* Elisabeth Filarski joined *The View*: She'd become Elisabeth Hasselbeck. In July 2002, just over a year after leaving the Australian outback, she married her college sweetheart. Tim Hasselbeck was an NFL player who was signed with the Philadelphia Eagles. In an instant, she was transformed from reality-star-turned-TV-host to reality-star-turned-TV-host/WAG. Marrying someone more famous than herself—a quarterback playing America's favorite sport—imbued her fame with a palpable sense of permanence. In the years that followed, Whos and Thems alike would find love on the football field with some regularity, but at the time there was a certain novelty to their love story, even though it pre-dated her first brush with fame. "In the US, we were not used to really taking people off reality shows yet," Brian Fons, the head of ABC Daytime at the time of Hasselbeck's hiring, told Setoodeh. But Elisabeth was, crucially, more than just a washed-up reality star; to those who cared about football, she was a *Hasselbeck*. (And to those who didn't? Well, they were probably already watching *The View* and would continue to do so no matter the lineup.)

Taking a risk on a reality star paid off. Hasselbeck's conservative Christian values made her a controversial figure on the left-leaning *The View*, and after a rough start, she and her paradoxical opinions led to captivating television for the better part of six years. Her tension with one particular co-host, the outspoken liberal comedian Rosie O'Donnell, reached a fever pitch in May 2007, when the two exchanged heated words during a debate about the Iraq War. It's almost quaint to revisit this nearly two decades later:

O'DONNELL: 655,000 Iraqi civilians are dead. Who are the terrorists?

HASSELBECK: Who are the terrorists?

O'DONNELL: 655[000] Iraqis—I'm saying you have to look—we invaded . . .

HASSELBECK: Wait, who are you calling terrorists?

O'DONNELL: I'm saying that, if you were in Iraq, and another country, the United States, the richest in the world, invaded your country and killed 655,000 of your citizens, what would you call us?

HASSELBECK: Are we killing their citizens or are their people also killing their citizens?

O'DONNELL: We are invading a sovereign nation and occupying a country against the U.N.

Not only did the moment dominate the headlines for a press cycle or two, it led to O'Donnell's early departure from the show. Just a month before their May tête-à-tête, O'Donnell had announced she would be leaving the show that coming June. But nine days after the fight, and a few weeks before her planned departure, she up and left, writing on her website: "When painting there is a point u must step away from the canvas as the work is done[,] anymore would take away." (She's always been a blogger at heart.) Hasselbeck, meanwhile, was living by the *Survivor* mantra—"Outwit, Outplay, Outlast"—with her new television venture, and by doing so she attracted as many haters as she did fans. Once O'Donnell departed, Hasselbeck grew more outspoken, and when she was fired from the show in 2013 for being "too extreme and right wing," she quickly found a home at, *where else?!*, Fox News, joining the cast of *Fox & Friends*.

By successfully dropping the "reality" from her title and becoming, simply, a television star, Elisabeth Hasselbeck became a case study for future generations of people who would treat the reality TV genre not as a mere blip in the story of their lives—fifteen minutes to savor and then, ultimately, put away—but as an entry-level job in a burgeoning industry, one that was new and exciting, with a rulebook that was being written in real time.

Reality stars still had no guaranteed way to extend their fifteen minutes to genuine Whodom (let alone Themdom), and Hasselbeck gave them a reason to believe such a thing was at least *possible.* Before she dominated two segments of network television in the aughts, the most notable extensions of reality-show fame could be found over on cable. Though it's been decades since MTV was known primarily for music videos—they killed the radio star before streaming killed them—they began experimenting with shows that ran counter to their name all the way back in 1992, just over a decade after launching. Before *Jersey Shore,* before *The Osbournes,* before *The Challenge*—before *Beavis and Butt-Head,* for chrissakes—MTV interrupted its music videos, music news, and music award shows with a humble reality show called *The Real World.*

WHEN IT PREMIERED on MTV in 1992, as videos for U2's "One" and Hammer's "This Is the Way We Roll" were in heavy rotation, *The Real World*'s conceit—placing seven non-famous young people into a single New York City apartment and asking them to live their lives together, on camera—was described as a "voyage of discovery," at least by the show's co-creator Mary-Ellis Bunim. Those first few seasons were indeed fascinating and groundbreaking television that introduced viewers to a young, telegenic, diverse, and opinionated group of people, including Pedro Zamora, who was one of the first people to disclose and speak openly about their HIV-positive status on television. Those early seasons were genuinely raw and revealing. Viewers watched the cast members learn from each other, fall in love with each other, grow to despise each other, and even slap each other through car windows—but nothing gold can stay. While Bunim's business partner, Jonathan Murray, had a background in news and documentary, she had come from the soap-opera world, and their show was on a channel for young people with shortening attention spans and a thirst for mayhem.

By the time *The Real World: Las Vegas* premiered in 2002, what began as a show about young people exchanging life lessons had lost most of its verité ideals and devolved into a shallow vessel for sloppy, if entertaining, behavior. (Try to *imagine* the things that Palms Casino Resort penthouse hot tub has seen . . . or don't.) Though comparisons to PBS's groundbreaking *An American Family,* the twelve-episode touchstone of the TV verité movement that chronicled the real-life troubles and triumphs of the Loud family in the 1970s, were apt in the mid-1990s, they all but vanished just a decade into its run.

The decline in the show's anthropological aspirations coincided with the rise of its spin-off series, *Road Rules,* effectively a gamified *Real World* on wheels. Three years after its 1995 premiere, Bunim and Murray had the brilliant idea to spin off *both* series into a show in which former cast members from *The Real World* and *Road Rules* competed for cash prizes. Originally called *Road Rules: All Stars,* the show was quickly renamed *Real World/Road Rules Challenge* and, later, *The Challenge.* But despite all the wonky title changes, the concept has remained relatively unchanged; for the past threeish decades, there has been a robust infrastructure by which people who rose to fame on MTV reality shows could stay both employed and (more important) famous without having to return to their former anonymous lives. We're shocked when a sitcom makes it more than a mere five seasons these days, but some of these contestants have spent a third of their life doing zip lines or whatever on camera. Chris "CT" Tamburello, whose first TV appearance was on *The Real World: Paris* in 2003, has appeared on twenty-one seasons of *The Challenge* since. Johnny Bananas (John Amadeus Devenanzio) debuted on MTV in *The Real World: Key West* in 2006. He's been in twenty-two seasons of *The Challenge* since! These men have better job security than a nurse practitioner. The idea of recycling reality stars may have begun on MTV, but it's since been copied by practically every network in the game. *Survivor* has its own All Stars seasons, as do *The Amazing Race* and *Big Brother.* Since Netflix entered the reality-show game in 2019, they, too, have discovered the benefits of bringing reality stars back for additional seasons of television. In a world where IP is king and original ideas feel increasingly less common, how is it any surprise that reality stars like Omarosa Manigault Newman (*The Apprentice, Celebrity Big Brother, The Surreal Life*); Harry Jowsey (*Too Hot to Handle, Perfect Match, Heartbreak Island*); and Kendra Wilkinson (*The Girls Next Door, Marriage Boot Camp, I'm a Celebrity . . . Get Me Out of Here*) are being treated like superpowerless versions of Batman, Wonder Woman, and the Hulk? It's grim, but the most reliable way for a reality star to maintain their fame (and a steady paycheck) after an introductory season of reality television is simple: Appear on another one.

Hasselbeck's initial post-*Survivor* job lasted just ten years. CT has been doing *The Challenge* for twice that long. In our increasingly precarious job market, where the number of reliable professions is dwindling at a rapid pace, it's quite something that reality stardom is one of the few fields that seems to be getting *more* secure.

That security, however, isn't accessible to every reality TV star. CT and Mr. Bananas treat *The Challenge* like their primary job. The show is unique in that respect—a world unto itself, not a chronicle of lives that exist outside its interactive gameboard. Compare that to *Survivor,* where even the show's biggest stars, like Parvati Shallow and Cirie Fields, can only appear on the occasional season that includes former cast members. Both Shallow and Fields have "real jobs," when they're not trying to impress Jeff Probst. (Shallow is a life coach and Fields works for a New Jersey healthcare company.)

BUT THE RISE of social media and influencer culture has allowed for a new generation of reality stars to learn from their forefathers and monetize their single season of television in a near instant. There's no need to return to the proverbial island, compete against Johnny Bananas, or even pivot to becoming an incendiary political commentator. Any first appearance on a reality show is this generation's version of "starting in the mail room." In the corporate world, you work your way up from assistant to manager, and maybe even to CEO. But not everyone can be a Kardashian (or marry into their family), so what's at the top of the hierarchy for the average reality star? Some start businesses like alcohol or lifestyle brands, while others make their businesses themselves through the monetization of memoir, meaning, *you know,* they start a podcast or a vlog.

The relative ease with which reality-show cast members are able to monetize and maintain their fame, becoming "working Whos," would not be possible without the blueprint created by the genre's First Family. While they represent the microscopic percentage of reality stars who worked their way up to become Thems, the Kardashians had a heavy hand in making it possible for other reality stars to become comfortable Whos. (And then, in rare cases, Thems.) In 2007, Kim Kardashian was famous only to the chronically online, which was more of a subgenre than it is today. Her father was the late Robert Kardashian, best known for being one of O. J. Simpson's attorneys during his 1995 murder trial for the killing of Nicole Brown Simpson and Ron Goldman, and the father of her half-siblings Kendall and Kylie is Caitlyn Jenner, an Olympic gold medalist turned inspirational speaker. But despite those famous-ish parents, Kim's big American family lived in relative anonymity in Calabasas, California, once merely an affluent city in the San Fernando Valley, before becoming an inescapable steamroller of popular culture. She grew up alongside some notable names—among them Paris Hilton (the great-granddaughter of Hilton Hotels founder Conrad Hilton, for whom Kim later worked in a professional capacity as a stylist-slash-closet-organizer) and Zoe Winkler (the daughter of Henry Winkler, aka "The Fonz")—but it wasn't until a sex tape starring Kim and Ray J Norwood (the brother of mononymous R&B star Brandy) was distributed by Vivid Entertainment that she became interesting enough to potentially lead a show. The origins of the tape, cheekily and/or ominously titled *Kim Kardashian, Superstar,* are muddy at best; Kim and her mother/manager, Kris, deny that she had any hand in brokering the tape's sale, while Kim's co-star Ray J disagrees. But for all the controversy surrounding the video's release, it was ultimately *Keeping Up with the Kardashians*' raison d'être; in fact, the very first episode is about the immediate aftermath of the tape's release.

In 2007, the only reality show about a famous family to have had any significant cultural impact was anchored by a much more famous person with a much more famous name: Ozzy Osbourne. The MTV series following the life of Ozzy and his family, *The Osbournes,* was a non-scripted sendup of classic family sitcoms from the middle of the twentieth century. The lead-up to the new millennium was a time rife with navel-gazing about how much the times were a-changin', and *The Osbournes* asked a question that reflected this general temperament: What if the twenty-first century's version of *Leave It to Beaver* starred the Prince of Darkness; his wife, Sharon; and their foulmouthed off-spring, Kelly and Jack? Were they the new portrait of the American family? Profane, loud, and . . . *British*? Eh, not really, but the show, as *The New York Times* put it at the time, "found resonance by delivering the opposite of everything MTV had represented since its inception in 1981. Instead of insisting that rock stars are inherently different from civilians—cooler, better-looking, more glamorous—it focused on how they are not." That *Us Weekly*'s regular feature "Stars—They're Just Like Us!" launched the same month as *The Osbournes* feels less like a co-incidence than a reflection of the way the general public's perception of fame was evolving in those early days of reality television and the always-on celebrity news cycle made possible by the internet. Famous people could now be presented as next-door neighbors from whom we could conceivably borrow a cup of sugar. Reality TV didn't just make fame feel more attainable, it made its resulting celebrities feel more ac-cessible. Their big, fabulous, affluent lives were *just* over the fence from our ordinary and utterly unfilmable ones. *The Osbournes* felt special at the time, and its success was at the forefront of TV host Ryan Seacrest's mind when he created *Keeping Up with the Kardashians* (*KUWTK*). "I loved watching *The Osbournes,* which was really the first show of [the genre], and started thinking about what another show could be like or who another show could be about," he said. After being introduced to the Kardashians, he was struck by their "chaotic" lives (also, you'd imagine, the sex tape of it all), and the show came together swiftly.

Early reviews of *KUWTK* were harsh, and not particularly prescient. Wrote *Variety*, "There's not much of a show here, and no discernible premise." But *The New York Times*' opening complaint has aged into something of a prophecy. At the very least it's a telling insight into the broader perception of reality stars at the time. "Kim," they wrote with obvious disdain, was "famous simply by dint of her aspiration to be." As in, if you wanted to be famous so badly, there were ways you could almost *will it to be so*. In 2007, becoming a celebrity through the brute force of a reality show, the most embarrassing and creatively bankrupt of genres, was as bewildering to audiences as it was maddening to those at the forefront of cultural criticism. Of all the people on this impossibly huge planet, why are we giving these eight rich weirdos the right to our attention when they didn't seem to have any discernible talents by which famous people had traditionally grown their fan bases? At least Kelly Osbourne wanted to parlay her reality stardom into a singing career, like her father had before her! Sure, it didn't work as well as she'd hoped, but the attempt was successful *enough*, and Kelly released a pair of moderately well-received albums before starting a career as a talk-show host and media personality like her mother. Kim and her sisters, on the other hand, didn't sing, act, dance, write, or have any interest in being talking heads outside of their own series, which is to say they didn't actively work to *create* anything entertaining. (Other than their show, which at that point they did not produce, write, or direct.) From the show's detractors, "famous for being famous" was lobbed as an insult. The Kardashians' job was appearing on a reality show, plain and simple, and if the mere act of being real meant they were *creators*, couldn't the same be said of literally everyone? The title proved prophetic. Like the apocryphal Joneses before them, the Kardashians would soon represent a lifestyle that everyone—from non-famous civilians to celebrities—seemed eager to keep up with. If one could make a living simply by being real in front of a camera . . . well, wouldn't that be nice?

In that first season, an eleven-year-old Kendall Jenner is chauffeured to various agencies by her mother as she attempts to land a modeling contract. Technically, it's a professional aspiration à la Kelly

Osbourne's singing career, but the scenes are as painful now as they were then, as she is, once again, *eleven years old*. The show presents those "go-sees" (shout-out once again to *America's Next Top Model*) as it does most of the family's absurd endeavors—such as the moment nine-year-old Kylie Jenner plays on her parents' stripper pole in the premiere episode, or the childish infighting following Khloé's DUI arrest in episode 5, even the *Girls Gone Wild* photoshoot that Kim, Khloé, and Kourtney try to hide from Caitlyn in episode 3—not as empathetic explorations of their goals but as vignettes chronicling their wacky, fame-hungry lives played for comedic effect. Back then, the juxtaposition between the family's privileged irreverence and the faux-relatable tone of the production was part of its charm: Why on earth would anyone actually want to *keep up* with these vapid, ridiculous people? But the family's willingness to endure ridicule resulted in nothing but success, even through life's "failures." For one, in 2011, Kim married NBA player Kris Humphries. The wedding was chronicled in a two-part episode during season 6, and made the cover of *People, Us Weekly, Hello,* and *Who? Weekly* (the Australian publication, not us), among others. Seventy-two days later, Kim filed for divorce. And when Kim's new boyfriend, Kanye West, joined the cast in season 8, the show's ratings were the highest they'd ever been.

But consistent Nielsen ratings were never the ultimate goal of *KUWTK*; rather, they were the means to a more capitalistic and unprecedented end. Though the show never received the curious critical acclaim of *The Osbournes,* it has lasted five times as long and, over the course of its run, evolved from being itself the entirety of the family's output to a marketing support system for their myriad external business ventures. In a 2015 interview with *Variety,* Kim revealed that one of her initial aspirations for *Keeping Up with the Kardashians* was to increase public awareness of Dash (a clothing store the sisters co-owned): "I was thinking [the series] might not last very long, but we'll grow a great business and expand online. I thought it would be great press. I didn't think it would turn into what it turned into." Though Kim, Kourtney, and Khloé's employment at Dash fueled minor subplots during the show's early seasons, the business never turned into a true retail empire, instead becoming more of a place for fans to engage with the show in person. Even a spin-off series dedicated to the store, 2015's *Dash Dolls*, ran just eight painful episodes. What Kim and her family seemed to be learning in real time was that their businesses didn't become famous by being chronicled by reality TV cameras.

It wasn't until 2009 that Kim became more seriously focused on extracurricular entrepreneurial empires. Without a blueprint, her early attempts at monetizing the family's fame beyond the show were technically successful but easy for the general public to ignore. Remember ShoeDazzle? Probably not. It was a subscription service in which users paid roughly $40 a month to get—forgive us—crap shoes, crap jewelry, or crap bags. The company still exists, currently rocking a 1-star rating on the Better Business Bureau's website. Later, she partnered with Lighthouse Beauty to launch a line of fragrances. In 2011, Lighthouse founder Chris Lighty said of Kim, "[She] has created her own brand, which has really be [*sic*] able to extend off-screen and out of the reality show arena it started in. She's not a one-horse show." The next horse in her show, to continue with Lighty's metaphor, would prove to be the most lucrative, at least up to a point. In 2014, Kim launched *Kim Kardashian: Hollywood,* an iPhone game in which users could simulate being a star of Kim's particular brightness. While it was free to download and play, spending real money allowed players (like, admittedly, both of us) to achieve their character's dreams more quickly—a gameplay feature that was so thematically on the nose that it almost hurts to think about. The game turned Kim into a respected businesswoman, as evidenced in a glowing *Forbes* cover in 2016 that labeled her one of the new "mobile moguls" for purportedly racking up over $160 million in sales through the game in just two years.

Kim Kardashian: Hollywood exemplifies the public's changing perception of reality stardom from its hilarious opening moments. Like most role-playing games, it begins with a character-creation experience, like *The Sims* or, for a more analog example, Dungeons & Dragons. But as you customize (or, as the game puts it, "kustomize") your avatar by selecting from the assortment of possible hairstyles, clothes, and accessories, it stands proudly on a red carpet, surrounded by stanchions and paparazzi. Before you craft any semblance of an identity, the game presents your character (kharacter?) as a star.

5 "Achievements" You Could Potentially Earn in *Kim Kardashian: Hollywood*

- Spotlight: "If you're afraid of large crowds and camera flashes, being a celebrity might not be for you."
- The Realest: "Stay in the public's eye by 5-starring reality projects."
- Illustrious in Italy: "1 in 10 Italians would give up espresso before giving up your show."
- Bundle of Style: "Babies appreciate nice clothes and hair just like everybody else. It's biological."
- Barfly: "The first step is to admit you have a problem. The next is to do booze-related things."

Back on TV, the other sisters quickly emulated Kim's strategy, beginning paradoxically with the youngest of the bunch launching a line of cosmetics called—what else?—Kylie Cosmetics, in 2015. Older sister Kendall's modeling career also reached new heights around this time; she landed her first *Vogue* cover in 2016 and solidified herself as part of the new class of supermodels, haters be damned. That same year, Khloé launched her denim brand, Good American. Even Kourtney, long characterized as the most traditional and family-oriented of the sisters, eventually launched a company. Her lifestyle website, the affiliate-link-filled Poosh, first began posting content in 2019. (Yes, a website can sometimes be a company!) All of their entrepreneurial successes merged with their personal dramas—from children and marriages to dramatic feuds with Taylor Swift—to continue to fuel the reality show. It's a vicious circle, and one that continues to make the Kardashians more powerful with every move they make. By its tenth year, *KUWTK* turned the idea of "famous for being famous" from pejorative to proven strategy; it was hard for a person to appear on any reality show, be it romantic (like *The Bachelor*) or competitive (like *Big Brother*), without believing that they were just one simple business decision away from parlaying reality stardom into a multimillion-dollar business. At the very least, they became acutely aware of the importance of having a social-media following. Even if you don't have the business acumen or connections to start, say, a beauty line, it doesn't take much effort to turn your highly followed social-media account into an advertising platform.

Re-premiering in 2022, the Kardashian-Jenners refreshed their reality show by switching networks from E! to Hulu and chopped off the first half of the show's title, the change implying that their most important work was finished. After years of myopic ridicule over their origin story, the world had finally caught up, and the show became, simply, *The Kardashians*.

BUT THERE'S A name we haven't yet mentioned, one that best, and most grimly, encapsulates the way reality television has fundamentally altered the way culture cultivates celebrity: Donald Trump. Though he was a famously despicable New York figure before the premiere of *The Apprentice* in 2004, the show—which followed eager businesspeople as they competed for a job in Trump's real-estate empire—catapulted the man from a mere fame-hungry New York celebrity to an embodiment of the American Dream. His show and its many spin-offs found a rabid fan base in people who believed they, too, could become millionaires—or even billionaires—if they were able to get in front of not just Trump but the cameras that followed him. Reality television allowed him to self-mythologize, to assert himself as America's most successful businessman. (Even if that description was never quite accurate.) The persona he crafted on a reality television show created by Mark Burnett, the same man who started the 2000s reality craze with *Survivor,* made Trump a respected, aspirational figure. And when he was elected to his first term as president of the United States in 2016, the genre that effectively began as a way to make television more cheaply had finally devalued an entire nation. Across his two terms—during which Trump and his family members launched a crypto-currency and social-media platform, and sold fragrances, shoes, books, watches, and countless red MAGA hats—the Trumps overtook the Kardashians as the first family of reality television. Because once a reality star becomes the most powerful person on earth, how can anyone possibly keep up?

Chapter 6

What's Love Got to Do with It?

Speidi, Bennifer & KimYe

In the airport, holding a copy of Sun Tzu's *The Art of War*;

Kissing through masks, during the 2009 Swine Flu outbreak;

At the supermarket, with two watermelons placed suggestively against breasts;

Atop a playground slide wearing matching Easter-themed bunny ears;

Eating a slab of bloody, raw meat out of a Ziploc bag;

Posing with shopping bags outside the 99-cent store amid the 2009 economic crisis;

Making out atop a pile of pumpkins at the pumpkin patch.

These are just a few of the many paparazzi photos that make up the nearly twenty-year relationship of Spencer Pratt and Heidi Montag, a couple so adept in celebrity that they have photographers on speed dial—paparazzi who are often amenable to catering to the couple's sartorial whims with the promise of tabloid magazine placement.

It's hard to remember a time when Spencer and Heidi weren't a couple—that there was a moment in history when "Speidi" wasn't an immediately recognizable, and utterly romantic, portmanteau—but they were in fact separate entities before appearing on the second season of MTV's pseudo-scripted reality show *The Hills*. Which itself was inspired by a piece of fully scripted drama, *The O.C.* That show made overnight Thems out of its leads—Adam Brody, Rachel Bilson, Ben McKenzie, and Mischa Barton—but more important, it inspired the MTV reality series *Laguna Beach*. Which naturally begat *The Hills,* continuing the story of *Laguna*'s protagonist, a rich California girl named Lauren Conrad, and introducing us to her pseudo-friends Stephanie Pratt and Heidi Montag, the latter of whom began dating the former's brother in the show's second season. Are you still with us? OK.

The most classic and expected pairing is Who + Who. These are the couples whose wedding photos occupy the bottom-left corners of *People* covers because everyone on the editorial staff knows they'd both be largely unrecognizable at five times the size. When people quantify their level of attractiveness on a 10-point scale, they tend to believe they belong with a similar number, meaning one that's not more than, maybe, two levels removed from their own. That is, 8's get with 6–10's; 6's get with 4–8's. Studies have shown that people tend to overrate their own attractiveness, meaning they see themselves as better-looking than people who are actually doing the looking. Fortunately, Who–Them is a binary that's more or less objective, given the fact that the two of us invented it. (It's actually crazy to invent something you can't bring onto *Shark Tank*.) So when we say a relationship consists of two Whos, there's really nothing to debate.

Compare the young and telegenic cast of *Laguna Beach* and *The Hills* to the young and telegenic cast of *The O.C.* The Hollywood machine—as well as its consumers—knew what to do with the actors on *The O.C.* (Skillfully cut out photos of them from magazines like *YM* and *Seventeen* and lacquer them to their wall like homemade wallpaper.) They were less certain of what to make of reality stars. From the moment the pilot of *The O.C.* first aired and the world heard a scary blond bully say, "Welcome to the O.C., *bitch,*" for the very first time, its cast benefited from the tried-and-true cultural narrative of young-adult TV stars. Hollywood responded to this newfound fame by inserting them all into its machine—from movies to magazines to brand sponsorships, all with varying levels of success and sustainability.

Brody landed roles in feature films like *Mr. & Mrs. Smith* and *Jennifer's Body* and received an Emmy nomination for his work on the hugely popular Netflix series *Nobody Wants This.* Bilson led the series *Hart of Dixie* for four seasons, later finding success in—surprise!—the world of podcasting. McKenzie starred in the successful crime dramas *Southland* and *Gotham,* and Barton starred in a slew of horror films. It even launched careers for its B-plot actors: Olivia Wilde went on to have her own story arc on *House* and later directed the films *Booksmart* and *Don't Worry Darling.* Despite their popularity among millennials (who were still in their teens and early twenties when both shows were on the air), the cast of *Laguna Beach* and *The Hills* were not afforded such obvious career paths after their shows ended. The influencer infrastructure that exists now, thanks largely to social media, was not available to reality stars in the genre's early days. Not long before *Laguna Beach,* there was no expectation of cultural longevity for people who appeared on shows like *The Real World* and *Survivor.* Their stars were *barely* even Whos by our definition, as they rarely made headlines after the cameras stopped rolling and instead retreated back to civilian life. But something was changing in the mid-aughts.

Brody and Bilson played an on-again, off-again romantic duo on *The O.C.* through its four-season run, while also (bonus!) dating in real life for the majority of that time. For those three and a half years, their fame levels rose at a steady, almost identical pace as they traversed the path of sudden Themdom with ease and momentum. There is something endlessly compelling about fiction that bleeds into reality—a love that transcends the TV or movie camera and sexual chemistry that breaks through the fourth wall. It still remains one of the go-to ways to sell a film, to make sure the two leads imply there's something *else* going on between them. When the world met Pratt, he was dating Montag on the second season of *The Hills*, having been introduced by his sister and Montag's friend Stephanie. Before reality stars could even imagine what being on TV might do to their real lives, these stars treated real life the same as their "fake life" on TV. There's a thrill in comparing an actor's scripted life to their private one that was, especially at that time, lacking in reality-star fandom. What you saw was, essentially, what you got. For updates on Brody and Bilson's real-life romance, you had to reach for the tabloids after turning off the TV. For updates on Pratt and Montag, in those early days, you waited for next week's episode. But when the shows ended, these reality stars didn't want their fame to run out. To maintain it, they looked to the blueprint.

Pratt and Montag love speaking to the media about the media, specifically their late-aughts/early-2010s pioneering mastery of it. In 2009, they released a book called *How to Be Famous: Our Guide to Looking the Part, Playing the Press, and Becoming a Tabloid Fixture*, in which they revealed some of their strategies for staying in the public eye despite not having a traditional reason for being there in the first place. ("Do you think either of us would be where we are today without the other person?" they write, a sentiment that's as mercenary as it is romantic. "It goes without saying that we wouldn't be. We reiterate: Speidi > Heidi + Spencer." Absolutely heartwarming.) Speidi are from the "famous for being famous" school of modern celebrity, pioneered by Kim Kardashian and Paris Hilton, the latter of whom Pratt has called out for being an influence on his approach to celebrity. "She was running the media game when we entered," Pratt told *Refinery29* in 2016. "So if it was anything it was definitely Paris—she gets all the credit." When MTV had no further use for them, they cannily used their connections to the tabloid press to sell photos and stories—many of which landed on the covers of magazines like *Us Weekly, People,* and *Life & Style*—that paid their bills. By maintaining a steady hum of public interest through their own manipulated media placements, they were able to stay on television, appearing in reality shows like *Ce-*

lebrity Wife Swap; I'm a Celebrity . . . Get Me Out of Here; and *Marriage Boot Camp: Reality Stars.* Sure, they never transcended Whodom—even Montag's music career, while allegedly lucrative, is more of an accidental peculiarity than the result of genuine stardom—but they got exactly what they wanted out of the whole decades-long order: lasting fame.

While Speidi found a way to embrace the permanent Who-y nature of their pairing, squeezing as much public interest and longevity as any two people possibly could without letting the prickly desire for Themdom get in the way, most Who + Who couples aspire to use their pairing at least in part to reach that next level. After all, plenty of magazine covers and splashy above-the-fold headlines should convince you that there are few better, more reliable ways to get press attention for any celebrity than to announce a new relationship with another famous person. But what's particularly fascinating about the public's fascination with celebrity couplings is that they don't seem to care whether they know who the couple consists of. Of course we're *more* interested if it's Ben Affleck and Jennifer Lopez, or Rihanna and A$AP Rocky, but what is it about less famous people named Chase Stokes and Kelsea Ballerini? There's a base-level interest there; we are drawn to the romantic escapades of hot, pretty people in the same way we are drawn to home tours of the rich and famous. Wouldn't it be nice to have a closet the size of a studio apartment? Wouldn't it be thrilling, even if only temporarily, to be in a relationship that made millions of people jealous?

THE 2023 SAGA of Sydney Sweeney and Glen Powell was a perfect storm of Hollywood synergy. The good-looking actors promoted a movie in which they played a couple by allowing the press to believe they were also one in real life, despite never receiving confirmation from either party that their relationship continued when the cameras weren't rolling. A classic! For months we saw production photos of them kissing in their swimsuits under the bright, hot Australian sun while reading conflicting reports about the status of their relationships with their respective partners: For Powell it was a model named Gigi Paris, and for Sweeney a random businessman named Jonathan Davino. *Is this an affair?* we wondered, despite knowing that these were actors whose job it was to sell an onscreen romance and then a real-life movie. *Are they cheating, or is it some sort of undisclosed ethical nonmonogamy?* we thought, ignoring everything but the vibes. *Is the rom-com actually back this time?!*

Real or fake, when Sweeney and Powell's movie, *Anyone but You,* finally came out, it made over $225 million on a $25 million budget.

The cynical, industry-centric assumption was that this was Sony Pictures' way of guaranteeing a rom-com's theatrical success. For years, especially those days of the Covid-19 pandemic, the trades hemmed and hawed over whether theatrical moviegoing was dead. Sure, "Barbenheimer" was a generationally significant cultural moment—a rare glimpse of the long-lost monoculture—but it was, unfortunately, an anomaly. As fans of movies and *moviegoing,* we were excited to see these sexy photos of relatively unknown sexy actors being sexy with each other on camera. To us, it seemed like a last-ditch effort to garner publicity for a movie that was expected to make little money because people by and large weren't going to the theaters unless those movies were superhero tentpoles or low-budget horror. This was an R-rated romantic comedy starring two people who not only hadn't been proven as movie stars but whose names were likely only known by fans of *Euphoria* and *Everybody Wants Some!!,* a low-budget Richard Linklater film that, while critically beloved, flopped at the box office seven years prior. Their romance—onscreen and, quite possibly, off—was the most intriguing part of the equation.

Those first photos from the set—the ones in which both Sweeney and Powell are in swimsuits and, to use *Daily Mail* parlance, *flaunting their assets in the sun*—were published by the press in March 2023, nine months before the movie was released. It's not just that the photos were sexy, which they were, but there was something . . . charmingly heteronormative about these two classically attractive people promoting their cliché-ridden rom-com with voyeuristic photos of them being sexy together. It harkened back to a time when successful movies actually did lead to off-screen romances between two stars—think: Humphrey Bogart and Lauren Bacall, Elizabeth Taylor and Richard Burton, and Jennifer Lopez and Ben Affleck, the latter of whom met on the set of 2003's *Gigli*. If the success of the film in which the couple met has any indication of the success of their real-life relationship, well, *Gigli* says it all.

The question, of course, became this: Would the public's sudden interest in these two sexy Who-lebrities persist, or would it be like most other viral stories, quickly forgotten? The latter was the likelier outcome, given the rapidly decreasing attention spans of the young audiences most necessary for the film's financial success, but the story of the relationship continued to evolve throughout the spring, summer, and fall, providing the movie with plenty of indirect marketing by way of gossip stories. Powell and Sweeney kept mum the entire time, rarely saying much of anything beyond flirty interviews (about the film, of course). But over a year after *Anyone But You* became a bona fide smash and both their previous relationships came to an end, a newly single Gigi Paris went on a podcast to tell her side of the story. It was what we might have expected: She told *Too Much* host Emma Paige that Powell allowed the speculation to continue despite Paris's frustrations in the hope it would make the movie more successful. Paris said she'd *hoped* Powell would say he would never cheat on her, but that denial never came. "It was serving them for their PR," she said, dripping with disdain. "I don't know if there was a relationship there or not, but then they came out to say it was all a PR scheme at the expense of our relationship."

There was something almost conspiratorial about the way Paris told the story to her friend. It was as if she couldn't believe—or didn't think anyone else would believe—that this sort of fake-relationship PR stunt was something that actually happened. That she could be the collateral damage in one of those movies about the person who ditches his "normal" girlfriend after tasting the sweetness of fame. To her, using a relationship as a means to become more famous was a thing that only happened *in* the movies. But there she was, over a year later, shaking her head in disbelief at how it all went down. Powell and Sweeney never actually confirmed a relationship ever took place, but they both booked plenty of leading roles in the months following *Anyone But You*'s release and have since transcended into Themdom. Had the ends justified the means?

A perfectly calibrated pairing of two Whos can act as a cultural launching pad. The Who + Who relationship is often a means to an end, a tacit agreement to allow the public to believe their relationship is real in the service of their mutual career growth. The Them + Them relationship is often portrayed as the end, *full stop,* despite the fact that it so rarely is. The public reacts with glee that two internationally famous Thems have definitively found their fame-appropriate match, and later reacts with indignant shock when they call it quits. We thought Jennifer Lopez and Ben Affleck, as two generational Thems, were MFEO (meant for each other) due to their mutual understanding of the struggles of Themdom; only Jen could understand someone like Ben, and vice versa. In our lifetimes, there are few Them + Them couplings more culturally significant than the ones between Beyoncé and Jay-Z, Brad Pitt and Jennifer Aniston, and the aforementioned "Bennifer." But the three relationships couldn't have evolved more differently: One endured plenty of rumored drama and inspired art from both while remaining as strong as ever; one set were introduced by managers and deemed the "golden couple" but were broken up by a love triangle; and, as far as the public knows, one fizzled out and reignited like a trick birthday candle decades later. But something they all have in common is the extent to which the relationship became a crucial part of each member's public persona. What was it about each of these three couples that stuck for us collectively? We couldn't believe that two super-famous people could be super famous and *in love with each other?* It felt too good to be true.

It's easy to imagine a conversation between a Them and their publicist just before a relationship with another Them goes public: *Are you sure you want to do this? Are you sure you want to double your exposure? Are you sure you want every element of your relationship to be scrutinized in every publication and TikTok comment section for the foreseeable future? Are you sure you want to risk the embarrassment of a messy breakup? Are you sure you want to risk marriage if all it leads to is legal fees and time in court?* But the likelihood of Shakespearean tragedy adds to the excitement, after all, for both the couple and their audience. Look at those two Thems who are willing to give true love the old college try even though precedent suggests that not only will it never last but it will end in otherworldly heartache. (And a ton of headlines.) One relationship cannot withstand two egos of that size, two fandoms of that fervor, two cultural objects with that virality. Nevertheless . . .

If a Them + Them couple breaks up like Bennifer or "Mr. and Mrs. Ross Vegas" (the name under which Jen and Brad allegedly used to book hotel stays) did, the public and press quickly separate them into villain and victim. Jennifer wanted it too much, and Ben wasn't emotionally capable of handling her love of fame; Pitt's on-set romance with Angelina Jolie during the filming of *Mr. & Mrs. Smith* created the narrative of a toxic love triangle. But if the couple stays together, as Jay-Z and Beyoncé have for over twenty years, the public and press will certainly, if quietly, seek out cracks in their foundation, eager to pounce on any rumor that suggests trouble in paradise . . . for paradise is a place that *cannot possibly exist.*

Any outcome of a Them + Them coupling will maintain a kind of cultural permanence. It's likely that for the rest of her life, Gwyneth Paltrow's divorce from Coldplay frontman Chris Martin will be brought up whenever she's written about at length. Give any writer a high-enough word count, and you'd better believe some version of "conscious uncoupling" will, like magic, appear in the draft. In a 4,500-word 2025 profile in British *Vogue* tied to Paltrow's cinematic pseudo-comeback, *Marty Supreme,* writer Giles Hattersley uses the word "uncoupling" not once but twice. Other words most likely found in long-form Paltrow features these days: "jade egg," "I wish you well," and "Hamptons bathroom."

Thems in love are the closest things we have to royals in American culture, but what of a royal who marries a commoner? Well, that's even better—that's a fairy tale. The coupling between a Them and a

Who is rife with intrigue: There's the rom-com-ready fantasy of someone who could theoretically "have anybody" choosing a relative "nobody," the rags-to-riches tale of the Who suddenly leveling up with regard to public attention and resulting career opportunity, and the Them deciding they've had enough of the artificiality of other huge stars and choosing someone who, in a way, *brings them back down to earth.* Hooking up with a higher-profile star can vault a Who to Them without even having to win an Oscar. When Tom Cruise jumped on Oprah Winfrey's couch in 2005 and declared he was in love with Katie Holmes, the tabloids went understandably nuts. He was a forty-two-year-old superstar; she was a twenty-six-year-old actor only a couple years out from having starred in the popular teen drama *Dawson's Creek.* Holmes, while engaged to actor Chris Klein, had even casually told *Seventeen* magazine years prior: "I used to think that I was going to marry Tom Cruise." (Foreshadowing!) Holmes and Cruise were first publicly spotted together in April 2005 and engaged by June. While Holmes co-starred as the romantic lead in 2005's *Batman Begins,* her Them status had already been secured by her high-profile romance. Even after their breakup in 2012, despite never having a bona fide blockbuster breakout of her own, Holmes remained steadily in Them territory. Despite the drama—mainly Cruise's longtime involvement with Scientology, which Holmes rejected for herself and their daughter, Suri—the simple power of getting involved with one of the only super Thems left in Hollywood fueled her own Themdom.

A THEM DATING a Who often results in similarly rabid coverage as a Them dating a Them. Perhaps the most rabid, in the worst sense of the word, coverage of a Who + Them relationship was the one between singer Britney Spears and a dancer named Kevin Federline. When they met at a club in 2004, Federline recalled to *People,* "I learned real fast how much of a whirlwind the press and everything was." Tabloids would chronicle the next three years of their lives in full, gratuitous detail. There was the music video in which Spears sings Bobby Brown's

"My Prerogative" in a sexy black wedding dress (while Federline slides a ring on her finger); the birth of their sons, Jayden and Preston; the clip from their brief reality show, *Britney and Kevin: Chaotic,* during which she waxes poetic about the possibility of time travel while eating takeout; Federline's admirable if unsuccessful attempt at pop stardom ("Popozão"); and, *finally,* their contentious divorce. As Spears's mental health declined, Federline was quickly, and surprisingly, painted as a savior—at least at first. Wrote ABC News during their custody battle: "By all accounts, Federline has successfully created a nurturing environment for his boys by enlisting the support of his parents, as well as Spears' parents, who visit their grandkids at his home." *The Sydney Morning Herald* was slightly less gracious: "Kevin Federline won't win any parenting awards, but the once-reviled ne'er-do-well has rehabilitated his reputation and is now seen by some celebrity watchers as a better parent than his ex-wife, pop star Britney Spears." It would take another fifteen years for Spears to pen a memoir that covered this time, *The Woman in Me*. By then she had finally been widely perceived as the victim of countless people in her life who took advantage of her illness for their own financial gain. And Federline's own memoir, *You Thought You Knew,* released two years later, would attempt to rehabilitate his image once more. But by then, no one cared—Federline's memoir has sold a few thousand copies, paltry compared to the millions Britney's has gone on to sell. The Them had already won, so it had always been written.

A Who + Them relationship might just be as well-covered as two Thems, because a Who needs to be not just defined but *explained* when they're dating someone more famous than they are. When Bebe Rexha, a Who, announced she was dating a filmmaker named Keyan Safyari, the central question was "Who are either of you?" When Ariana Grande, a Them, started dating Pete Davidson, the questions were myriad. Beyond "Who's he again?" were "Wait, can you repeat that?"; "Since when?"; and "Is this a joke?" The answers, in brief, are: "A former *Saturday Night Live* cast member from Staten Island"; "A former *Saturday Night Live* cast member from Staten Island"; "Since May 2018"; and "No."

Bossip was the first publication to report on the singer and former *SNL* cast member's relationship, sharing the news with this master class in headline writing: "Did Ariana Grande Dump Mac Miller to Let THIS *SNL* Actor Chop Her 4 Octave Cakes to Smithereens?" ("Chop Her 4 Octave Cakes to Smithereens" being simultaneously phrasing you don't want to look up and also one that should win a MacArthur genius grant.) After the chaos that quickly ensued due to the rumor's sheer unbelievability—why would one of the most successful young pop stars of her generation date someone best known for being a stoner archetype and second- or third-tier cast member on *SNL*?—*People* promptly confirmed *Bossip*'s reporting, sharing that the relationship had "just started" and was "very casual." The extent to which the public was shocked by the randomness and asymmetry of their fame level, perceived talent, and upward trajectory exemplifies why the Who + Them pairing is such a discombobulating cultural event. More than Who + Who or Them + Them, it recontextualizes both sides of the equation, forcing fans and journalists alike to reconsider not just who they are, but who they wish to be.

5 All-Timer *Bossip* Headlines

- "Kondomless Klown King Tristan Thompson Kries Krocodile Tears to Khloé over Infant Indiscretion, Apologizes for Rampant Raw Doggery" (2022)
- **"Bae of the Day: 'WAGS Miami' Star Darnell Nicole Is Beautifully Stacked Like a Dolphin" (2017)**
- "Caucasity Audacity: Soft-Boiled Ostrich Egg Taylor Swift Gets Buried, Burned and Blown Away for Earth, Wind and Fire Cover" (2018)
- "Poon-Sizzling Villain Bae Michael B. Jordan Is Destroying Dashiki Drawls Across Wakanda" (2017)
- **"In White Folks News: Bradley Cooper and Irina Shayk Have Reportedly Called It Quits" (2019)**

It wasn't just the pairing of Grande and Davidson that got the media riled up but the speed at which the two barreled toward holy matrimony. Spoiler alert: they didn't make it all the way there, but Davidson got three Grande-inspired tattoos on the way to their inevitable breakup. A lot of painful tattoo-removal lasers were in his future, but by dating Grande, Davidson instantly transformed from a featured *SNL* cast member with few, if any, memorable characters to the most intriguing young man in comedy. A photo of the couple went viral in June 2018 because it flipped the Who + Them dynamic on its head. The two are holding hands on a sidewalk. Grande is staring up at Davidson as she coyly licks a lollipop, while the dominant figure in the image faces forward, his eyes covered by a hoodie, his own lollipop stashed in his mouth behind locked lips. By gazing up, enthralled by his seemingly uninterested and half-shrouded face, Grande drew the rest of the world's eyes to Davidson; what she saw in him was a mystery to us, which made speculation about his character, personality, and . . . *physical attributes* a sort of game during the early stages of their relationship. *Well, he must be sensitive and a good listener because he's suffered significant trauma over the tragic loss of his father, an FDNY member who died saving lives during the 9/11 terrorist attacks. And he must be more talented than we could tell from his four-season stint on* SNL, *given Grande's track record of dating critically acclaimed artists.*

It was a line of thinking that led to the term "big dick energy," popularized in part by writer Allison P. Davis in *The Cut*. So rarely does new slang enter the monoculture with the speed of BDE. We were so utterly desperate for an explanation for this couple, and suddenly, here it was. "BDE is a quiet confidence and ease with oneself that comes from knowing you have an enormous penis and you know what to do with it. It's not cockiness, it's not a power trip—it's the opposite: a healthy, satisfied, low-key way you feel yourself," Davis wrote. Let's return to that original paparazzi photo that prompted the acronym's initial usage: Davidson is in a hoodie, dressed as casually as any straight man might be when walking down the sidewalk on his day off, but Grande is staring at him like he'd just satiated her every desire—even ones she didn't know she had. It was the most unforgettable photo of the singer since she was captured on CCTV licking donuts, saying "I hate America," and one that shot Davidson from niche Who-lebrity to full-on Them.

Grande was a reliable, established pop star when she and Davidson started dating, but the blatantly autobiographical music she released in the wake of the relationship's demise proved to be some of the most popular of her career. "Thank U, Next," a song Grande named after something she tweeted after she and Davidson called it quits, was a chart-topping smash. "*I'm so fuckin' grateful for my ex,*" she sings, providing Davidson with the parting gift of grace. As writer Hanif Abdurraqib wrote in *Pitchfork,* "The twinkling chorus is steeped in a kind of corny but joyful gratitude, for the past but also for the present self. Crooning ever so angelically, Grande reminds the masses that we choose to love people for a reason, even if that love is brief." Grande released her fifth studio album, also called *Thank U, Next,* just before Valentine's Day 2019. Davidson had inspired the bestselling and most critically acclaimed album of the singer's entire career.

But Thems aren't the sole beneficiaries of a Who + Them relationship. Without the sudden spike in public awareness thanks to his high-profile relationship with one of the country's biggest pop stars—not to mention the chart-topping tribute to their brief time together—Davidson likely wouldn't have transitioned from bit player to leading man with such speed. During an appearance on *Hot Ones,* one of a few chicken-centric talk shows, Davidson himself acknowledged this in no uncertain terms by telling host Sean Evans, "It's really annoying because I live in Staten Island and [paparazzi photographers] come there now 'cause, like, Ariana Grande made me all famous and stuff." Thanks to his newfound celebrity, Davidson hopped over a few rungs on the ladder of fame, and, within a few months of the breakup from Grande, his Judd Apatow–directed comedy *The King of Staten Island* was in production. This wasn't an adaptation of an *SNL* character, as are most breakout movie roles for the show's storied alums, but a pseudo-biographical origin story co-written by Davidson and Apatow. Would anyone have cared about Davidson's origin story if he weren't a Them? Apatow has never claimed Davidson's spike in celebrity was a factor in getting the movie made. But would he have gotten anyone to pay for it if not for Davidson's recent rocket to stardom? Feels unlikely.

Oddly enough, Davidson's next high-profile relationship connects us to another variation of Who + Them couplings—one considerably more unpleasant and resulting in no chart-topping pop music. In October 2021, Kim Kardashian hosted *SNL* for the first time. When she kissed Davidson onscreen during a sketch in which they played famous lovers Princess Jasmine and Aladdin, fans and celebrity reporters alike remained cautious about calling the two an item. In *Vulture*'s coverage of the sketch, writer Alejandra Gularte ignored all speculation, instead focusing on the costumes: "This isn't the first time Kim Kardashian West has dressed up as the Disney princess. Back in 2016, she dressed up as Princess Jasmine for Halloween alongside her daughter North West." Good to know. But Kardashian and Davidson's public appearances continued after the episode aired, most notably in a photo of the two of them holding hands on a roller coaster at Knott's Scary Farm in California. It was clear: The two were dating, and Davidson had once again found someone considerably more famous than he, despite being a newly minted Them. If fame disparity in relationships were measured with the calendar, like age gaps, Davidson and Ariana would have been a February/September romance. Davidson and Kim? They were your classic May/December. To our collective surprise, the relationship lasted a full nine months, and it was notable not only for the surprising visual and conceptual pairing of Davidson and Kardashian—he wasn't her "type" as far as the public knew—but because Davidson was her first high-profile relationship after the dissolution of her roughly seven-year marriage to Kanye West. (Although post-BDE, we'd learned that Davidson might somehow be *everyone's* type.) He was more than just a rebound; he was great press, a sympathetic funny guy who brought a kind of absurd levity to Kim's public image, which had grown considerably unpleasant during the harrowing final years of her marriage.

A few months into Kardashian and Davidson's relationship—during the early days of a celebrity relationship's post-journalistic confirmation, but before an initial red-carpet appearance—West was spotted at a party in Miami with Julia Fox, the actor and model best known for her role in the Safdie Brothers' 2019 thriller, *Uncut Gems*. Alongside two suspiciously clear photos of the couple—as if taken by someone within earshot—*Page Six* wrote that West and Fox "appeared to be having a good time in each other's company as they dined at Carbone." Four days after the images went viral, *Interview* magazine published a series of photos chronicling Fox and West's night in Miami alongside a two-paragraph introduction, penned by Fox:

> After dinner Ye had a surprise for me. I mean, I'm still in shock. Ye had an entire hotel suite full of clothes. It was every girl's dream come true. It felt like a real Cinderella moment. I don't know how he did it, or how he got all of it there in time. But I was so surprised. Like, who does things like this on a second date? Or any date! Everything with us has been so organic. I don't know where things are headed but if this is any indication of the future I'm loving the ride.

The accompanying photos do indeed chronicle a moment that looks straight out of a fairy tale, with West standing by fitting racks filled with beautiful garments for Fox to try, like Julia Roberts in *Pretty Woman* or perhaps more so the vibe of Daniel Day-Lewis and Vicky Krieps in *Phantom Thread*. In one photo of them together, she's smiling. In case the audience was questioning whether the relationship was merely a platonic one between artist and muse, there's a photo where they're kissing up against a wall. Alas, a month or so later, West and Fox broke up. Eighteen months after that, in October 2023, Fox published her bestselling memoir, *Down the Drain,* in which she wrote compellingly about the "whirlwind romance" for the first time. The chapter chronicling their brief affair is titled "Sudden Starfall," and she never names West explicitly; instead, she refers to him only as "a famous artist" and "the artist." She describes meeting him at a particularly dark moment of her life, during an emotional and financial battle with the father of her child. When "the artist" first speaks to Fox on the phone, he listens. Fox writes, "He breathed a new life into me." Before long, she's visiting him in Miami for their first proper date. When she receives a phone call from *Page Six* the following morning asking for comment on the "heavily Photoshopped" images they'd just published of the two, she fears "the artist" is the one who leaked them. What follows is a harrowing account of Fox's realization that "the artist" was using her for his own game, treating her as expendable. West needed someone more or less unformed in the public eye—someone he could mold into precisely the rebound he needed at the time. (When he asks, unprompted, if she'd like him to pay for her to get a "boob job," she politely declines.) He needed a Who, and once she figured out she was being used as a publicity stunt, it was too late. By breaking it off with "the artist," she loses a "million-dollar" deal with an Italian denim brand, as it was "contingent" on the couple being together. Unlike Davidson, Fox would never argue that the relationship helped her career. On the contrary, she characterizes it as a deeply regrettable period in which she was given a crash course in the darker (and NDA-filled) side of celebrity.

ULTIMATELY, WHEN AUTHENTICITY is king, falling in love is one of the most genuine things a celebrity (be they a Who or a Them) can do. We understand love as something you simply can't control—we crave the dream of an on-set hook-up, be it temporary method-induced romance, cunning showmance, or *the real deal.* All options are a kind of cheat code for rapid fame and attention. It's also why we experience an all-too-intense degree of collective heartbreak when things don't work out. And the odds are stacked against these Whos and Thems, no matter our high hopes and fantasies.

It should be no surprise that the Who + Them relationship is the riskiest combination. A power dynamic spread to both ends of the celebrity spectrum allows for both kinds of Cinderella stories, the ones that end in riches as well as the ones that end back in rags. When the playing fields are more symmetrical, as they are in Who + Who and Them + Them pairings, even parasitic relationships tend to end with both parties receiving some quantifiable gain. Maybe that's why so many older celebrities tend to abandon famous partners altogether and choose wealthy civilians. Look at Salma Hayek, Miranda Kerr, and even Brooklyn Beckham. The math is actually quite easy: When all else fails, just find yourself a normal, everyday billionaire.

Chapter 7

Fame Means Always Having to Say You're Sorry

PR Statements, Talk-Show Appearances & Notes-App Apologies

"There's no such thing as bad publicity," P. T. Barnum once said. (Allegedly.) And while Barnum was one of the first to employ a publicist—or "press agent," as he called it, a marketing marvel named Richard F. "Tory" Hamilton—you have to wonder what these guys would've made of cancel culture. That P. T. Barnum quote has been repeatedly attributed to Oscar Wilde, which makes sense if you've read any Oscar Wilde, and so has this one: "There's only one thing in the world worse than being talked about, and that is not being talked about." There's no proof he said either, but RuPaul did once say to *The Hollywood Reporter*: "In showbiz, there's no such thing as bad publicity as long as they spell your name right." At least we've got one properly attributed quotation. Now that public pressure spreads faster (and louder!) thanks to the internet, "bad publicity" could actually be quite damaging to a celeb. It could cause them to lose valuable promotional deals; brands simply don't want their Instagram-based spon to fill up with negative comments. And now that so much more of a celeb's income is likely to come from product marketing, fear of cancellation is much more of a primary concern. If they were alive today, maybe Barnum and Hamilton would've eventually come around to pushing the same advice given to many celebs who find themselves in hot water: *Say nothing at all.*

One of the reasons we launched *Who? Weekly* was to bemoan the access celebs were starting to deny to journalists in the mid-2010s. The trend coincided with a new wave of broad skepticism toward the media. Celebrities never quite trusted magazines to tell their story—or, sometimes more accurately, the story they'd *like* to be telling. A magazine profile would demand days (or weeks!) of time spent with a subject—perhaps even enough time to expose warts and all, rather than a curated snapshot. On the other hand, while one of the journalistic tenets is, naturally, to report the truth, there's no way a good writer isn't always inadvertently inserting their own opinion into the action. (There's a reason good magazine profiles are fun to read, and it's because they're not just a list of facts!) The intention behind the term "clickbait" was around long before there was anything to click; if something is written that perhaps embarrasses a celebrity (no matter its accuracy), it's quite easy to just deem it clickbait. Why risk having something to complain about when you could just deny access? It'll become the ultimate payback to bad press.

With media getting increasingly less access to celebs, fan attention moved away from tabloids and toward social media. Once celebs had total control of their own platforms, they could announce their own pregnancies, post their own promotional movie trailers, and even . . . *apologize*. Celebs asked their audiences to follow them for the "real deal" and were therefore obligated to provide it. But when you're given the platform to say whatever you want, whenever you want, to tens of millions of people at once (and you're a public figure who may be slightly sheltered from criticism, perhaps a pop star living in a world of yes-men, or a child star homeschooled on the set of, let's say, *The Wizards of Waverly Place*), there's a good chance you might say something that demands apology.

Before celebrities had to speak for themselves, they paid teams to speak for them. The first press release was not over a drunkenly uttered slur or a forty-eight-hour Vegas elopement. It was published in 1906, after a Pennsylvania Railroad train crash killed more than fifty passengers, prompting Ivy Lee (who had co-founded the nation's third public relations firm, Parker and Lee, just two years earlier) to directly give reporters a statement from the perspective of the railroad. On October 30, 1906, *The New York Times* published it word-for-word. It wasn't quite an apology, more so an explanation, but the company still took responsibility for the tragedy: "The Pennsylvania Railroad Company is leaving nothing undone to get at the cause of the accident. The coroner has already gathered a jury and is making a thorough investigation; the officials of the company are giving him every assistance in their power."

The reaction to Lee's statement was overwhelming. People loved how proactive and sincere the statement felt, praising its "openness and honesty." Before that, reporters were regularly banned from accident sites, so this felt like something new. Was the release completely accurate? Of course not. Lee also invented PR spin and ushered in a new era of publicity and of crisis management. He would go on to work with John D. Rockefeller (after a worker strike led to 1914's bloody Ludlow Massacre) and companies like American Tobacco (where he collaborated with doctors to release endorsements saying smoking could help reduce stress).

Just as magazines and other media now push back on lack of access, so did newspapers to Lee's newfangled press releases, reducing them to advertisements. (They'd still publish them anyway.) But Lee sought to redeem his missives by issuing an additional one in 1905, calling it his "Declaration of Principles": "This is not a secret press bureau," he wrote. "All our work is done in the open. We aim to supply news. This is not an advertising agency. If you think any of our matter ought properly to go to your business office, do not use it . . . In brief, our plan is frankly, and openly, on behalf of business concerns and public institutions, to supply the press and public of the United States prompt and accurate information concerning subjects which it is of value and interest to the public to know about."

With the advent of TV, apologies could be told to the world directly—but, naturally, with precise and pre-written preparation. After Hugh Grant was arrested for lewd contact when he was caught soliciting sex from a sex worker in Los Angeles, it was a question whether the incident would hurt the actor's career. This was in 1995; he'd just starred in the wildly successful *Four Weddings and a Funeral,* was in a flashy relationship with buzzy actor Elizabeth Hurley, and was poised for Themdom, his floppy haircut and piercing blue eyes leading the way to leading man. Luckily, the same hair and eyes and cheeky shrug led Grant to *The Tonight Show,* where he'd apologize for the incident to Jay Leno (and subsequently the world). "Let me start with question number one," Leno says. "What the hell were you thinking?" The audience goes berserk with laughter. (It's a late-night show, after all. They're poised for comedy!) Grant stutters but does so in his signature ever-so-charming way: "Well, it's not easy . . . People give me tons of ideas on this one. I keep reading new psychological theories and stuff like that. You know, I was under pressure, I was overtired, or I was lonely." He continues with a nimble precision, delivering what were certainly prepared remarks as if they're off the cuff. "But I think that would be bollocks, really, to hide behind something like that. I think you know in life, pretty much, what's a good thing to do and what's a bad thing. I did a bad thing, and there you have it." He'd star in back-to-back crowd-pleasing blockbusters *Notting Hill* and *Bridget Jones's Diary* in the following years.

Not all are as successful as Grant on *The Tonight Show*. In 1989, R&B duo Milli Vanilli were caught lip-syncing, thanks to a malfunctioning backing track during a live performance on MTV. (Hard to imagine that an artist lip-syncing back then could lead to so much drama! Now you'll catch good singers lip-syncing merely because they don't feel like singing that day. Or because they're battling acid reflux, like Ashlee Simpson.) But the scandalous reveal led to an even bigger one: They hadn't been the ones singing on the original recorded tracks at all. Eight months after they won a Grammy for Best New Artist, the National Academy of Recording Arts and Sciences revoked the award, the first and only time in the history of the Grammys that a winner has been forced to return their trophy. The duo claimed their producer, Frank Farian, had barred them from using their own voices on the tracks, and that they could actually sing and they'd attempt to prove it at a press conference in Los Angeles. More than one hundred journalists sat and watched the two warble the chorus to "Girl You Know It's True" as if anything (even the most beautiful vocals!) could persuade the masses from turning away from Milli Vanilli. Well, especially not an (almost) hour-long press conference filled with excuses and passing the blame. As far as apologies went, this was too much. The two never recovered.

In 2013, Lance Armstrong took his doping apology directly to Oprah Winfrey, whose line of direct questioning perhaps made his admissions way less palatable. Despite all the media training in the world, Armstrong's apology came off as less an apology than a list of excuses. "All the fault and all the blame here falls on me," he begins. It's a good start! But then he keeps going: "Behind that picture and behind that story is momentum. Whether it's fans or whether it's the media, it just gets going. And I lost myself in all of that. I'm sure there would be other people that couldn't handle it, but I certainly couldn't handle it." That's where he started losing steam. It was as if he *had no choice* but to dope illegally, blaming "the culture": "I didn't invent the culture, but I didn't try to stop the culture, and that's my mistake." It turns out all he needed was time: After fifteen years of lying low in Aspen, Colorado, he moved back to Austin, Texas, and now hosts podcasts, runs a venture capital firm, and appeared in Season 1 of the Fox reality show *Stars on Mars* in 2023. You know, the things famous people do once their careers start flailing.

EVENTUALLY, CELEBRITIES REALIZED they could skip the press tours of traditional public apologies and instead keep their words of regret siloed in their own hermetically sealed personal media environments. In lieu of awkward conversations with Oprah, their messages could be delivered in a new form: written on the iPhone's Notes app, screenshotted, and posted directly to Instagram. (To note: Notes-app apologies also made their way onto Twitter, which is a place people used to care about a lot more in the 2010s. *Always be cross-promoting!*) The best Notes statements follow the same guiding principles of any good apology: Get in and quickly get out; be direct; don't try too hard to defend yourself; and (for extra credit) maybe say what you're doing to be a better version of yourself moving forward. For example, when the internet resurfaced old tweets model Chrissy Teigen had written that weren't the kindest ("Is it okay to call a small child cocky?" she wrote of nine-year-old Oscar nominee Qvenzhané Wallis), she wrote a 1,127-word apology essay on *Medium* (a social-media/blogging platform for those who have "more to say" than what would fit on Instagram), ending it with an action item: "I'm going to keep working to be the best version of myself for EVERYONE. Everyone deserves better—even my detractors."

Gone were the days of press releases to magazines. Even further gone were the days of that *Chicago*-style Roxie Hart press conference on the courthouse steps. (Unless you were fresh out of some legal proceeding. In that scenario, the courthouse would have to do.) The celebs now had an easy way to skip whatever "misinterpretation" any publication could twist into their communication. They finally had a chance to speak out entirely on their own terms, and they grew addicted to speaking directly to their fans (or, as they'd often put it, "haters").

Who could forget the grainy security-camera footage seen round the world in 2015, when Ariana Grande was captured licking a donut and saying, inexplicably, "I hate Americans. I hate America"? It actually makes you think: What would be worse for one's career now, a stealthy, unsanitary donut lick or a seemingly random unpatriotic outburst? Well, how about both? She followed that up with an apology video sent to *TMZ* ("Not here to make any excuses or justify my behavior, because I can't . . . I'm just here to apologize"), as well as an apology written with the Notes app: "What I said in a private moment . . . was taken out of context and I am sorry for not using more discretion with my choice of words." Both of these statements have since been smartly wiped from the web.

In 2017, Ja Rule took to his Notes app to apologize on Twitter for the mess that was Fyre Fest, a fraudulent music festival that fooled thousands of excited ticket buyers: "I truly apologize as this is NOT MY FAULT . . . but I am taking responsibility I'm deeply sorry to everyone who was inconvenienced by this." Is there anything funnier than putting the words "NOT MY FAULT" into your apology?

Will Smith's Instagram apology for the infamous Oscars slap he gave Chris Rock in 2022 was more measured: "I would like to publicly apologize to you, Chris. I was out of line and I was wrong. I am embarrassed and my actions were not indicative of the man I want to be." He ended his missive with the relatable cliché: "I am a work in progress."

"I've seen the messages, tags, comments, and concerns, and I want to respond," read a 2021 Instagram-posted Notes apology written by Justin Timberlake. What he'd seen was a much-belated (but wholly deserved) backlash to his Super Bowl performance from way back in 2004, in which Janet Jackson accidentally popularized the term "wardrobe malfunction." It continued: "I am deeply sorry for the times in my life where my actions contributed to the problem, where I spoke out of turn, or did not speak up for what was right." His apology conveniently came one week after the release of *The New York Times Presents: Framing Britney,* a documentary on Timberlake's ex-girlfriend Britney Spears's conservatorship. Thus, Timberlake decided to bundle together *two* apologies into one Notes statement: "I specifically want to apologize to Britney Spears and Janet Jackson both individually, because I care for and respect these women and I know I failed." It turns out that two wrongs and one wordy screenshot do not make a right, but by using the Notes app he was able to avoid any visible awkwardness that inevitably would have come from a sit-down interview with a TV journalist like Gayle King.

There's Justin Bieber's 2019 contribution to the genre, where he apologizes for making "every bad decision you could have thought of" (namely, doing drugs, disrespecting women, and being generally aggressive). YouTuber Tati Westbrook issued a two-slide Twitter apology (posted as a Notes screenshot) for calling out fellow YouTuber James Charles in an epic video takedown (the oft-quoted, forty-three-minute masterpiece of the form, titled "Bye Sister"): "I was attempting to explain my upset and concerns so that everyone would understand my position and end the speculation that it was all over vitamins." Believe it or not, Armie Hammer apologized (pre–cannibal scandal) in 2018 via Notes on Twitter for calling out *other actors* for posting "grief selfies" responding to Stan Lee's death: "While attempting to provide some unnecessary social commentary about the current selfie culture, I . . . inadvertently offended many who were genuinely grieving the loss of a true icon." YouTube prankster-turned-wrestler Logan Paul even used the Notes app to ask forgiveness for inadvertently taping (but *advertently* posting) a video of a dead body in Japan: "I'm often reminded of how big of a reach I truly have & with great power comes great responsibility . . . for the first time in my life I'm regretful to say I handled that power incorrectly . . . I should have put the cameras down and stopped recording what we were going through." A reminder that it's also smart to share what you could've done otherwise.

But you know who has bigger reach than Logan Paul? The Dalai Lama, whose team used a Notes-adjacent apology to reach legions of Lamaheads, after a video appeared of the spiritual leader kissing a young boy on the lips in 2023: "His Holiness often teases people he meets in an innocent and playful way, even in public before cameras. He regrets the incident." (If you're wondering, celebs also use the Notes format to ardently *not apologize* for things, as well. In 2018, after Cardi B announced she'd secretly married fellow rapper Offset, she posted one to Twitter that read, in part: "Well now since you lil nosey fucks know at least ya can stop saying i had a baby out of wedlock.")

With so many decidedly bad apologies being posted directly online, you have to wonder where these celebs' publicists were. Did these hired pros—experts in the art of maintaining proper public profiles and sweeping celeb snafus under the proverbial rug—actually approve (or worse, *write*) any of these grand gestures of apology? Or is the *appearance* of genuine authenticity more valuable than a buttoned-up statement?

5 Silly Things a Celebrity Had to Apologize For

- Joey Graziadei mixes up Ruth Bader Ginsburg and Gypsy-Rose Blanchard: "I'm so sorry. I know I won't live that one down. I know how much of a legend she is, and how much she's done for equal rights and women's empowerment." (TikTok, 2024)
- Tyler Posey pretends to come out as gay while standing under a sign for Gay Street: "I am truly sorry to the people I've offended or lessened how big coming out is. I just want to spread love in this world." (Twitter, 2016)
- Angela Simmons carries a handgun-shaped Casze Atelier purse to the BET Awards: "It was a mistake that does not define who I am or my commitment to ending gun violence. To anyone who was hurt or offended by my actions, I offer my deepest apologies." (Instagram, 2024)
- Pierce Brosnan walks in an off-limits "thermal area" at Yellowstone National Park: "I deeply regret my transgression and offer my heartfelt apologies to all for trespassing in this sensitive area. Yellowstone and all our National Parks are to be cared for and preserved for all to enjoy." (Instagram, 2024)
- Lorde apologizes for posting a photo of a bathtub alongside a lyric from a Whitney Houston song: "Extremely extremely poorly chosen quote. I'm so sorry for offending anyone—I hadn't even put this together, I was just excited to take a bath. I'm an idiot. Love Whitney forever and ever. Sorry again." (Instagram, 2018)

AUTHENTICITY HAS ALWAYS been a kind of currency to public figures, but the casual intimacy of social media made it easier for them to grasp. Entire teams of professional publicists had worked to keep us firmly at arm's length, but there was now a way to be up close and personal. It feels insane to imagine suggesting to a public figure these days that they willingly take up a habit of daily tweeting, but not that long ago a single tweet from Shaquille O'Neal or an Instagram comment reply from Rihanna could generate a press cycle of its own; back then, the closeness, *the realness* was a novelty. I (Lindsey) once even received my own version of what had to be the same as a coveted signed headshot: Mariah Carey responded to a question I'd jokingly thrown at her on Twitter about the usage of a word she'd clearly (and charmingly) made up—"bleakosity"—to which she replied: "@lindseyweber define 'bleakosity'?.OK.Bleakosity:..the state of being bleak and or drab..the opposite of festive." *The thrill of a lifetime!* I felt strongly then (and, honestly, still to this day) that Mariah had written it herself. That authenticity is why she has legions of fans (they call themselves "lambs") who not only flock to support her music but also celebrate her uniquely prima donna personality. It takes her from successful musician to absolute icon.

We'd just about die for a celeb retweet. (Or some form of online acknowledgment—remember Taylor Swift's Tumblr era? Some of us do.) It's the same reason a stan proudly places "noticed by CELEBRITY NAME on SOME SPECIFIC DATE" in their bio, and the same reason why an intentionally "casual" screenshot posted online was believed to work better than what had been done for years and years before.

We might even be past the era of written apologies. The Notes apology (much like the rest of media) is undergoing another change: pivot to video. (Cyclical, if you consider the aforementioned Lance Armstrong on Oprah or the Milli Vanilli press conference.) If screenshots could no longer be seen as the peak of sincerity and authenticity, how about something visual? Even *The New York Times* weighed in, specifically digging into the aesthetic of these repentant videos: "These videos appear off the cuff—hair disheveled, faces uncharacteristically makeup-free, weird lighting—but they are likely curated to elicit empathy, down to the cozy, intimate locations, any hint of far more opulent surroundings out of the frame, according to public relations experts."

Now celebrities were reaching beyond the humble Notes (found on any old iPhone) and presenting themselves candidly, makeup-free, posed strategically away from any flashy art or appliance. (God forbid they subject themselves to the brutal aftermath of March 2020's Covid-era "Imagine" video.) But ultimately, no matter the effort, these videos will be picked apart by eagle-eyed fans looking for loose ends, for easy evidence of inauthenticity, or worse: exorbitant wealth. There was a video of Ashton Kutcher and Mila Kunis explaining why they wrote supportive letters for the convicted rapist (and their former co-star) Danny Masterson. They're positioned against a simple, rustic backdrop—one that was quickly exposed as the exterior of a poolside guesthouse on the couple's six-acre estate, KuKu Farms. It wasn't hard to find. The couple's home had also been the subject of a 2021 *Architectural Digest* feature with the headline "Step Inside Ashton Kutcher and Mila Kunis's Sustainable L.A. Farmhouse"—which detailed the "sprawling French Neoclassical mansion" that Kutcher bought in 2007 for $8 million. Only a week later, Drew Barrymore would post a discomfiting, earnest video responding to allegations of scabbing on her talk show during the guild strikes of 2023: "I know there is just nothing I can do that will make this okay to those that it is not okay with. I fully accept that. I fully understand that," she says in a now-deleted video. She's sitting, casual and clean-faced, in her New York City apartment—a place once deemed "surprisingly normal" by a *BuzzFeed* headline. ("Why is drew barrymore's tv so small and bad. What's going on. I'm unsettled," once tweeted writer Rebecca Shaw, sharing a video of Barrymore watching *The Wedding Singer* on an unexpectedly small television. Relatable!)

Jason Momoa took the video apology to new heights. While filming *Fast X* in Rome, Momoa posted photos online that he'd taken inside the Sistine Chapel (a sin the Catholic Church will go out of their way to make tourists feel guilty about) and was hit with a wave of criticism. As penance, Momoa "addressed the comments in an exclusive video for JustJared.com." Momoa provided the site with a no-frills video shot in what appears to be someone's home gym as Red Hot Chili Peppers blasts in the background. After dropping two hefty weights, the actor follows with his apology, quite plainly and *seemingly* off-the-cuff: "I just also wanted to say, if you ever felt that I disrespected your culture, it wasn't my intention . . . I would never want to do anything to disrespect someone's culture. If I did, I apologize. That wasn't my intention. I love you. I'm sorry if I offended you." The only comment left on *JustJared*'s post covering the apology is from a user named AngelSoe that reads, "You have to apologize for breathing nowadays. Geez."

That's not to say the sleuths only come out to critique video. One of the best moments in Notes-app history was when Demi Lovato announced a breakup (2016's split with known Hollywood playboy Wilmer Valderrama) in a screenshot that revealed she'd done so within a folder titled "Poems." Fans also once dug into a Taylor Swift Notes statement in a similar fashion, calling out during the 2016 Kim Kardashian / Kanye West "Famous" fiasco that a screenshot Swift posted had kept the "Search" indicator up top, implying she'd searched for the statement in the app. If that means nothing to you, well, *good*, but it meant to a legion of Swifties (and their detractors) that the pop star had *inauthentically* prepared her Notes post like a press release—by writing it in advance.

ULTIMATELY, NOTES APOLOGIES have taught us that the medium is far less important than the sentiment. The public is willing to forgive their favorite stars if they actually *believe* they are sorry. Figure out how to apologize well, and you can post it anywhere. But that's easier said than done (which is perhaps why celebs still retain publicists). Publicists aren't necessarily going anywhere; their jobs are just expanding to catch up with the times. It's not just apologies they're dealing with these days, it's full-blown reputation management. That ranges from "how to apologize" all the way to what reportedly went down between Justin Baldoni and Blake Lively during the filming of *It Ends with Us*. Thanks to filed documents from an ongoing court battle, we know that Baldoni's publicity team went so far as to contact a third-party reputation-management professional to strategically place comments with "anti-Lively sentiment" throughout the internet, egging on already existing fan narratives that spun around the feud-turned-legal-battle.

That's not to say celebs won't fall back on old tried-and-true publicity techniques, like a press release, or come up with something entirely new. Perhaps an ideal medium for celebrities looking to apologize (but not have their apology linger for eternity) is Instagram's next-generation posting mechanism: the disappearing story. Sure, a tabloid or fan could (and if you're famous enough, no doubt *will*) screenshot your apology and republish it, complete with an accompanying SEO-optimized headline: "James Kennedy Apologizes for Posting Photo with the Tate Brothers: I 'Condemn Their Beliefs' "; "Pitch Perfect's Ester Dean Apologizes for Writing Beyoncé Diss on Keri Hilson Remix: 'It Was Childish' "; "Benson Boone Apologizes for 'Aggressively' Grabbing Crotch after Grammys Performance." The "disappearing mechanism" most of us relish doesn't quite apply here.

If a good apology is so rare, then why attempt one at all? More cynically, if the news cycle now moves faster than it ever has before—thanks to the internet—wouldn't you quickly move on and hope others do too? Scores of now-deleted Notes apologies across both Instagram and Twitter suggest that the best tactic is perhaps waiting for things to blow over. Even more diabolical, imagine drawing attention to a flub that someone wasn't even aware had happened. Given the nature of our splintered celebrity landscape, one might read about an apology *before they've even heard about what is being apologized for*. Something, perhaps, the guilty could've swept under the proverbial rug?

Now everything has its very own "Streisand effect"—named for the singer in 2003 when she sued photographer Kenneth Adelman for $10 million after he "distributed" pictures of her mansion in Malibu. (The photos allegedly revealed how to gain access to her private residence.) At that point, the offending photos had been downloaded a total of six times, including twice by Streisand's own lawyers. Of course, the case was picked up by plenty of news outlets, causing the photo in question to be published over and over and over again. Adding insult to injury, Streisand lost her lawsuit and was ordered to pay Adelman's legal fees, clocking in at $177,000. A more recent version of the Streisand effect occurred when the Foo Fighters' Dave Grohl posted that he'd "become the father of a new baby daughter, born outside of [his] marriage." *It was news to us!* In fact, the story of Grohl's infidelity and subsequent new baby (at that point) hadn't gone beyond the community of Foo Fighters fans at the time he first addressed it publicly. It wasn't until Grohl posted the apology that the story was picked up by the greater media, making its way into our sight line.

But luckily, the internet has a funny way of making something last forever—or magically disappear from the public consciousness. Somehow, it's either one or the other. That reads like nonsense, but the internet only eternalizes culture for those of us who go looking. Otherwise, our collective memory is short.

Chapter 8

From Selling Out to Selling Crap

Hair Gummies, Waist Trainers & Nespresso

In the right context, the phrase "sold out" refers to a best-case scenario, an unequivocal success. It means a band has filled every seat at the venue where they were booked, that a movie theater has run out of tickets for the 8:40 showing, or that a novel has demanded another printing because bookstores can't keep a story about five queer teenage werewolves/punk rockers who travel through time solving the cases of murdered women on the shelves. In short, it means demand has exceeded supply. But in another context, the phrase can be used for shade; just add a narrowed eye, a disdainful tone, or a short video clip of a drag queen saying literally anything at all to another drag queen. Seen from a certain angle, there's nothing more shameful than selling out. Though its sting has dulled over the years, there was once a time when being deemed a "sellout" was something so cruel, so painful, so existentially humiliating that the thought alone would make any artist shiver.

How the term arrived at its shadier meaning requires a brief history lesson. So let's travel back to the Gilded Age—not the HBO series (though no one throws shade quite like Carrie Coon's Bertha

Russell)—a moment characterized by excess, greed, and political corruption. William "Boss" Tweed was a multihyphenate before his nickname was popularized by singers who act, dance, *and* have liquor brands—*entrepreneurs*! He was a member of the U.S. House of Representatives, a member of the New York State Senate, the director of a railroad, the owner of a hotel, and the founder of Casamigos, the best-tasting, smoothest tequila and mezcal that didn't have to be covered up with salt or lime. Scratch that last one, we're confusing him with somebody else. In any case, Tweed was hugely powerful in his home of New York City, and like most hugely powerful New Yorkers, he was also hugely corrupt. He had an army of minions doing his dastardly bidding, which included inflating documented prices for public works projects and skimming money off the top. It's shocking to learn that this once happened in the "*concrete jungle where dreams are made of*," but it did. During his heyday in the early 1870s, Tweed's misdeeds were often covered by *The New York Times,* and while doing so, the paper would often criticize the scandal-ridden *New York World* for accepting payments from Tweed in exchange for publishing articles supporting the "mission" of Tweed's Democratic Party.

In one piece, the paper puts it more plainly:

> And this grand achievement of the New York Democracy is a practical illustration of what the *World* calls the 'mission of the Democratic Party.' To fulfill this 'mission' it is only necessary to do all over the country what it does here—eschew 'affirmative issues,' hold no fixed principles, and sell out . . . to the highest bidder.

Over the next century, the phrase evolved from an accusation from a purportedly virtuous bastion of the free press to an unethical tabloid rag to an insult lobbed by teenagers to their former idols when they felt like the music had gone from an underground show to something your retired mother plays casually in her car. An epithet that was once reserved for those complicit in the undermining of American democracy became an easy way to disparage artists who started making art the public deemed embarrassing.

By the middle of the twentieth century, in a postwar world where consumerism was reaching new heights (mostly thanks to everyone starting to watch a ton of TV), calling someone or something a sellout had reached the mainstream. Artists began to openly fear the allegation. In 1967, English rock band the Who (no relation) began working on a new album with a peculiar concept, one meant to satirize the deep ties between popular music and commerce—but in a way that would also make *them* money. In a piece for *The Guardian,* Alexis Petridis writes that Who frontman Pete Townshend felt conflicted over his band's participation in a series of Coca-Cola commercials, making them "the first band to record a British ad" for the American beverage company. Afterward, Townshend told *NME* that the future of music was "groups not afraid to make concessions and mock the whole process." In other words, it's OK to sell out, as long as you're aware that you're doing it. And the Who were definitely aware; they'd named the album *The Who Sell Out.*

"The Who may run into legal problems upon the release of their forthcoming album," fretted *Rolling Stone* at the time. "The album is like an extended commercial: all the songs are about people who solve their problems by using brand-name products." On the cover were two images: one of lead singer Roger Daltrey lying in a bathtub filled with Heinz Baked Beans, and another of Townshend applying some Odorono deodorant to his armpits. (Both are positioned so the brands' logos are more prominent than the men's faces. Now a well-worn admonishment for influencers: *Label facing out.*) There were more brands featured in the liner notes, as well as parody ads for Medac acne cream, Jaguar automobiles, and others littered among iconic songs like "I Can See for Miles" and "Sunrise." Co-producer Chris Stamp told *Rolling Stone,* "We have a song about a girl who's worried about B.O. For some reason [deodorant brand] Odorono didn't like being referred to in connection with sweat." Audiences and critics, however, loved it. The album was a hit.

Nearly four decades later, singer/songwriter Jewel surprised fans of her first albums with a likely Who-inspired sellout of her own. During the eight years following the 1995 release of her debut album, *Pieces of*

You, Jewel topped the charts with moody and pensive folk rock like "Foolish Games" and "Hands," accompanying her distinctive sound with an aesthetic that painted her as a mysterious poet—perhaps one who's been living alone in the woods for a few years. *She was strange! She was adored by Bob Dylan! She grew up in Alaska!*

By the time her fifth album, *0304,* was released in 2003, the world had spent almost a decade getting used to Jewel's signature "girl who once lived in a van" style. From its first single, "Intuition," listeners expected perhaps a black Nissan Sentra with a Lilith Fair bumper sticker on the back in album form. What they got was a brand-new Ford Mustang. In hot pink. (Perhaps even pimped out by Xzhibit and his West Coast Customs crew.) Musically, the song is also shocking: a masterfully produced piece of up-tempo, purposely radio-friendly pop. But lyrically, it's classic Jewel: a raw, poetic take on a personal struggle—in this instance, consumerism. Coupled with a tongue-in-cheek video that parodies the objectification and monetization of celebrities by following Jewel as she turns every moment of her life into a moneymaking opportunity, the experiment worked and the album was a hit. She wasn't *really* selling out; she was just making art about how embarrassing it is to sell out! *Don't you get it?* After she performed the song live on former MTV VJ Carson Daly's long-running yet easily forgettable NBC talk show, *Last Call,* Daly, nearly speechless from horniness, asks, "Jewel, what the hell is going on with you? I've known you like, almost ten years, and now all of a sudden you reek of sex . . . This whole thing, where is this coming from?"

After scoffing at the cruel and inappropriate suggestion that she'd never been sexy, Jewel responds, "It's a contrived, marketed adventure."

"Is it?" Daly asks skeptically.

"Yeah," Jewel says, her hands on her hips.

That defiance carried over through a minor controversy that resulted when "Intuition," the very song that made fun of people who sold out, instead made out with a bucket of cash. Not long after the single was released, it was used in a $70 million ad campaign for Intuition, a new Schick razor targeted at women. Both Jewel and Schick denied that the song was written with Schick's razor in mind, but that didn't shut down the campaign's critics. *Slate*, a relatively new online media outlet at the time, published an op-ed maligning the perceived hypocrisy that summer. Columnist Rob Walker writes: "This seems so blatantly contradictory that it undercuts not just Jewel's message, but her status as an endorser: Presumably that status had something to do with the idea that she's more 'authentic' than some flash-in-the-pan pop tart, but it's now pretty hard to argue this with a straight face. In fact, the idea of 'trusting your intuition' has rarely been so roundly mocked." A little razor burn, you could say.

The public admonishment of Jewel's partnership with a razor blade was as much a result of sexism as it was fallout from the musical trends of the '90s. As two millennials who came of age at the turn of the century, a fear and loathing of selling out was endemic to our cultural existence, thanks in part to the anticonsumerist and antiestablishment messages in punk and hip-hop. Green Day, a band formed by Billie Joe Armstrong and Mike Dirnt, added the "pop" to "pop-punk" with international fame and success in the mid-1990s, and hits like "Basket Case," "Longview," and "Good Riddance." By the early aughts, the aging band's fans wondered if Green Day's monstrous success would in any way compromise their artistic integrity. Would they start making music directed at the masses? Was it really "punk" to make music that parents enjoyed just as much as teens and young adults? Would they soon be spun by Delilah, the Queen of Adult Contemporary radio, instead of being put on the playlist by the most stoned person at the party? "Warning," reads a headline from a 2001 edition of the *Las Vegas Sun*. "Don't Call Green Day a Sellout." In the piece Dirnt declares: "Selling out is compromising your musical intention. And I don't even know how to do that."

Twenty-three years later, Green Day slapped their logo (a hand holding a heart-shaped grenade) on the Keurig® x Green Day *American Idiot* Anniversary Edition Brewer Bundle. It came with a tumbler emblazoned with the logo for their coffee brand, Punk Bunny (a deranged-looking rabbit, sometimes depicted with straight-edge-style X's over its eyes). As of this writing, the brewer bundle is listed as "OUT OF STOCK DUE TO POPULAR DEMAND" on Keurig's official website. Some 150 years after the saga of Boss Tweed, the only risk of selling out is that you could literally sell out. What happened since Jewel soundtracked the introduction of a gendered razor blade to take us from a world where celebrities were ashamed to be seen as shameless, money-hungry capitalists to a time when the act of compromising one's artistic integrity has been lovingly rebranded as "hustling"?

IN 2003, THE fear of being labeled a sellout was the plot of a hit Oscar-winning film. *Lost in Translation* follows an American movie star named Bob Harris (played by Bill Murray) in the waning years of his career who travels to Tokyo to shoot advertisements for Suntory whiskey. Directed by nepo-baby auteur Sofia Coppola (daughter of Francis Ford Coppola), the film presents the act of shilling for a brand to be the nadir of a famous person's career, something so humiliating that it must be done thousands of miles away from home, in another language (even amid a career downturn!). Throughout the film we watch as Bob drinks alone at the hotel bar, resentful of a jazz musician who is able to share her creative gifts with the world without having diluted her talent with commerce. So when Bob holds up his whiskey-filled glass, smiles, and says, "For relaxing times, make it Suntory time," we're not meant to laugh at the aging star as he sinks to what he considers to be a career low, but to pity him. Thank God for Charlotte, played by Scarlett Johansson, who jolts Bob out of his existential misery. By the end of the film, when he's on his way back home to the United States, we're left to believe that he may soon crawl out of this depressive rut. Maybe Charlotte inspired him to take his art seriously again; maybe he'll get another role worth respect.

More than two decades after its release, we wonder if the film resonates as strongly with new audiences, when the concept of "selling out" is all but unexplainable to younger generations who came of age during a time when art and commerce are all but indistinguishable. Perhaps they'd even cheer Bob on: *Get that money while you still can!*

Compare the fictional Bob Harris to the real-life George Clooney, who has been shilling for the European coffee brand Nespresso for more than twenty years. Clooney, of course, shot to fame on NBC's long-running medical drama *ER* and quickly transitioned into international movie stardom. It was an unlikely jump back then—fans weren't always ready to see their favorite TV stars take on a bigger screen. After he left *ER*, getting a dose of George Clooney was no longer as easy as flipping on free, ad-supported programs on your television. You had to travel to the theater and pay for a movie ticket to see *From Dusk Till Dawn*, or go to Blockbuster and risk late fees if you didn't return *Out of Sight* on time. Being more inaccessible made you more alluring, and being in a television commercial—especially in the days before subscription-based streaming made ad-free the norm—made you more accessible than ever. So when Clooney had the chance to supplement his acting income with Nespresso money, one imagines that part of the appeal must have been that the spots would only air overseas, far from his primary audience. The first one ("What else?") premiered internationally in 2006, playing off the actor's suave demeanor. But since 2013, Clooney's Nespresso ads have aired all over the world, Clooney now playing up his involvement in the brand's Sustainability Advisory Board, reading voiceovers like "When you hear Nespresso talk about sustainability, it's about the people as well as it is about the coffee bean and the plant." Perhaps Clooney was learning more about the coffee industry and wanting to do more "good"; perhaps now that his ads would be playing un-siloed (and online), he felt the need to reposition his involvement.

In 1994, the year *ER* premiered, Phil Dusenberry, then-CEO of the advertising agency BBDO, said it was difficult to convince famous actors to accept brand deals unless there was a bit of anonymity baked into the project. Voiceovers, he said, were an easier way in for actors like Martin Sheen, Whoopi Goldberg, and Jeff Goldblum. "High-priced, superstar actors feel that they are above and beyond commerce, that they have to transcend that kind of commerciality, that it would in some way distort the public's perception of them as artists," he said. "It keeps them anonymous, yet it's still a payday." Going overseas, an ocean or two away from American audiences, offered celebrities interested in a little second-or-third-house money a similar kind of anonymity in the '90s. Their faces were in advertisements, but their primary audiences (Americans) only saw them on vacation, or ideally not at all.

Beyond the accessibility argument, one can't necessarily blame Clooney and other megastars for thinking advertising gigs were beneath them, or a sign that they had "sold out," at least not back when acting jobs were considerably more siloed. Before Nicole Kidman began appearing in every single Hollywood production in a Shake-N-Go wig, TV shows were for TV actors, theater was for theater actors, and commercials were for, well, commercial actors—which usually meant professionals who could convincingly play normal people, or, if a brand was lucky, aging stars of yesteryear for whom bigger roles had all but dried up. When we think of the most iconic coffee commercials in contemporary American history (at least the ones that frequently go viral in nostalgic posts on social media) it's gotta be the uncomfortably intimate relationship between a brother and sister who love drinking Folgers, or midcentury Thems Joe DiMaggio and Lauren Bacall praising Mr. Coffee and the decaffeinated deliciousness of High Point, both long past their respective career peaks. At the height of one's celebrity, *they* are the product, the dom of their own professional life. To shill for another product is to suggest you're a sub.

Unless, of course, the shilling is eventified. Four years after Ridley Scott's film *Gladiator* made nearly half a billion dollars at the box office and won the Oscar for Best Picture, Pepsi premiered a *Gladiator*-themed Super Bowl commercial starring three of the biggest pop stars of the time, Britney Spears, Beyoncé Knowles, and Alecia Beth Moore-Hart (aka Pink, or P!nk if you're nasty). Back then, in the direct shadow of *Lost in Translation,* Thems could loudly and proudly participate in marketing if the advertisements themselves were—to co-opt an iconic Oprah line, market-*ed.* Pepsi's Super Bowl ad was an event, one that came with behind-the-scenes footage and much fanfare. Directed by Tarsem Singh, who began his career with music videos and transitioned into art-house peculiarities like *The Cell* (starring Jennifer Lopez) and *The Fall* (starring Lee Pace), the commercial was as much a product as the product it was selling, and none of its three stars were knocked down a single peg in the press for participating. The ad, soundtracked by a new rendition of Queen's classic hit "We Will Rock You," spawned a single ("We Will Rock You—Pepsi 'Gladiator' Sound Track Remix 2004"), and even a pseudo-sequel starring Megan Thee Stallion and Travis Kelce tied to the release of *Gladiator II* twenty years later.

But the ubiquity of high-speed internet, capable of streaming endless amounts of video content, changed media consumption in ways not seen in culture since the dawn of TV. (And not just in an *Oh yay, we can watch* The Simpsons *on our phones whenever we want* way.) It was harder to make an event out of anything, let alone ads, when everyone was watching different things on different screens. This tectonic shift not only meant Clooney's once region-locked Nespresso ads were viewable (and lampoonable) around the world, but so were his films and television shows. The home-video royalties he and countless other actors found so reliable for more than a generation dried up seemingly overnight thanks to a fundamental shift in media delivery. In short, streaming was great for consumer convenience but disastrous for an actor's bottom line. The bar of shame would soon get a little lower for most Thems . . . but not before Whos took advantage of its sudden descent first. And where better to start selling than on their own highly followed social-media accounts?

AS PEOPLE WHO worked in advertising before going into celebrity journalism, we know firsthand that there are few things a brand loves more than a new platform on which to advertise their products. When we both worked at VH1 in the early 2010s, ads would have to be formatted specially for the channel's social-media accounts. We can't tell you the number of ads we had to rewrite for *Love & Hip Hop, Mob Wives,* and long-forgotten game shows hosted by Mark McGrath. (Have you tried fitting a synopsis *and* tune-in date into 144 characters or less? It isn't easy!) But it made sense why fans would want to follow a brand like VH1—they wanted to watch trailers and bonus content, and be reminded when new episodes were released. As other brands joined the maelstrom while working with more traditional advertising agencies, we couldn't help but wonder (in a Carrie Bradshaw sense), *Why the hell would anyone want to follow State Farm's Facebook page?* The early 2010s were a total mess for advertisers; they spent those years with one foot in the past and the other hovering nervously in the future. Print media and network TV weren't dead, but they weren't pulling in the audiences they once did, meaning advertisers began looking elsewhere to spend their money. Once celebrities started gaining significant followings on Instagram, brands couldn't help but see those accounts with hundreds of thousands—even millions—of followers as micro-platforms. Audiences needed to be met where they were. And they were on Kim Kardashian's Instagram grid.

In 2014, Kim was the second-most-followed person on Instagram (after Justin Bieber), with 12.1 million fans. She had three hallmarks of Whodom: reality stardom, a semi-famous family, and a love of attention at any cost. In the much-imitated *Paper* feature from 2014, "Break the Internet," which pairs a profile by writer Amanda Fortini with provocative photographs by Jean-Paul Goude, Kardashian is asked whether she would exist without social media. "I don't think so," she answers. No one would ever accuse such a person of selling out, because selling out inherently requires the person doing so to have artistic integrity to forfeit in the first place. Her single "Jam (Turn It Up)" unsurprisingly failed to make any impact beyond an abundance of punch lines on social media. So how, exactly, can one sell *out* when their entire job is selling *themselves*?

As a reality star, she made for great television. As a social-media star, she made for great ROI. Before Instagram was an algorithmically controlled, video-centric hellscape, it was a place to post photos for people who followed you, and a place to view photos from people you followed. That's it! The end. Kim's millions of followers were a goldmine to advertisers (before the algorithm began ordering posts, those were guaranteed eyeballs) and she was among the first high-profile celebrities to pepper her Instagram feed—which normally consisted of the kinds of selfies that made it into her 2013 photography collection, *Selfish*—with images of her posing alongside a product she was being paid to promote. In the middle of the decade, it was hard to flip through her feed without seeing endorsements for modern corsets unpleasantly known as waist trainers, a brand of gummy supplements that purported to make hair shinier, and "skinny tea" (synonymous with "laxative juice"). One of her most notorious Instagram posts was shared in 2015. It was a photo of Kim holding a drug for morning sickness called Diclegis. In the image, she can be seen holding a medicine bottle while staring fiercely into the camera, alongside a caption that reads, in part,

> OMG. Have you heard about this? As you guys know my #morningsickness has been pretty bad. I tried changing things about my lifestyle, like my diet, but nothing helped, so I talked to my doctor. He prescribed me #Diclegis, and I felt a lot better and most importantly, it's been studied and there was no increased risk to the baby. I'm so excited and happy with my results that I'm partnering with Duchesnay USA to raise awareness about treating morning sickness.

Within days, the FDA sent a letter to the drug's manufacturer that accused Kardashian's caption of failing to meet FDA guidelines. The post was quickly deleted, revised, and reuploaded to bring it up to the agency's standards. The new caption was much longer, and seemed to have been constructed by multiple partners at a law firm, reading in part,

> #CorrectiveAd I guess you saw the attention my last #morningsickness post received. The FDA has told Duchesnay, Inc., that my last post about Diclegis (doxylamine succinate and pyridoxine HCl) was incomplete because it did not include any risk information or important limitations of use for Diclegis. A link to this information accompanied the post, but this didn't meet FDA

requirements. So, I'm re-posting and sharing this important information about Diclegis. For US Residents Only . . .

We'll stop there, but the conciliation went on for a further 244 words that covered all necessary legal bases.

It was a humiliating press cycle for Kim, but one she and her family were able to handle deftly. Perhaps it even planted a seed in their minds about all the social-media advertising they'd been doing. Sure, they were getting paid well to tell their followers to buy other people's stuff, but wouldn't it be even more lucrative to use Instagram to tell their followers to buy *their own* stuff? Cut to the present day, and Kim is the founder of Skims, a shapewear brand worth $5 billion. As we've already discussed, there's an intrinsic synergy (and, thus, free advertising) happening in the Kardashian-Jenner family: They all love to promote each other's brands.

IN 2019, THREE YEARS into the run of our podcast, the singer-songwriter/canonic Who-lebrity Bebe Rexha revealed a new partnership with Lay's. The press release declared: "Lay's Partners with Bebe Rexha to Create Perfect Harmonies with First-Ever Music-Inspired Chip Flavors That Unlock New Custom Songs." That's baseline hilarious on its own, a discombobulating mishmash of promotional-speak that confidently announces something inexplicable as if it makes all the sense in the world. "First-Ever Music-Inspired Chip Flavors"? *Sure!* In a video cross-posted to both Rexha's and Lay's Instagram accounts, the singer does her best to explain what it means to create harmonies for chip flavors that unlock new songs. "Flavor and music can trigger such powerful emotions," she says. "Different genres of music can get me feeling certain ways, and the same goes for different flavors. So what if you paired the two together? Now, that would be a *crazy* sensory experience." While the camera captures Rexha and a troupe of other songwriters/producers (read: actors pretending to be songwriters/producers) chatting in a recording studio, she takes two quick bites—*crunch, crunch*—of Lay's Flamin' Hot Dill Pickle Remix-Flavored chips to the beat of her own song, "Right Here, Right Now." It was brilliant camp; we laughed about it for hours.

5 Notable Things Celebs Have Tried to Sell Us

- **Vanessa Hudgens:** #ad Tomorrow is @MyLittlePony Friendship Day! Don't forget to #FrienditForward and do something nice for your bestie. #FriendshipisMagic
- **Danielle Brooks:** So elated to finally share this news with you all. I'm happily pregnant! #ClearblueConfirmed #clearbluepartner.
- **Antoni Porowski:** Happy #NationalGuacamoleDay! I'm partnering with WHOLLY GUACAMOLE, the brand that makes it easier to enjoy delicious guac anytime—no mashing or prep needed. It's made with real ingredients like hand-scooped Hass avocados and no added preservatives. Get a FREE coupon using the link in my bio. Today only, while supplies last.
- **Paula Abdul:** #paidpartnership / I am ecstatic to announce my newest partnership with @psychics1on1, a modern platform where you can connect with expert, vetted psychics through video chat or audio call. I've been helped through incredible spiritual advisors who have been so spot-on, and have helped me navigate my way throughout my career and my love life. I have found spiritual advice offers wonderful lessons that are yours for the taking if you allow yourself to be open minded enough to seek that spiritual guidance.
- **Kristen Chenoweth:** #ad Making my #DipForDinner dreams a reality tonight with NEW Town House Crackers Dippers. My dip game is strong but I have a feeling these buttery beauties won't break under the pressure.

Bebe Rexha is an objectively successful artist, but even she would likely agree that most of her top songs are as the featured artist behind someone much more famous—artists like G-Eazy, Louis Tomlinson, and David Guetta—or even further behind the scenes as a songwriter. She has crafted a huge number of hits, but they were broadly credited to the artists who sang them, like Rihanna, Selena Gomez, and Nick Jonas. So it's no surprise that the product she sold in 2019 was confusing: three brand-new and limited-edition flavors of potato chip, paired with a painfully convoluted brand message asking audiences to remember that Lay's Wavy Electric Lime Sea Salt equals pop music, Lay's Flamin' Hot Dill Pickle equals hip-hop, and Lay's Kettle Cooked Classic Beer Cheese equals rock music. Oh, and she paired *those* pairings with a new song called "Right Here, Right Now," but you could only listen to each remix if you scanned the QR code on the bag of the flavor that represented the corresponding genre. (Rexha was using QR codes well before they became Thems during Covid-19.) All George Clooney did was look into the camera and tell people to drink Nespresso.

When listeners call in to our podcast with questions, comments, or concerns, they often sign off with Rexha's melodic "*crunch, crunch,*" which, they understand like we do, is a perfect distillation of everything we find hilarious and charming about the lives of Who-lebrities, especially the way they changed the landscape of sponsored content. In a world where Thems were traditionally expected to hide from blatant sponsored content, Whos like Bebe Rexha proudly accepted outlandish offers and posted them to their Instagram grids, where they could quickly be pushed down the feeds and obscured by more organic, non-sponsored content. By the end of the 2010s, it seemed like every reality star, aspiring actor or musician, and TikTok influencer was supplementing their creative income with a post promoting a vibrator, supplement, gambling service, or alcoholic beverage. And because the Whos walked through those early days of social-media sponcon, Thems finally decided they were ready to take the baton and run.

For celebrity-adjacent Instagram commerce, the anonymity of a Who was a kind of immunity, providing a collective ability to fight all the way through the Wild West of early social-media marketing. As audiences rolled their eyes and pointed out all the ways they allegedly "sold out," the Whos kept at it. Jennifer Aniston, one of the most famous television stars in the history of the medium, resisted Instagram for years. When she finally joined in 2019, it was to subtly promote a *Friends* reunion on HBO. She posted a grainy, abysmally lit selfie with her co-stars and the caption "And now we're Instagram FRIENDS too. HI INSTAGRAM 👋." It was a charming (if brief) glimpse into the personal life of one of our most private celebrities. The purity of her feed was short-lived, however. Today, you can see ads for Skinny Pop popcorn among those intimate photos with friends because now everyone is free to sell *stuff* in this brave new world, without the fear of selling out.

THERE IS PERHAPS no celebrity who has more successfully (and shamelessly) straddled the line between selling himself and selling products than Ryan Reynolds. After spending more than a decade in a purgatory between Themdom and Whodom, during which he had one of the titular roles in the popular-ish ABC sitcom *Two Guys and a Girl* (né *Two Guys, a Girl, and a Pizza Place*) and starred in a handful of relatively successful comedies like *Just Friends* and *The Proposal*, Hollywood began giving Reynolds the kinds of leading roles that suggested they saw he was primed for Themdom. Big studio swings like the superhero flop *The Green Lantern*, the high-concept dump *The Change-Up*, and the disastrous ghost cop action vehicle *R.I.P.D.* failed to make him a household name; nevertheless, Reynolds persisted. In 2016 he produced and starred in *Deadpool*, a Marvel Comics adaptation and passion project of sorts that quickly became the highest-grossing R-rated film in U.S. history. It even spawned not one but two blockbuster sequels. When he married Blake Lively in 2012, *she* was the more bankable star. By the end of the decade, Reynolds had eclipsed her, finally the A-lister he'd always dreamed of becoming. But instead of using this as an excuse to become more private and discerning, as a Them may have done twenty or even ten years prior, he added yet another hyphen to his title. Two years after the release of the first

Deadpool film, Reynolds purchased the Portland, Oregon–based alcohol brand Aviation Gin. In a press release, the brand said Reynolds wouldn't just be a financial backer but would "play an active role in the day-to-day business and oversee creative direction as part of his mission to introduce the world to the great taste of Aviation."

Now, we've read enough press releases to know that the phrase "creative director" doesn't necessarily mean that you're either of the words of which it is composed. It's the marketing equivalent of receiving an honorary degree, something that sounds pleasant to the ear and looks nice on a press release but tends to be given away without asking for anything in return. In the past two decades we've watched with narrowed, skeptical eyes as Thems like Lady Gaga, Will.i.am, and Victoria Beckham became the "creative directors" of Polaroid, Intel, and Range Rover, respectively, without ever convincing the public that they were in any way responsible for a single piece of creative output that they allegedly "directed." When Alicia Keys became the creative director of BlackBerry in 2013, the company was in steep decline as Apple overtook the cellphone market share; her hiring appeared to be a Hail Mary pass at maintaining relevance in the telecommunications space. The only substantial press Keys received while holding the title was when, less than a week after earning it, she was caught sending tweets from her iPhone—*not a BlackBerry.* ("Started from the bottom now were [*sic*] here!" she wrote, the words "Sent from my iPhone" blaring beneath her message.) Keys departed the company within the year. Even more bizarre was Justin Timberlake's brief stint as creative director of Myspace, which began after he and Specific Media Group purchased the company for $35 million in 2011—years after we forgot the passwords to our long-dormant accounts. If you're wondering what he actually *did* there, well, that depends on whom you ask. In a statement released at the time, Timberlake said his role was to help Myspace reach its full potential. But a mere two years later, the company's COO, Chris Vanderhook, said Timberlake didn't have a title, or even an office at their building. The "SexyBack" singer's job, Vanderhook said, was "pretty broad." In short, he didn't "direct" any "creative" at all, and instead was a humble investor—a canny one at that, as Time

Inc. eventually purchased the company for more than double what Timberlake and his partners paid. The title had been an honorific, just as most people suspected from the start.

Which brings us back to Ryan Reynolds. The same year he bought Aviation Gin, Reynolds co-founded—and was named (or named himself?) creative director of Maximum Effort, a hybrid film production company and marketing agency. Unlike Keys and Timberlake, Reynolds seems to have taken his job title seriously. Sure, many of his clients are brands and films in which he holds a financial stake (*Deadpool*, Aviation Gin, Mint Mobile, and his famously sober wife Blake Lively's alcohol brand, Betty Booze), but he has developed advertisements for companies like Peloton and Heinz. Reynolds, it seems, wants to be perceived as the rare Hollywood celebrity with the charisma of a movie star and the brain of a businessperson, a staunchly capitalist, modern-day version of Paul Newman, appearing in ads as himself and speaking to the press about his role as an "Ad Man" in ways that would make Don Draper proud and Newman shake his damn head. "I feel like there's no reason we can't have Super Bowl–level advertising all year round," Reynolds told *The Hollywood Reporter* in 2022. "You can make a tremendous impact in the marketplace when you're moving at the speed of culture." Ah, the lyrical emptiness of an advertising professional is truly something to behold.

For a celebrity whose slow, detour-filled rise to the Themdom has been a central part of his narrative, one can't help but think that the Ryan Reynolds we know now wouldn't have happened had his career reached its current peak back in the aughts. Back then, audiences likely would have rejected this particular kind of multihyphenate, and the butterfly effect of finding huge success before actors were allowed to be influencers could very well have been that we wouldn't see Aviation Gin on the top shelf of bars today.

Our podcast would probably be out a little cash too. Mint Mobile, bless their hearts, is a regular advertiser on *Who? Weekly*.

Chapter 9

The Plight of the Nepo Baby

Jane Fonda, Gwyneth Paltrow & John David Washington

"Shocker! Daniel Day-Lewis Quits Acting (EXCLUSIVE)," reads a June 2017 headline in *Variety*. The three-time Academy Award winner announced his retirement just months before the release of *Phantom Thread,* his second collaboration with writer/director Paul Thomas Anderson, with a plainly worded, publicist-written statement: "Daniel Day-Lewis will no longer be working as an actor. He is immensely grateful to all of his collaborators and audiences over the many years. This is a private decision and neither he nor his representatives will make any further comment on this subject." *Phantom Thread* had been released to huge critical success, earning him a sixth Oscar nomination. Who could blame the guy for wanting to go out on top?

But much like Cher and the band KISS, eight years later, the following headline appeared in the very outlet where the actor's retirement was first announced: "Daniel Day-Lewis Comes Out of Retirement After 8 Years in Family Drama Directed by His Son." And you thought the man was done acting! Just because he had said so! One of the most reclusive and sought-after actors of a generation was back at work. All it took was a little nepotism.

We've had nepo babies for as long as we've had celebrities who choose to procreate, but we'd never had a sticky name for them until this decade. Sure, the root word "nepotism" has been there the whole time, but terms like "beneficiary of nepotism" or "product of nepotism" don't exactly roll off the tongue; they're too formal, and maybe even (God forbid) *legitimizing*. Using "beneficiary of nepotism" is like using a scientific name instead of a colloquial one: No one at a zoo calls that lumbering, humped creature a *Camelus dromedarius*; it's a dang camel!

Nepotism comes in many shapes and sizes, but when we talk about nepo babies, we're talking about the *celebrity* children of *celebrities*. To us, nepo babies are children of celebrities who become as famous as their parents or more famous than their parents ever were; children who are tabloid fixtures for their entire adult lives but who also make headlines well outside the entertainment sphere, who monetize their fame in new and perhaps unexpected ways, all while remaining unapologetic about their last names. These are people who are afforded not just a foot in the door but a stampede of famous and otherwise powerful bodies breaking it down for them. How can an aspiring actor who just hopped off the plane at LAX with a dream and a cardigan (the non-Cyruses among them, anyway) compete with someone who shares an agent, publicist, and lawyer with their Oscar-winning parent?

When searching for the blueprint, or patient zero, for the *contemporary* nepo baby, one has the impulse to start hunting in the early days of Hollywood. We're talking (or not talking) about the silent era. The first dynasty that might pop into your brain is the Barrymores—that storied showbiz family whose name was synonymous with entertainment from the late nineteenth century to the early twentieth century. But even the many branches of the Barrymore family come up short when it comes to presenting a nepo baby on par with the ones prevalent today. After the third generation of Barrymores (siblings Lionel, Ethel, and John) found success in Hollywood in the 1920s (and well into the '50s), the family didn't produce another huge star until 1982, when seven-year-old Drew, John's granddaughter, appeared in *E.T.* (She'd also go clubbing at Studio 54 at nine, write the iconic memoir *Little Girl Lost* at fourteen, and eventually host an eponymous talk show at forty-five.)

A more reasonable argument could be made for John Huston being the blueprint for the modern nepo baby. On paper, it's *almost* there: He was the son of early Hollywood superstar Walter Huston, his directorial efforts (like *The Maltese Falcon*, *The Treasure of the Sierra Madre*, and, duh, *Annie*) were massive hits, and he had plenty of high-profile affairs and marriages—his lovely memoir *An Open Book* contains several stories about his personal life being fodder for the gossip papers—but ultimately John was a writer/director, not an actor. And in the celebrity hierarchy, actors trump directors *every single time*.

When it comes to true modern-day nepo babies, there really is no one like Jane Fonda.

IN THE JANUARY 9, 1958, installment of "Just for *Variety*," Army Archerd's long-running, wildly influential column covering Hollywood gossip, nightlife, news, and general goings-on, twenty-year-old Jane Fonda gets her first-ever mention. It's a manically formatted, ellipsis-filled, stream-of-consciousness recollection of every remotely celebrity-adjacent bit of news that Archerd heard in the previous twenty-four hours. In other words, it's a riot. While reading down the page you'll encounter items about a "Distinguished Achievement" award won by Kirk Douglas (whose son Michael was just thirteen at the time); the upcoming wedding of Jayne Mansfield and Mickey Hargitay (they'd welcome Mariska six years later); and, under the subhead "AFTER DARK," a party celebrating the premiere of Tennessee Williams's off-Broadway production of *The Garden District*, which was made up of two brand-new one-act plays: *Something Unspoken* and *Suddenly Last Summer*. (The latter's film adaptation starring Elizabeth Taylor would be released the following year.) At the Williams soiree were, among others, Aly Khan (son of Sir Sultan Muhammad Shah, the forty-eighth imam of the Nizari Ism'aili), who brought Eugenia, the stepdaughter of Mervyn LeRoy (the producer of *The Wizard of Oz*), who came with *her* stepbrother Warner LeRoy, whose grandfather was one of the four original Warner brothers (not Albert, not Sam, not Jack, but *Harry*). Archerd writes that Warner "squired" Jane Fonda, who was described as, simply, "Hank's sprig." While it may make most modern readers raise an eyebrow in confusion, those in 1958 certainly understood Archerd was saying that Jane was the child of Henry Fonda, one of the most beloved and successful stars of Hollywood's Golden Age.

These days, a party report featuring four children of the rich, famous, and/or powerful would have a pithy headline like "NEPO NIGHT OUT." Back then it was more of an intriguing novelty. "The movies" as we know them now had only been around for three decades at the time of Jane's first film role, placing her among the first wave of actors to have fully grown up in or around the version of the business that's still recognizable today. We just didn't have a great term for what she and other famous children of celebrities *were* until she was in her mid-eighties.

After skyrocketing to fame not long after that first "night out" with one-fourth of the Warner brothers' grandsons, Fonda's career quickly became the model for the kind of Hollywood nepotism the media (and the public) seems to be the most invested in—meaning, we care less about family businesses if the family business doesn't involve someone we love watching onscreen or listening to on the radio. Is anyone out here talking about what happened to Warner LeRoy, or any of the Warner brothers' children's children? *Not really!* But we can't get enough of Tony Goldwyn, who nepo-babied his way from grandchild of iconic movie producer Samuel Goldwyn to one of Hollywood's most reliably sexy villains. The rest of the family? *Who cares!* But Tony played the villain in *Ghost* and the president who romanced Kerry Washington on *Scandal*. To everyone who would argue on behalf of other second-generation nepo babies of the era like Liza Minnelli (child of actor Judy Garland and director Vincente Minnelli), Michael Douglas (aforementioned child of actors Kirk Douglas and Diana Douglas), or Jamie Lee Curtis (child of actors Tony Curtis and Janet Leigh), we have three words for you: *Jane Fonda's Workout*.

With that bestselling series of workout tapes sold on VHS during the rise of home video, Fonda predicted the result of a suffocatingly large nepo-baby conversation that would be had decades later. Here she was, a politically outspoken nepo baby and two-time Oscar winner, sharing her workout routine for $59.95 a pop *in the '80s*. (That's roughly $200 in today's money.) From her career-spanning refusal to stay silent about the wars in Vietnam and Iraq in an environment where keeping one's mouth shut was the celebrity status quo to selling astronomically expensive videotapes that taught people how to exercise in their living room, the general public had every reason to find Jane Fonda insufferable. But she kept at it, powering through every storm and refusing to go away. It is arguably the kind of dedication that stems from privilege, specifically Hollywood privilege. Henry Fonda was beloved from the 1930s to his death in 1982, so why wouldn't his daughter share the same fate? This isn't to say blind, all-encompassing self-confidence is exclusive to the children of famous people, but it's gotta help.

Every few years, a single topic overtakes the typically diverse and non-homogenous landscape of modern celebrity journalism and discourse. Though usually fractured and fine-tuned for every conceivable niche or micro-fandom—with actors talking about their acting, musicians talking about their music, and models talking about their morning routines—there is an occasional topic that becomes a major talking point for nearly everyone in Hollywood. Typically, these discussions stem from cultural events that highlight systemic problems in the industry, be they a spotlight on the racism inherent to awards shows (the focus of #OscarsSoWhite, a hashtag created by media strategist April Reign in 2015); the open secret of rampant sexual abuse and misconduct (the focus of #MeToo in 2017); or the ways in which productions fail members of their guilds (the focus of both major guild strikes in 2023). During these moments, celebrities are roped into sharing their opinions with not just their peers but their public, and the public is happy to join in! During #OscarsSoWhite, stars like Lupita Nyong'o, George Clooney, Viola Davis, and Reese Witherspoon spoke out through personal channels and professional interviews, happy to join a conversation started by civilians in order to make awards more inclusive. Much has been written about how the women who bravely shared their stories early on in the #MeToo movement inspired countless others (celebrities and non-celebrities alike) to do the same, all in the hope of making the industry a safer, more functional place to have a career. Even the guild strikes, despite their inside-baseball technicalities and language, led the general public to celebrate or condemn celebrities who either supported the guilds or openly scabbed. But not every viral movement mobilizes both celebrities and their adoring fans with the hope of enacting change. Sometimes we all just simultaneously find something, well, interesting! Perhaps worthy of a laugh, or even simply a raised eyebrow. At the very least, something we can all agree on being worthy of conversation. In 2022, that something was the nepo baby.

FROM THE HEADLINE ("She Has Her Mother's Eyes. And Agent. Extremely Overanalyzing Hollywood's Nepo-Baby Boom") to the illustrations of the adult heads of pseudo-recognizable young stars who look like their more famous parents copy-pasted onto the bodies of newborn babies in the nursery of a hospital, *New York* magazine's December 2022/January 2023 cover story and accompanying package on nepo babies was a hit. The term itself is no doubt condescending but somehow also gentle, like a schoolyard insult one could easily brush off. They put adult heads on the bodies of newborn babies—how serious could it be? Writer Nate Jones charts one of the earliest uses of "nepo baby" to a 2020 post on the blog *Pop Culture Died in 2009.* (Shout-out to a true chronicler of aughts culture.) Jones argues that the term first went broadly viral two years later, in mid-2022—thanks to a tweet by Meriem Derradji that read, "Wait I just found out that the actress that plays Lexi is a nepotism baby omg 😭 her mom is Leslie Mann and her dad is a movie director lol." The "Lexi" to whom Derradji referred in her tweet is Lexi Howard, a character on the HBO drama series *Euphoria* played by Maude Apatow. Apatow's mother is Leslie Mann, a successful comedic actor, and her "movie director dad" is Judd Apatow, the man behind basically every R-rated comedy with an ensemble of white people released between 2004 and 2015.

A casual Twitter observation that started inescapable chatter? It was like "The Dress" all over again. (It was blue and black, by the way. Case closed.) People began to seek out nepo babies like Easter eggs, as though these brightly colored objects filled with money, power, and a Rolodex were surreptitiously scattered across every movie, album, and TV show. But it was an easy hunt. Actor Denzel Washington's son John David would soon be headlining an action tentpole despite having little experience; producer/director J. J. Abrams's daughter, Gracie, was giving Taylor Swift a run for her money when appealing to the sonic appetites of tweens; musician Lenny Kravitz's daughter, Zoë, was a well-liked actor who seemed to be friends with basically everyone in Hollywood; and actor Melanie Griffith's daughter Dakota Johnson was somehow so powerful that she single-handedly destroyed the reputation one of the most beloved comedians of a generation. (There were other factors at play, but "Actually, no, that's not the truth, Ellen," made it OK for the real work to start.)

The discourse caused a kind of Baader-Meinhof effect, because once you start looking for nepo babies, you'll find them everywhere. To open TikTok during that time was to experience a deluge of nepo-baby content, with floating heads of strangers breathlessly revealing nepo babies hidden throughout culture like conspiracy-theorist food influencers ranting about the secret prevalence of seed oils. *Euphoria*? Nepo babies! The Marvel Cinematic Universe? Nepo babies!! The DC Universe?! Nepo babies!!! The co-star of Best Picture nominee *The Substance*? She's a "secret" nepo baby (or so writes *The Sun*), because her surname doesn't match her famous mother's!!!! In the months immediately following the publication of *New York*'s Nepo Baby issue, it seemed like every media outlet decided to join in on the conversation. *Cosmopolitan* published a piece titled "I Present: All the Celebs You Didn't Know Were Nepo Babies," many of whom were already featured in *New York*'s issue. *People* first published their running list of

"Nepotism Babies" in August 2022, around the time Derradji's tweet went viral, and the post is *still* being updated today. Even other industries joined in on the discourse, with *Business Insider* publishing a list of nepo babies in corporate America and *The Takeout* publishing a list of "nepo babies of the food world."

THESE LISTS CAST as broad of a generational and notoriety net as possible, creating adjacencies that are often outright comical. In a Yahoo! piece titled "53 Celebrities You Forgot Were 'Nepo Babies' from Famous Families," celebrities like Maya Hawke (the MTV Movie & TV Award–nominated daughter of actors Uma Thurman and Ethan Hawke) are found alongside Eva Amurri (the actor-turned-blogger and child of director Franco Amurri and actor Susan Sarandon). In a piece for *The Wrap* called "All the 'Nepo Babies' on 'The Pitt' and Their Famous Parents," Taylor Dearden, the daughter of Emmy-winning TV star Bryan Cranston, is presented as equally privileged as Fiona Dourif, the daughter of the man who voiced Chucky, the killer doll from the *Child's Play* franchise. (No offense to Chucky, whose offspring, Glenda Ray, starred in 2004's *Seed of Chucky*. Nepotism much?) In its nascent stage, the nepo-baby conversation implied that the children of famous people sat comfortably atop the hierarchy of Hollywood, with all of them dumped into the same lofty bucket, rattling around like bingo numbers.

Fallout from the discourse's first stage—the TikToks, the tweets, the seemingly endless barrage of published lists—was soon felt by nepo babies on the promotional circuit. For months, if not years, no celebrity with a famous parent (or sister, or brother, or even, in the case of pop star Sabrina Carpenter, an aunt who voices Bart Simpson) could sit down for an interview without expecting a question about their nepo status. Many came prepared for the conversation, locked and loaded with thoughtful, humble responses. When interviewed about his series *Lessons in Chemistry*, Lewis Pullman (son of actor Bill Pullman) called himself "undeniably fortunate." Similarly, while promoting her role in *The Last of Us,* Nico Parker (daughter of actor Thandiwe Newton and writer/director Ol Parker) said, "I think it's incredibly important to recognize that with your parents being prevalent in the industry, it's way easier to get in the room."

5 Nepo Babies Who Tried to Fool Us (But Didn't)

- Angelina Jolie (born Angelina Jolie Voight, child of Jon Voight and Marcheline Bertrand)
- Malia Ann (born Malia Obama, child of Barack and Michelle Obama)
- Louisa Jacobson (born Louisa Gummer, child of Meryl Streep and Don Gummer)
- Nic Cage (born Nicolas Kim Coppola, child of August Coppola and Joy Vogelsang)
- Norah Jones (born Geethali Norah Jones Shankar, child of Ravi Shankar and Sue Jones)

Some celebrities tried to wave away the discourse by offering up a history lesson. Many nepo babies compare their career choices to more run-of-the-mill "family businesses," like dentists raising children who then grow up to be dentists, or, as Zoë Kravitz put it in an interview with *GQ*, "It's completely normal for people to be in the family business. It's literally where last names came from. You were a blacksmith if your family was, like, the Black family." (They were actually the Smith family.) The profile immediately follows this by sharing how "proud" Kravitz is to come from such a storied, successful family of entertainers. And how could you not be proud to have Roxie Roker as your grandmother? Before you ask: Al Roker is Lenny's second cousin.

Others took a more defensive stance. Sam Nivola (son of actors Emily Mortimer and Alessandro Nivola) said his appearance on *The White Lotus* had nothing to do with his parents, telling *Variety* he was "proud" to have gotten acting roles *without* using his father's agent:

"Other than my genes, I don't think I can attribute much of my success to my parents . . . I did it by myself." Actor Dan Levy (son of actor Eugene Levy) told *Page Six,* "I never really turned to my dad for anything . . . out of fear of the label of nepotism." Perhaps to his surprise, the label came anyway. Even director Destry Allyn Spielberg (daughter of director Steven Spielberg and actor Kate Capshaw) rejected the idea that her father, arguably the most famous director on planet Earth, had any role in shaping her career. Destry tweeted, "People can argue nepotism, but I know deep down that I worked hard to get where I am, and it wasn't easy." Would it surprise you to know she deleted the tweet not long after it was posted?

One of the funniest responses to the nepo-baby line of questioning came from someone who benefited from a slightly atypical form of nepotism: the child of a powerful showbiz producer. In August 2007, a thirteen-year-old Ben Platt posted on the "Addicted to Wicked" Facebook group, "Hello, I'm Ben Platt and my dad is marc platt [*sic*] the producer of Wicked." The screenshot of Platt's post tends to resurface on social media anytime Ben is a trending topic—as if it succinctly encapsulates what it means to grow up as the child of someone you believe can help get your foot through any elusive door. In December 2016 the musical *Dear Evan Hansen* opened on Broadway. Platt (who was twenty-three at the time) played the titular Evan Hansen and won a Tony for the role the following spring. The show's writer? Naturally Ben's dear old dad, Marc. While Platt was promoting 2023's *Theater Camp*, a film he produced, wrote, and starred in, *Rolling Stone* writer EJ Dickson asked how it felt to be featured not just inside but on the *cover* of *New York* magazine's nepo-baby issue. Their exchange is more memorable than anything that happens in *Theater Camp*.

EJ: You were on the cover of *New York Magazine's* Nepo Baby issue. I'm curious, what was your response to that? And what do you make of that whole discourse?

BEN: We're going to skip right over that if we can.

EJ: No comment?

PUBLICIST [INTERVENING]: If we could just focus on *Theater Camp,* that would be great. Thank you.

The following year, Platt was given the opportunity to atone for his defensiveness in an interview with *Elle*. He said he regretted giving the question of nepotism "too much power," and went on to deliver the kind of eloquent, thoughtful statement that has since become the norm: "Of course, I acknowledge I'm an absolute nepo baby through and through by definition. My dad is a producer. I did grow up with an understanding of the business and an access to it. I will say that was the benefit, more so than it has been getting individual jobs as an adult. I think it really helped me to give me the tools and the foundation to build my career." We'll stop there, but note that Platt went on for a further 225 words. He had messed up before, and he came to this interview *ready*.

Gwyneth Paltrow (the daughter of actor Blythe Danner and producer/director Bruce Paltrow) accidentally delivered what would become the most widely acceptable template for a nepo baby responding to the Nepo Baby Question in July 2022, just a few months before it started being asked ad nauseam. On an episode of Hailey Bieber's bizarre, short-lived YouTube interview series *Who's in My Bathroom,* during which she interviewed other celebrities in her bathroom for absolutely no reason (even more confounding, it was a set that was made to look like the star's bathroom), the two nepo babies discussed being nepo babies. (Hailey Bieber is, in case you forgot, the child of actor Stephen Baldwin and niece of his more famous brother, actor Alec Baldwin. Now she is a model, a beauty mogul, and the wife of pop star Justin Bieber.) Despite being mere feet away from a non-flushing toilet, the conversation grew more serious. Paltrow says, "As the child of somebody, you get access other people don't have. So the playing field is not level in that way." *Correct!* "However," she adds (*cue record scratch*), "I really do feel that once your foot is in the door, which you unfairly got in, then you almost have to work twice as hard and be twice as good. Because people are ready to pull you down and say you don't belong there or you're only there because of your dad or your mom or whatever the case may be." While less objectively true than the first half of her response, it's worthy of argument. And taken as a whole, a reply that both acknowledges privileges while also doing a bit of defiant chest-thumping in the process, it stands as the perfect way for every nepo baby to respond in her wake: both proud and humble in the same breath. (If only so many nepo babies hadn't taken months to realize the right answer had been there in the archives of Hailey Bieber's bathroom-based interview show all along.)

BUT ENOUGH ABOUT actors for a moment. As the successful-producer-parent-to-successful-actor-child pipeline suggests, nepo babies exist across the spectrum of cultural influencers. Sometimes, when an actor mommy and director daddy love each other very much, they do a special dance that results in a nepo baby who decides to become a Rhodes Scholar and journalist. We're talking, of course, about Ronan Farrow, the child of director Woody Allen and actor Mia Farrow, who herself is the nepo baby of actor Maureen O'Sullivan and director John Farrow. (We don't have to get into the fact that Ronan's paternity is the subject of Reddit conspiracy theories that suggest his *real* birth father was Frank Sinatra, but take a look at some side-by-side photos and decide for yourself.) Hollywood is in Farrow's genes, no matter who you think his father is, but instead of seeking a career in film, like his parents, he decided to jump into the world of journalism. Before he rose to national fame thanks to his industry-rattling reporting at *The New Yorker* on Harvey Weinstein's decades-spanning sexual abuse, his photogenic looks and famous last name were used in a handful of failed attempts to make him a television news star. He had a show on MSNBC called *Ronan Farrow Daily* (which lasted just one year) and, later, a segment on NBC's *Today* called "Ronan Farrow Investigates." Perhaps the intention was to make him the next Anderson Cooper, another nepo-baby journalist who entered the world of journalism thanks to *his* telegenic looks and, as the child of Gloria Vanderbilt, famous parent. But Farrow didn't find true success until he took cover in the shadows of real, boots-on-the-ground reporting. Americans didn't need their news to come from someone whose name they recognized; they just needed news they could trust, regardless of it was being given by someone whose mother is best known for delivering the child of Satan in a film directed by the type of sexual predator Farrow is known for exposing.

As a Pulitzer Prize–winning journalist, Farrow is more of a nepo-baby *media figure* than nepo-baby *celebrity*. Resentful discourse about his privilege is typically ignored due to the fact that his cultural output—his work on #MeToo, especially—is so much bigger than him.

When it comes to conversations surrounding the privileges of nepotism, some of the most illuminating were had in the modeling community. At first glance it's easy to dismiss such a superficial industry as having an equal playing field, as it requires qualifications one is "born with" at an even more fundamental level than parentage. Skin color, body type, height, facial features—these are all written in one's DNA. Whether or not one has the "look" of a model (whatever that may be at the current moment) is determined by one's genes long before they're even born. This is something that can be used as both a defense and an admonishment of nepotism: Isn't it fair to assume that the child of someone whose body fits the definition of "model" would have a leg up, so to speak, in an industry that's largely about appearance?

In November 2022, model-turned-actor Lily-Rose Depp (daughter of actor Johnny Depp and model Vanessa Paradis) shrugged off the nepo-baby label during an interview with *Elle* promoting her starring role in the short-lived and uniquely horrendous HBO series *The Idol*. "I can definitely say that nothing is going to get you the part except for being right for the part," she says. "Maybe you get your foot in the door, but you still just have your foot in the door. There's a lot of work that comes after that." The backlash to her dismissive reply was near instantaneous. Several models spoke out about their own roadblocks in the industry that would have likely been removed if they had famous parents. Model Vittoria Ceretti shared a post on her Instagram Stories that, while not explicitly directed toward Depp, seemed to be a direct response to the remarks: "Yes, I get the whole 'I'm here and I work hard for it,' but I would really love to see if you would have lasted thru the first five years of my career," she wrote. "Not only being rejected, because I know you have an experience with it and you can tell me your sad little story about it (even if at the end of the day you can still always go cry on your dad's couch in your villa in Malibu)." (It's true that in 2012, Johnny Depp did buy a $4.4 million Malibu home for his daughter.)

Model Nyagua Ruea agreed with Ceretti. She added that her race makes the fact of her non-nepo-baby status even more of a struggle. "I will speak for my fellow Black/African models. Our reality is completely different because I don't even think there's any one Black model who has benefitted from nepotism," she wrote on her Instagram Stories. "Each and every single one of us has had to build & work for everything we have from scratch." A handful of Black nepo-baby models do exist, namely Aoki Lee Simmons (the daughter of model Kimora Lee Simmons and music producer Russell Simmons) and Lori Harvey (daughter of comedian Steve Harvey), but they're among the few exceptions to the rule.

The discourse, while often annoying, was less about changing the way capitalism often works than it was about allowing people to air their long-simmering frustrations to an audience that was newly receptive to it. It's no surprise that the nepo-baby conversation first blew up in the years following other profound cultural reckonings. While nepotism is by no means an issue as urgent as the #MeToo and Black Lives Matter movements, or the myriad inequalities laid bare during the Covid pandemic, those conversations laid the groundwork for a conversation about injustices to be had with full-throated confidence. And in just a few months, perceived missteps by models like Depp were clearly being used as promotional learning moments for her peers. Sisters Gigi and Bella Hadid are two of the highest-paid models of their generation, and their success is a helpful encapsulation of what makes nepotism both understandable and frustrating for those without familial connections. That they are *qualified* for the job isn't necessarily up for debate. As the children of a successful model, they were born with the looks of one. But beautiful people who stand five feet, eleven inches tall and have symmetrical faces aren't that rarefied as a group; the lobby of any modeling agency is proof. Getting noticed is, at minimum, half the battle. It helped that both Gigi and Bella grew up around people with major influence in the business. After model-turned-reality-star Yolanda Hadid gave birth to Gigi in 1995, it took just two years for her to reap the benefits of Punnett squares and familial connections. She attended preschool with a daughter of Paul Marciano, the founder of fashion brand Guess, and their respective parents "became really good friends." Marciano then "discovered" her, Gigi says, and before long she "started shooting Guess Baby and Guess Kids." Gigi had a foot in the door—in this instance, the home of Marciano—roughly around the same time she learned how to walk. When asked to comment about her status as a nepo baby by *The Times,* Hadid displayed the sort of self-awareness and humility that was, roughly six months into the nepo-baby discourse, finally becoming the norm. "Technically I'm a nepotism baby," she said, before writer Ellie Austin even had a chance to ask the question. "My parents came from very little [but] I've always acknowledged that I come from privilege. My parents told me, 'Just because you have parents who were successful, it doesn't mean that you shouldn't walk into the job being as nice and as hard-working as you can be.' "

WHEREAS GIGI SEEMINGLY learned from the mistakes of others when forming her own thoughts on the privilege that comes with being a nepo baby, others, hilariously, learned from themselves. Some of the most cogent and entertaining responses to the question came from one of Hollywood's most successful and beloved nepo babies, Jamie Lee Curtis, an actor known for her brutal candor in interviews. The height of the nepo discourse coincided with Curtis's promotional tour for the film *Everything Everywhere All at Once.* As Curtis campaigned for various Best Supporting Actress awards throughout that season, competing directly against the more critically acclaimed performance by Angela Bassett in *Black Panther: Wakanda Forever,* her approach evolved from righteous indignation to a more measured acknowledgment of privilege. In December 2022, eight months after *Everything Everywhere All at Once* was released, she wrote in an Instagram post, "There's not a day in my professional life that goes by without my being reminded that I am the daughter of movie stars. The current conversation about nepo babies is just designed to try to diminish and denigrate and hurt." During an interview on the film podcast *Little Gold Men,* she presented her nepotism as a warm story about the family business, telling host David Canfield, "[My parents] found their way to the top of the pile of this industry, and both of them were nominated for Oscars. And all of a sudden they were my parents, and they were welcoming me." Upon learning of her Oscar nomination, she found comfort in knowing "how thrilled" her parents would be for the accomplishment. During her acceptance speech for the SAG Award for Best Supporting Actress, Curtis said, "I know you look at me and think, *Well, nepo baby, that's why she's there,* and I totally get it. But the truth of the matter is: I'm sixty-four years old, and this is just amazing." (Curtis's evolution was chronicled that spring in a piece published by *Vanity Fair* with the headline "Jamie Lee Curtis Loves Being a Nepo Baby.") Oh how far she'd come in just one short month. While accepting her first Oscar that March, she ended her speech by addressing her late parents: "And my mother and father were both nominated for Oscars in different categories," she said before gesturing up toward the sky, as if their spirits were hovering over the sea of glitterati. "I just won an Oscar!"

While it's unlikely that a nepotism-related gaffe would have torpedoed Curtis's chances at the Oscars, it's still impressive that she was able to weather the storm throughout all those months and bring home the trophy. Many called her win a de facto "lifetime achievement award," more an honor of her career than the performance she gave in *Everything Everywhere All at Once,* a film whose *actual* breakout star was non–nepo baby Stephanie Hsu. But the same was also said when it came to Angela Bassett's likelihood of winning. Her "Oscar narrative" involved decades of snubs, and arguably more critical acclaim than Curtis. Didn't she deserve a "lifetime achievement award" as much as Curtis? It was hard to watch Curtis, who is the white child of Oscar-nominated actors, accept that award without feeling—even if only slightly—that what made her triumph over her Black peer (the child of a non-famous social worker) was some frustrating combination of nepotism and race. After all, we live in a country where whiteness and family connections are two of the most powerful forms of privilege.

It's doubtful that people *actually* want nepo babies banned from working in Hollywood. Like most forms of privilege—be it race, gender, sexuality, wealth, or anything else—acknowledging one's inherent advantages tends to be a first, and perhaps even final, step toward snuffing out any resounding criticisms. And while nepotism by no means guarantees Themdom, which (typically) requires both talent and tenacity, it gives its beneficiaries a running start of inherent Wholebrity. Like Ceretti and Ruea suggested with their Instagram posts, it's painful to feel gaslit by the privileged when they imply that everyone is playing with the same game pieces—even the same rules. Watching people have fame and money effectively handed to them is, beyond the jokes, wildly frustrating as the middle class continues to disappear and the gulf between the haves and have-nots becomes ever wider. That's all the nepo-baby conversation ever really was, a rare moment when the regular-degulars with no generational wealth or familial connections to Hollywood could lament their dull, ungilded birthright by making people with more resources and opportunities squirm, even if only a little. We had found their Achilles' heel, and it was just two words.

Chapter 10

Fandom Isn't Enough, It's Time to Stan

Barbz, Swifties & @ClubChalamet

Even after the *Merriam-Webster Dictionary* added the word "stan" in 2019 (along with "EGOT," "buzzy," and "snowflake," if you were wondering where the culture was at the time), there was still some disagreement on whether the word was simply a reference to the tragic titular subject of Eminem's 2000 single "Stan"—which some say is a portmanteau of "super" and "fan"—or something more sinister: a portmanteau of "stalker" and "fan." From the jump, Eminem was pretty clear that his Stan was a dark figure (despite being embodied in the music video by a bleach-blond Devon Sawa): At the end of the video, during which he scribbles out increasingly worrying letters to his musical idol, he drives himself and his pregnant girlfriend off a bridge. If we were at all curious how Eminem felt about his most diehard fans, well, it was now clear. He was scared shitless of them. Nas even followed up "Stan" in 2001 with his own take on the term: *"You a fan, a phony, a fake, a pussy, a Stan."* The term made its way outside the rap genre in 2002, with the Pet Shop Boys' "The Night I Fell in Love," which tells a story from the perspective of someone who, upon meeting a musician backstage at their concert, is asked, *"Hey, man! Your name isn't Stan, is it?"* In song, the term implies a Stan is a person who is threatening—or at the very least makes people uneasy. The *Merriam-Webster Dictionary* put it slightly more gently, defining "stan" as "an extremely or excessively enthusiastic and devoted fan." Sure, it's less pointed than "phony, fake, pussy" but nevertheless resoundingly negative.

When put this way, how could anyone *want* to be a Stan?

In his book *Convergence Culture,* Henry Jenkins writes about a time pre-standom: "The culture industries never really had to confront the existence of this alternative cultural economy because, for the most part, it existed behind closed doors and its products circulated only among a small circle of friends and neighbors." In a way, by "behind closed doors," he means *offline*—because without the internet, there was only so big a stan community could grow. *Star Trek* conventions aside, fans weren't able to shift into powerful bodies of influence until they were able to connect with one another quicker, and en masse. "A man with one machine (a TV) is doomed to isolation, but a man with two machines (TV and a computer) can belong to a community," Marshall Sella wrote in *The New York Times Magazine,* discussing the rise in popularity of TV recaps on websites like Television Without Pity. By the early aughts, culture had become deeply social in nature. From the moment something became consumable, it would also become shared.

When shared, the same culture could also inspire the formation of a new community. Before stans took over the internet, a fan might exist solely in a one-sided relationship with their celebrity of choice—inspiring trend pieces like 2024's "How the Loneliness Crisis Is Fueling 'Stan Culture,'" which responded to a 2021 American Perspectives survey that concluded Americans were having fewer close relationships than they did in the past. "Could it be that stan culture is the result of us replacing in-person friendships with the mirage of celebrity ones?" the writer asked. Is that still true? Or were the stan communities transforming these deeply parasocial relationships with their idols into real-life, reciprocal relationships with fellow stans?

At some point, "stan" went from noun to verb, for example: *No, you don't understand I've BEEN stanning Zara Larsson from the beginning; The way she's fully aware that she's an obnoxious bitch I kinda have to stan now;* and the dreaded *We have decided to unstan.* No longer were we that original desperate Stan about to drive ourselves and our pregnant girlfriends off a bridge; we were simply *stanning.* It was immediately a lot less severe: totally stanning versus being a total Stan. The first recorded use of "stan" as a verb (according to the *Oxford English Dictionary*) was in 2008, when @AuraAintGotTime replied to a tweet with: "I stan for Santogold. I may even like her more than MIA." (Santigold originally went by Santogold.) Notably, @pauljeffries responded to that tweet over ten years later to see if @AuraAintGotTime perhaps meant to type "stand" but missed the "d," which perhaps would have made more sense at the time. *But no matter!* However, the sentiment stands: She stanned then, and we all *really* stan now. Today's stans dedicate themselves to causes across the cultural landscape, from Rihanna to *Severance* to Dunkin' Donuts. (And if you have an issue with the last example, take it up with Ben Affleck.)

Long before @AuraAintGotTime stanned Santigold, there was Beatlemania—a well-known phenomenon that involved teenagers screaming for (and sometimes *at*) the Beatles. Before Beatlemania there was Lisztomania: not merely the title of a 2009 Phoenix song, but a term coined by German poet and essayist Heinrich Heine in 1844 to describe the fervor around pianist Franz Liszt. "And what tremendous rejoicing and applause!—a delirium unparalleled in the annals of furor! And what is the real cause of this phenomenon?" Heine wrote in *Lapham's Quarterly.* "The solution of the question belongs rather to the province of pathology than to that of aesthetics." Basically, the girlies were going absolutely *bonkers* for this guy: "They stamp unceasingly with their feet, producing a dull and persistent sound that is punctuated by isolated, involuntary screams," wrote a reviewer at a conference in Paris. So bonkers that Heine spoke to a doctor:

> A physician whose specialty is the disorders of women and with whom I conversed as to the magic which our Liszt exercises on his public, smiled mysteriously and told many things of magnetism, galvanism, electricity, of contagion in an overheated hall, in which are a vast number of wax candles, and as many perfumed,

> perspiring mortals, of histrionic epilepsies or stage fever, of the phenomena of tickling, of musical cantharides, and other ticklish subjects, which have, I believe, relation to the mysteries of the Bona Dea.

Sure, it could've been Franz (he was a great pianist!), but it could also be merely *the vibes*—that is, the beginnings of a collective standom at work.

THE EFFECT OF a collective worked then as it works now: The stans congregate online, deeming themselves Lambs for Mariah Carey or Barbz for Nicki Minaj or, unfortunately, Arianators for Ariana Grande (no hate to the Arianators, but y'all really could have come up with a better name). There are Megatrons (Meghan Trainor), KatyCats (Katy Perry), Harries (Harry Styles), even Rexhars (Bebe Rexha). Sometimes the names imply violent action—the Britney Army (Britney Spears) or Rihanna Navy (Rihanna, *duh*)—while others would probably embarrass their idol. (Did you know Ellie Goulding's fans go by the Gould-diggers?) Sometimes the names are coined by the idol themselves, like Lady Gaga's Little Monsters, while others make more lyrical sense: Justin Bieber's fans are Beliebers; Blackpink fans are BLINK. If you've heard any stan name in popular culture, it's no doubt the Beyhive for Beyoncé's most ardent supporters. Or maybe the *Eras Tour*'s proliferation of self-identified Swifties, aka those willing to shell out thousands to see Taylor Swift live.

5 Standoms You Maybe Haven't Heard of (Until Now)

- McAvoyeurs (James McAvoy)
- Fanilows (Barry Manilow)
- Kellebrities (Kelly Clarkson)
- Zswaggers (Zendaya)
- Sexy Souls (Ricky Martin)

Each standom grows to have its own hive mentality, one that will usually mimic whatever character their idol is performing. (Let's say "performing," because we really only see what they want us to see, right?) So many of the antics attributed to the Barbz (doxxing, threats, harassment) are dictated by Minaj herself. In 2021, mid-pandemic, she posted this now-storied tweet: "My cousin in Trinidad won't get the vaccine cuz his friend got it & became impotent. His testicles became swollen. His friend was weeks away from getting married, now the girl called off the wedding. So just pray on it & make sure you're comfortable with ur decision, not bullied." Critics pointed out the clear misinformation but also naturally poked fun at the casual usage of "swollen balls"; journalists attempted to reach out to Minaj's cousin for clarification—something that she did not like, tweeting at a reporter ("BITCH YOUR DAYS ARE FUCKING NUMBERED YOU DIRTY HOE") while also sharing their and other journalists' contact information as a pointed doxx. It was a call to action, and the Barbz descended. (Only two years later would Minaj, glaringly while promoting an upcoming album, ask her fandom to lay off the haters: "Dear Barbz, Be sure to never threaten anyone on my behalf. Whether on the internet or in person. Whether in jest, or not. I don't & never have condoned that.")

The Beyhive is perhaps one of the few fandoms that act more aggressively than their focus: Queen Bey has never commanded her worker bees to go after any target. (These days, the pop star barely speaks publicly at all.) Perhaps that's why fans feel as though they need to act as the voice for the implicitly demure pop superstar? When Beyoncé alluded to a "*Becky with the good hair*" in "Sorry" from the album *Lemonade* (which was a seemingly personal account of her husband Jay-Z's infidelities), the fandom was determined to figure out who Becky was. Did the song provide *just* enough information for them to find out? No, Beyoncé might've thought. Or perhaps we're underestimating her intentions, alas. But she certainly underestimated her industrious fans. They flooded the Instagrams of "Becky" suspects like fashion designer Rachel Roy and Rita Ora with hateful accusations. Some even mistakenly went after celebrity chef

Rachael *Ray*, who is an unlikely pairing for Jay-Z, but an exciting one nonetheless.

K-pop fans are known to fill the replies of their enemies with pointed spam, a mix of fancams (videos cleverly cut together that highlight the talents of their idol) and encouragements to "stan [INSERT FAVORITE] instead." They're annoying to sift through, but these fan-led guerilla-marketing movements sometimes work: In 2014 a K-pop group called EXID received a big career boost when a fancam featuring one of its members, Hani, dancing to their single "Up & Down" went viral. The fancam aesthetic has since become so effective as to become a joke-turned-meme in itself: "I'm sorry there's a Judas x Jesus fancam set to My Tears Ricochet??" @kellwhyyy tweeted in 2024, attaching a video made by TikTok user @jesustaylorsversion, in which clips from the 2017 Christian series *The Chosen* are mashed up and soundtracked with Taylor Swift. Honestly, it works: "*'Cause I loved you, I swear I loved you / 'Til my dying day,*" she sings as actor Jonathan Roumie, playing Jesus, is led to the cross.

They say there's an audience for everything out there—but now there's a standom too.

EVENTUALLY, ARTISTS STARTED to see their devoted stan communities as marketing assets (or, at least, their record labels did). Before Minaj was commanding her Barbz to go after her adversaries, it was just a goal to get "noticed" by your idol. That meant a "like" on Twitter, perhaps a question replied to in the Instagram comments—this wasn't something Barbra Streisand was doing at the peak of her fame in the '60s. (Although Babs fan clubs certainly exist today and have gone strong for years, and while the star herself definitely replied to a few fan letters in her day, this was more of a one-on-one experience.) Meanwhile, the minute Ariana Grande had fans to speak of, she was replying to them on Twitter—for all with Wi-Fi to witness. It also helps when the star is of the younger generation and as obsessed with the internet as their fans. "It was easier to get noticed by her back then because she wasn't as big as she is now," wrote the moderator of a Grande stan account on a Reddit message board. And once they were noticed, fans understood they also might have a bit more power—especially as a community.

If you thought Taylor Swift and Beyoncé fans were intense, may you never experience the ire of a Johnny Depp fan. After his ex-wife Amber Heard lodged abuse allegations against Depp, he filed a complaint of defamation against her, claiming at least $50 million in damages. In return, Heard filed counterclaims against Depp claiming $100 million in damages. Throughout the two-month trial, a legion of Depp fans ("a very large fan base that appears to be a combination of OG actor fans, Harry Potter stans, and true crime aficionados," noted *BuzzFeed* at the time) aggressively organized against Heard across the social-media landscape. Notably on TikTok, where clips of the livestreamed trial went viral alongside commentary, memes, and the hashtag #justiceforjohnnydepp; it felt like fans began the movement and then the immense virality of the content inspired those perhaps less passionate about *Pirates of the Caribbean* to hop on the hate train. The result was hundreds of supercuts from trial footage, edited to make Heard's accusations seem unfounded. Wrote Jessica Bennett in *The New York Times*: "The reviling of Ms. Heard has created some strange bedfellows, bringing together men's rights activists, Depp superfans and those who simply don't believe Ms. Heard and claim she's hurting 'real' victims of abuse—some of them self-proclaimed feminists—in the cesspool of the internet misinformation machine."

By organizing into large stan groups, fans could go from mere cheerleaders (and consumers) to consultants, weighing in on what their star could (or *should*) do next. They could have a real impact on a star's next album on the charts or film at the box office. Since the trial, Heard has mostly stayed out of the spotlight: She moved to Spain in 2023 with her daughter, took a small role in the sequel to *Aquaman*, and starred in a low-budget indie called *In the Fire* and a play at the 2025 Williamstown Theatre Festival.

■ ■ ■

IF MUSIC STANDOM is about *Billboard* charts and fancams, Hollywood standom is about hard news. Accounts across Twitter and Instagram, with display names like "Matt Bomer Files," "Dunst Archive," "Millie Source," "Joseph Quinn HQ," and "Glen Powell Central," present like spin-off magazines dedicated to a singular topic, much like that *Titanic*-themed magazine you might've seen in the checkout aisle, as if people still aren't quite sure what happened there. But "Ewan McGregor Daily" is devoted to keeping us updated on every aspect of Ewan McGregor's public life—"Looks like our guy was hanging out at some boat show in Southampton . . . in our favorite cardigan 😄 ," they tweeted alongside pictures of the actor. While "Best of Hailey Bieber," whose bio reads "Updates & media content about Hailey Bieber. Posting videos, pictures, updates, gifs, and more. ((Not impersonating))," vacillates between updates on the model-turned-entrepreneur's whereabouts ("Hailey Bieber at Sushi Park") and breathless proclamations of her beauty: "this face card is INSANE"; "Hailey Bieber is so classy"; "MOTHER." If you're up on your internet-speak, that last assertion manages to be both an accurate fact and an excited hyperbole.

Most important, they know what's going on with their subject—at all times. Thanks to the internet, that's a lot easier than it used to be, but these accounts are doing some serious on-the-ground reporting when necessary. Bebe Rexha told *Entertainment Weekly* that she's sometimes learning things about herself from the Rexhars: "They're like, 'Bebe Rexha is performing in Bulgaria on this date,' and I'm like, 'I am? I have no idea!'" The singer Raye once tweeted that she goes on Twitter to check her stan account instead of checking with her label, adding: "i love it this way and raye updates you are the truth you mean so much to me and i love you."

These accounts will fill their feeds with photos of their subjects at premieres, casting-news retweets, and just general all-purpose lustiness ("madelaine petsch is so stunning," says "best of madelaine petsch"; "This man right here. Look at him!" says "best of paul mescal"). They also know they have to keep their feeds populated—even if their subject isn't busy promoting something that would provide the content they so desperately need. To combat that issue, stan accounts will dig into the archives to post old photos of their subject—"throwbacks," if you will—or find newsworthiness in their romantic partners or co-stars for perhaps a bit of cross-promotion with other stan accounts. If you've ever worked for a newspaper or online magazine/blog, you'd be quite familiar with the editorial calendars of these accounts. And *don't you forget* topical holidays and anniversaries: "Happy 20th anniversary to Princess Diaries 2," tweeted @AnneHathabae in August 2024; "Happy Pride month," tweeted @GoslingSource in June, alongside photos of actor Ryan Gosling in the film *Murder by Numbers,* which did have *a bit* of homoerotic energy. "First Monday of may [*sic*] but for Dianna's fans it's just another Monday," writes @Agron_Updates, a particularly funny stan account whose gripes mostly appear in the form of consistently begging actor Dianna Agron to appear in more projects. (Here, specifically, they were griping that she wasn't attending the Met Gala.) After years of what the account deemed to be disappointing work (or, more accurately, "not work") from their subject, @Agron_Updates closed up shop. The account signed off dramatically, with a long goodbye statement: "During these eight years, we tried to make people fall in love with Dianna, as we did back then and we still do. When I think about legacy, I sure hope that's the one we're leaving behind."

We once DMed the now-retired @Agron_Updates to get a sense of the person behind the stan account. She revealed herself to be a pretty normal thirty-two-year-old Brazilian woman whose love of Agron began with *Glee* and who launched the account with a friend in 2016. "It's a nice environment," she said of the Agronation. (We made that name up. It doesn't appear that Dianna Agron's fandom has a stan name as of the writing of this book.) "But sometimes, within the same fandom, egos can get in the way." And when asked if she had any tips for others wanting to start a stan account, she answered: "I think the main lesson I've learned, and I've learned it the hard way, is that you have to know how to log off. I've updated the account while drunk [at] parties and festivals, that's not healthy."

One of @Agron_Updates' most telling tweets was posted when Agron was "in the news" after a video clip of her speaking in a confusing accent (one that was decidedly *not* her own) went viral. "The comments on TikTok," @Agron_Updates tweeted in response to the sudden flurry of negative attention. "What do you know about Dianna Agron? Only me and her other 10 fans are allowed to make fun of her, it's our job." The account's jabs—maybe of note to journalists like us, who hadn't seen a stan come for their favorite like that before—stemmed purely from love. At the end of the day, a stan is a celebrity's ultimate ally.

A select few take their role as chronicler more seriously—in fact, they will go far to hold their idol accountable. This is relatively controversial in the world of standom, where the expectation is to defend your subject at all costs, even go after the haters if the opportunity arises, which it often does. When actor Ansel Elgort faced allegations of sexual assault in 2020, the dormant stan account @ElgortUpdate came back to life, tweeting: "Sike. We condemn the actions that pig has made towards every single victim, and stand with girls coming out with their stories. We see you. We believe you." In 2017, a Jenner sisters stan account, @knjdaily, got press for calling out the Jenners' "penchant for unapologetic cultural appropriation," tweeting: "why we decided to unstan: a thread." The thread detailed fourteen examples of bad behavior, including Kendall Jenner's controversial Pepsi ad, which saw her ending police brutality and systemic racism by presenting an armed officer with an ice-cold can of Pepsi, and the sisters' clothing line selling T-shirts with the likeness of rapper Notorious B.I.G. without his estate's permission (or knowledge). "[Kendall] has young fans that are impressionable and that need to learn about it, not protect her," one of the former stans (appropriately named Ann) told the online publication *The Outline*. The account has not been updated since July 2017.

"This Sky Ferreira Stan Account Is Losing Hope," headlined *Paper*, covering a stan account called @SkyFUpdates that had repeatedly stated that if the singer's comeback wasn't as imminent as she'd promised, they were going to officially shut down operations. "I will always respect her and the choices she makes. This is a me issue. I'm starting to grow past the 'stan twitter' fiasco we all live in," they wrote in a Notes-app statement. In 2021, @JamesMcAvoyUpdates wrote: "This account was initially to help me let my feelings out and sometimes rant but my antidepressants have started working and they helped me realize I actually do not like James McAvoy as much as I thought I did." There's even a well-circulated screenshot of an Instagram post where a user who goes by "BTSArmy222777" wrote: "SORRY I HAVEN'T BEEN POSTING ON HERE A LOT GUYS I STARTED TAKING A MOOD STABILIZER AND NOW I'M NOT OBSESSED WITH BTS ANYMORE." They caption their statement with "Still love them though♥," as if to imply that they've simply moved from being a stan to being merely a fan. (For what it's worth, we checked the *Diagnostic and Statistical Manual of Mental Disorders* and are happy to report that stanning is not an acknowledged form or symptom of mental illness. Yet.)

"I don't believe in blind stanning," Anthony aka @ArmasUpdates told *MEL* in 2020. This was after the account received press for noting that actor Ana de Armas was going on a plethora of "pap walks" with her then-boyfriend, actor Ben Affleck, despite a shelter-in-place order in Los Angeles at the peak of the pandemic. "Ana de Armas & Ben Affleck get early morning coffee and walk their dogs together while finally wearing masks when outside," @ArmasUpdates tweeted in the spring of 2020; "Ana de Armas & Ben Affleck walk their dogs outside instead of praying for the pandemic to go away on Easter Sunday," the account tweeted two days later. Naturally, this break in character delighted the internet, which immediately picked up on the account's cheeky outrage. Or was it earnest outrage? Well, "Ana de Armas & Ben Affleck hopefully telling each other to go back inside," reads a bit more cheeky than it is CDC-aligned. However you read @ArmasUpdates, Anthony had taken a break from straight stanning his idol and veered off into a newer, more opinionated position than we'd seen these accounts hold before. If this had been a local paper filled with news about actor Ana de Armas, suddenly that paper had an op-ed section. And by the end of April 2020, the actor blocked the account dedicated to her own updates: "BREAKING: Golden Globe nominee and movie star Ana de Armas has recently blocked us!" the account tweeted with glee, in almost the same tenor as they might announce that the actor had "noticed them" with a like or a retweet.

"It's definitely a persona I've put on her," Anthony told *Jezebel*. "I think it's a self-aware one because we're all in dark times right now, and I feel like this account is something funny to put out there . . . At the end of the day, it's just light-hearted sarcasm. I mean no offense towards her at all." And Anthony did not choose to unstan de Armas. He even eventually met her in 2022 at the Venice Film Festival. "THIS IS HER LOOKING AT ME," he tweeted with a picture of de Armas looking not at all terrified. (It's kind of a half-smile/half-grimace, but completely unclear if she's reacting to the overwhelming number of fans clamoring for an autograph/selfie, or the realization she's finally meeting the stan who shook up her pandemic fling with his critical coverage.)

Anthony's decision to speak up but not fully shut down is a post-cancel-culture nuance that stan accounts are just now starting to express. After Sydney Sweeney was rumored to be dating music executive Scooter Braun (enemy number one of Swifties everywhere, thanks to his devious purchase of the master recordings of Swift's first six albums from her former label, Big Machine Records), the internet went hard on the actor, who had already racked up a slew of criticisms (including the cursed American Eagle "Sydney Sweeney Has Great Jeans" campaign). But if the stan accounts had survived her previous faux pas (and the general suspicion that she held conservative political beliefs), this wasn't the last straw. Unlike Sweeney, who doesn't have to speak on her personal life if she doesn't want to (and no good PR person would advise her to do so!), the stan account "Sydney Sweeney Daily" felt it necessary to comment: "I feel like not posting it would make me look selective when it comes to sharing Syd updates." (That's some journalistic standards right there!) "I also don't think what she's doing is a crime, but personally I don't celebrate it . . . I've always wanted this account to be a place where you can find news about Syd, and even if I don't always like what I have to report, I hope I can keep fulfilling that goal." In other words, Sweeney coverage will continue *despite* the account's personal belief system clashing with the object of its standom's belief system.

FOR A WHILE NOW, these stan accounts have been relegated to the realm of those who are not just online the way most people are now online, but rather "terminally online." That is, the stan accounts are run by a niche group of self-selecting people who share and even *enjoy* the output. Their posts are like private jokes between pop-culture obsessives or alternative ways for the community of Pedro Pascal lovers (*before* he went full Them) to keep in touch with one another. It's not often that they "break out" of that space and receive attention beyond Twitter. Until, that is, Club Chalamet stepped into the, uh, *club*.

"Meet the 30-Year-Old+ Super Fans of Timothée," a 2019 *Refinery29* headline proclaimed, pointing out what was initially most novel about the "Club Chalamet" community: their ages. In 2019, the promising boyish, mop-headed actor, age twenty-four at the time, was coming off a big role in Greta Gerwig's *Little Women* (in which he played every March sister—*just kidding,* but what if . . .) and his fandom was led by a loud and pervasive leader: then-fifty-two-year-old writer Simone Cromer, who also moderated a Facebook page for "mature fans" of the actor. "I want to help carve out a niche fanbase of mature, well-balanced adults in support of his career," she told the website, which really could have been the end of the story right there. Older fans of a younger actor? Maybe it was worth a blog post, but this really wasn't anything unusual! If anything, it was an early sign of Chalamet's star power, which would continue to grow, earning him leading roles in big projects like *Dune* and the Bob Dylan biopic *A Complete Unknown.* But really, could *anyone* have predicted the virality of Chalamet's press tour for *Marty Supreme,* which began with the release of a scripted marketing meeting with A24 and culminated with Chalamet standing atop the Las Vegas Sphere, whose screens had been turned orange to simulate a giant Ping-Pong ball?

It wasn't until Chalamet started dating Kylie Jenner (which was first reported in April 2023, but likely began a bit before) that Cromer—now fully realized as @ClubChalamet on Twitter and Instagram—reached the true masses. "If you're feeling distressed by the video, it's ok. But please take care of yourself. Step away from social media for a couple of days," the account posted on Instagram, giving the clear impression that she was more distressed than any of her followers. Like Timmy, Cromer even took to livestream, hosting a Twitter Space where she spoke for over fifty minutes about the blackmail she believed to be behind the actor's new romance. "We've never even seen them go to Olive Garden," she says, implying that Jenner would be an unlikely, if not terrible, girlfriend for Chalamet. "Timothée loves Italian food. Why not just go to Olive Garden, or something like that?"

Upon first glance, you might assume this is the work of a lovelorn stan, as it would be in line with other stan accounts. But Cromer's motivations are of a new generation of stan account, much like the accounts that track the chart movements of their favorite pop star. Her main goal is to see Chalamet win an Oscar. She won't make the direct connection, but what perhaps worries her the most is the threat Jenner poses to the young actor's chances at reaching his prestige potential. "The most generous interpretations of Club Chalamet's fear of Kylie Jenner's presence in Timothée Chalamet's life is that she sees any distraction from his career . . . as a possible roadblock for his now self-proclaimed goal to become one of the greats, a goal Miss Club knew about before we, or he, did," wrote Jodi Walker for *The Ringer*.

Turns out, Chalamet did not bring Jenner to the Screen Actors Guild Awards, where he ended up winning Outstanding Performance by a Male Actor in a Leading Role for *A Complete Unknown*. He *did*, however, bring her as a date to the 97th Academy Awards, where he was nominated for his performance in *Marty Supreme*.

Was Club Chalamet onto something there? Can the stan know more than the star? And does it even matter if they do? Maybe Jenner was simply busy that night. Post-*Unknown*, CC wasn't done with her work as self-appointed Chalamet-whisperer, having published a four-point mini-manifesto on Instagram as to how the star could "finally" win his Oscar for a (then) upcoming role in *Marty Supreme:* "Timothée should attend events with a friend and business associates, or his family so that they are not only there for moral support, but they are not a gossip distraction where, frankly, immature displays of 'affection' don't take away from the legitimate reason why Timothée is at these awards events."

Despite all that unsolicited advice, a year later Chalamet did not win his first Oscar. Not that Club Chalamet cared. By that point, months after Chalamet's Oscar campaign had started, she'd splintered her interest and had officially started supporting a new up-and-coming star: *Heated Rivalry*'s Connor Storrie. Hey, the heart stans what it stans.

Beyond all their rabid, near-obsessive complimentary posting and their militarization as coordinated units able to do a star's bidding (or what they may perceive to be a star's bidding), stans are, fundamentally, admirers of art. It's deeper than patronage. Fandom is something intangible, a purely emotional response to an artist and their work. But standom is its own kind of work, and an art form in and of itself.

Chapter 11

Stop Giving Celebrities Podcasts!!!

Anna Faris Is Unqualified, SmartLess & The Lohdown

When we started *Who? Weekly* in 2016, the biggest stars podcasting were Anna Faris, Marc Maron, and Shaquille O'Neal. (Before you name others, well, *do you consider Adam Carolla a celebrity?* If so, then yes, he was podcasting back then too!) This is to say that back then, the podcasting ecosystem wasn't awash in celebrity to the extent that it is today. It barely had the ability to *turn* someone into a celebrity, let alone attract an already-famous person to the microphone. In 2016, *Forbes* noted a "rise" of celebrity podcasting, listing notables from "Steve Austin to real housewife Heather DuBrow to Maria Shriver." One could hardly call that a boom, but it was certainly prescient.

It's now harder to name the influencers, actors, singers, reality-TV stars, and retired politicians who *don't* have podcasts than those who do.

The celeb-on-celeb interview goes back long before *Variety* took journalists out of the equation by setting up cameras and calling the conversations "Actors on Actors." And who are we kidding, journalists are *still* writing the questions that the actors are asking each other, but the format is immediately more appealing to the viewer, who instead of hearing directly from one of their favorite celebs is hearing from two! Meanwhile, *Interview* magazine's been publishing conversations between celebrities for years. Who needs a professional journalist when you could just read Kristen Stewart fielding questions from Justin Bieber, or Cindy Sherman in a tête-à-tête with Grace Jones?

Maron and Faris had quite a lot to do with ushering other celebs to podcast, if only because their formats required them to quite literally introduce their fellow famous friends to the format. When Faris launched *Unqualified,* the premise was that she was doling out "not-great relationship advice from completely unqualified Hollywood types." Not a bad idea! But unsurprisingly, listeners wanted less advice and more behind-the-scenes celeb banter, and the show slowly pulled away from its original premise and toward a chat show between Faris and famous guests, which included everyone from Tony Hawk to Lena Dunham to Faris's now-ex-husband, Chris Pratt—who was at that point way less famous than Faris herself.

No matter the quality of jokes Faris was making, listeners remained way more engaged with small, revealing details about her personal life. Their relationship with the actor went from fandom to parasocial: "I'm in love with you Anna!" an Apple review reads. "Not creepy at all, but really thank you, every morning my dog and I enjoy your voice. And your shoes." The beauty of a podcast was that it gave even the most untouchable stars the ability to at least attempt to appear relatable. And the Whos who were already quite, uh, touchable? They could turn that existing relatability into a type of deeper, albeit one-sided, emotional connection with the consistency of regular missives.

While Faris's pre-pod stardom pushed listeners to tune in to her show, the success of Marc Maron's *WTF* undoubtedly brought him more celebrity as a podcaster than he'd had as a comedian. Once a niche comedian's comedian, Maron went on to book high-profile acting roles on shows like *Louie* and *GLOW,* and even to star in his own *Curb Your Enthusiasm*–style, semi-autobiographical comedy, *Maron,* which ran for four seasons on IFC. In so doing, he became the first "celebrity" to parlay his podcast into broader fame by altering what people thought podcasting was capable of. Just six years later, President Barack Obama took a seat in Maron's recording-studio garage.

Obama would eventually host a series of conversations with Bruce Springsteen as part of his own Spotify deal. By then, it was just a thing that celebrities did—even if (or especially when?) they were former presidents.

Marc Maron once told *The Guardian:* "I'm not a journalist, I don't write down questions. So, you know, go fuck yourself, I'm having a conversation, following my own instincts about what's interesting to me." Is he the most notable celebrity podcaster decrying any sort of journalistic tutelage—or, more important, responsibility? That title might be best suited to another comedian, Joe Rogan, who would launch his podcast, the wildly popular and even more wildly controversial *Joe Rogan Experience,* in 2009—the same year Maron launched *WTF.*

Though both Faris's and Maron's podcasts are no longer airing, they formed the blueprint for other celebs who always fancied themselves capable enough to play journalist. Or clever enough to know that something other celebrities might want out of an interview is a fellow famous person to agree to their hard limits. We call those types of questions softballs.

WHY MIGHT A celebrity launch a podcast now? Dax Shepard, another actor perhaps now more well-known as a podcaster, launched *Armchair Expert* in 2018. His wife, the more famous actor Kristen Bell, was the show's first guest. "What qualifies me for such an endeavor?" Shepard writes on the show's website. "More than a decade of sobriety, a degree in Anthropology and four years of improv training . . . I will be, in the great tradition of 16th-century scientists, an Armchair Expert." Notably, the show offers its guests the option to cut parts of the interview after it has been recorded. ("Interviewees frequently take them up on this," wrote *The New York Times* in 2019.) Perhaps this is Shepard's gesture toward a fellow famous person—attempting to cultivate a safe space where a celeb wouldn't feel as if they might be misconstrued or set up to fail. Or so that no one "of note" would have the opportunity to get mad at him?

Notably, the podcast would soon become more lucrative than Shepard's acting career: *The Wall Street Journal* reported that in July 2024—seven years after his last attempt at leading a studio comedy, 2017's *CHiPS,* flopped at the box office—Shepard signed an $80 million podcasting deal with Amazon's Wondery platform. While most celeb hosts aren't signing $80 million deals, they're likely making solid payouts from ad reads. Nothing to scoff at, but relatively small compared to other types of more traditional Hollywood projects. Plus, brands tend to get a much better deal seeking an ad read from a celebrity podcaster for their show versus offering them a more traditional brand partnership (a linear commercial, or some sort of fake "creative director" situation).

Celebrities also start their own podcasts as a way to keep themselves in the conversation—if no one's talking about them, maybe they should just talk about themselves? Actors Jason Bateman, Sean Hayes, and Will Arnett started the podcast *SmartLess* together in 2020, reportedly out of mid-pandemic boredom. And when the pandemic came to a close, the podcast had become such a success—the most lucrative of their careers, in fact—that despite having actual acting work, they kept recording it. Their podcast agent, CAA's Josh Lungren, said in an interview, "The podcast might be called *SmartLess,* but they're actually three very smart guys. They're smart about money. They're smart about the work and where they put their time. They understand the media landscape. Together, I think we saw this opportunity. The north star became to build this into a media company—more than just the one podcast, which is a juggernaut." Perhaps the three actors didn't envision their new podcast to be about seeking profits in a flailing industry, but their agents saw dollar signs.

But it's not always merely about the money. Reality stars are known to launch podcasts after their seasons air as a way of telling their sides of the story without the intervention of television editors. What's more, a podcast is a great way to attempt to stay in the headlines and extend your fifteen minutes of fame. "Scandoval" was a cheating scandal in 2023 that unfolded on the reality show *Vanderpump Rules* and unexpectedly broke out beyond the show, giving its stars fifteen minutes that they each turned into various opportunities: sponsorships, hosting gigs, and . . . *so many podcasts.* In fact, "Scandoval" was covered extensively on each of the current (and even former!) cast members' pods: *Balancing Act with Kristen Doute and Luke Broderick;* Stassi Schroeder Clark's *Stassi;* Katie Maloney and Dayna Kathan's *Disrespectfully;* Jax Taylor and Brittany Cartwright's *When Reality Hits with Jax and Brittany;* Scheana Shay's *Scheananigans;* Tom Schwartz's *Detox Retox;* Lala Kent's *Give Them Lala;* and by the show's newly crowned villains, Tom Sandoval (on *Everybody Loves Tom*) and Rachel "Raquel" Leviss (on *Rachel Goes Rogue*). The only cast member without a podcast on which to address the scandal? The betrayed party: Ariana Madix, whose hero status had her zooming past podcaster and straight to contestant on *Dancing with the Stars* and eventually earned her a gig hosting *Love Island.* Rather than reviving her own short-lived podcast, *Earth to Ariana,* which came and went long before Scandoval broke, she decided she'd take her story to other people's bigger podcast platforms, like *Call Her Daddy* and *Chicks in the Office.*

While so many stars dream of themselves in the Johnny Carson late-night seat, it may be more lucrative (although certainly less glamorous) to pursue a podcast route instead. Take former late-night host Conan O'Brien—who launched *Conan O'Brien Needs a Friend* in 2018, while his TBS talk show, *Conan,* was still on the air. It took convincing: "Someone said, 'You should do a podcast.' And I was sarcastic, like, 'Oh, really? Because I've been on television for, at that point, 25 years. So a podcast is what I should do, you think? That's good thinking,'" he told *Adweek.* Unsurprisingly, despite the hesitation, O'Brien's has become one of the biggest podcasts out there. "His weirdness translates well to the casual intimacy that's come to define the podcast as a platform for performance, and his default stance of efficient self-deprecation makes the show feel accessible in ways that other comedy podcasts, fronted by needier ids, may not," wrote Nicholas Quah in a *Vulture* piece simply called "Conan O'Brien Is the Perfect Podcast Host." O'Brien may have never seen himself as a podcast host, but suddenly he was a perfect one.

Most celebs are far from perfect podcasts hosts. In fact, celebs don't need the expertise or excuse of a theme or premise—let alone a degree in broadcast journalism—to launch a podcast where they simply chat with their famous friends; that alone is enough to get people to tune in. They don't even bother trying to convince you there's some sort of connective tissue: "I'm Justin Long and I've been an actor for most of my life, so I'm used to getting inside the heads of the characters I play," reads the description of Justin Long's podcast, *Life Is Short with Justin Long*. While the pod name's pun is on point, its premise isn't fooling anyone: "I want to peek inside the heads of real people to learn how they find meaning in life. I'm also very curious what their favorite snack food is, and what emoji they use most often—ya know, the REALLY important stuff." Actor Rachel Bilson's favorite emoji is the "melting face," in case you were wondering. She appeared on a December 2022 episode of Long's podcast not long after launching her own chat show: *Rachel Bilson's Broad Ideas,* where she and her best friend Olivia are "joined by old friends, young friends, and some friends they haven't met yet to have fun, casual conversations about the same kind of broad topics you'd find yourself discussing with your girlfriends." Bilson has appeared on *Off the Vine with Kaitlyn Bristowe,* a former *Bachelorette* star, who has in turn appeared on *The Nikki & Brie Show,* a podcast co-hosted by WWE star Nikki Garcia and her twin, Brie. (Garcia has popped up on both model Ashley Graham's show *Pretty Big Deal* and Paris Hilton's pod, *I Am Paris.*) We could go on forever: Kevin Hart's *Gold Minds;* Minnie Driver's *Minnie Questions; Literally! With Rob Lowe; Now What? with Brooke Shields;* Jessie Tyler Ferguson's *Dinner's on Me;* Ellen Pompeo's *Tell Me;* Julia Louis-Dreyfus's *Wiser Than Me*—all of these podcasts have the same concept, celebs gabbing with other celebs, and they often share the same guests.

Celeb-on-celeb chat shows might be the most lucrative sell for a celeb pod, and the lowest lift might be the "celebrity talking to one of their best friends" podcast—employing the "let's just chat" model and adding a Nah who happens to already know everything about them. Relatable! We all have best friends who get us, so why wouldn't I want to tune in to *Scrubbing In* with *The Bachelor*'s Becca Tilley and her BFF, Tanya Rad, or *Impaulsive* with Logan Paul and his friend Mike

Majlak or *Forbidden Fruits* with Julia Fox and her pal Niki Takesh? Instead of a celeb having to do any sort of research or prep to chat with someone they might not be as familiar with, they'll just have their best friend ask *them* questions under the guise of a chat show. It doesn't get any easier than that, and is additionally a great way to perform the very *Entourage*-esque charity of giving your childhood friends work. You'd be surprised how much of Hollywood still works as *Entourage* foretold.

5 Actual Episode Titles of Real Housewife of New York Bethenny Frankel's Podcast, *Just B*

- "Martha Stewart Hates Me" (February 14, 2023)
- "I'm Glad You're Mad" (January 23, 2024)
- "Lashify Tried to Come for Me—Now They're Getting ROASTED" (February 26, 2025)
- "No One Wants to Go to Your Thing" (September 16, 2025)
- "A Colonoscopy Is No Excuse for Bad Fashion" (August 19, 2025)

Other concepts are more challenging. Take the "celebrities talking to an expert in something" genre, often sold as the "I have intellectual curiosity!" genre. This is compelling to celebs, who are always working to convince us that they're more than how we've previously pigeonholed them. *Getting Better* (which was once called *Getting Curious*) with Jonathan Van Ness has the *Queer Eye* star chatting with neuroscientists and psychotherapists. *Wholly Human* with singer LeAnn Rimes introduced her to intuitive and spirituality experts and life coaches. *The Real Heal* with Alicia Silverstone ran for just eleven episodes, with one called "Protecting Our Oceans with Ali Tabrizi." These celebrities are humbling themselves before us; they want us to know that much like us, they still have plenty to learn—and let's do it together, why don't we?

Equally humbling is the celebrity podcast genre that feels more ominous than enlightening: "celebrity couples talking to each other." *Couple Things* with Olympian Shawn Johnson and her husband, NFL player Andrew East; *The Best Podcast Ever* with actor Raven-Symoné and her wife, Miranda Maday; *Double Date* with Marlo Thomas and Phil Donahue; *The Squeeze* with Taylor Lautner and his wife, whose name is also . . . *Taylor Lautner*. (She used to be Taylor Dome but took her husband's name as a cruel joke on us.) The downside? It's not that hard to imagine. When actor-turned-singer Jana Kramer's husband, Mike Caussin, cheated on her, they naturally discussed it on their podcast, *Whine Down*. (This was after *Us Weekly* broke the news that Caussin cheated with multiple women, and he subsequently entered treatment for sex addiction.) The two got back together before officially calling it quits in 2021. Kramer's podcast is now called *Whine Down with Jana Kramer*. Caussin is no longer a podcaster as of the publishing of this book.

There's also the safer version of this where celebrities talk to members of their family—mostly their siblings or parents: *Sibling Revelry* with Kate and Oliver Hudson; *Brotherly Love* with the Lawrence brothers (Joey, Matthew, and Andrew); *Sorry We're Stoned* (now *Sorry We're Cyrus*) with Miley Cyrus–adjacent mother-daughter team Tish and Brandi; and *Workin' On It* with "All About That Bass" singer Meghan Trainor and her brother, Ryan. One of the most charming versions of this equation is singer Jessie Ware's podcast with her mother, Lennie, called *Table Manners,* a show where Lennie has unexpectedly become the breakout star: Celebs like actor Jonathan Groff, Geri Halliwell-Horner, and Cyndi Lauper are showing up to chat with *her*.

A genre that's not as ominous as it is reeking of desperation is perhaps an even lower lift than simple chat shows, and that's the podcast "recap" phenomenon. This applies to TV stars whose big hits are firmly in the rearview, which is totally fine if your memory holds up. Thanks to streaming, new audiences find old TV shows every day and would love for the stars of *Boy Meets World* to reunite for a podcast called *Pod Meets World,* where Topanga (Danielle Fishel), Shawn (Rider Strong), and Eric (Will Friedle) discuss every episode. There's *9021OMG* with Jennie Garth and Tori Spelling; *Fake Doctors, Real Friends* with Zach Braff and Donald Faison; *Back to the Beach* with Kristin Cavallari and Stephen Colletti; *Boneheads* with Emily Deschanel and Carla Gallo; *Wizards of Waverly Pod* with Jennifer Stone and

David DeLuise . . . In fact, if there's a long-running TV show, it's almost guaranteed there's a companion celeb-hosted recap podcast to go along with it. The pioneer of the genre is no doubt *Office Ladies* with Jenna Fischer and Angela Kinsey, which was so successful in its recapping that even after the ladies ran out of episodes of *The Office* to recap in October 2024, they continued on their podcast journey, transitioning to a new format they're calling *Office Ladies 2.0*. If you already guessed that the new format involves Fischer and Kinsey interviewing other celebrities, *Ding-ding-ding*, you're correct!

IF EVERY FUNNY MOMENT, every behind-the-scenes peek, every insurmountable challenge, every game night at Questlove's is now monetizable . . . well, who needs a memoir? Barbra Streisand's *My Name Is Barbra* took her reportedly fifteen years to write and ended up almost one thousand pages long ("I wanted two volumes," she told *The New York Times Magazine*. "Who wants to hold a heavy book like that in their hands?"), and yet you could never imagine her releasing a weekly podcast. Memoirs will always win out over podcasts in prestige points: the advance money, the opportunity to use a ghostwriter (less work!), and the built-in editorial filter of the book-writing process, one that makes it a lot less easy for things to accidentally "slip" into the public forum. And is there anything classier than showing off the book you just wrote? Even our most shameless reality stars will often opt for the long-tail process of writing a book—even if they *already have a weekly tell-all podcast*. Can the best of both words be claiming your fifteen minutes and expanding it into eternity?

At one point we might've been worried that these celebrity podcasts might eat up our listenership. Who wants to listen to two aging millennials gab about celeb hypotheses when they could hear it straight from the horse's mouth? Would you be surprised that more than half the podcasts we've mentioned in this chapter are no longer releasing new episodes? Maybe not. What happens when a celeb realizes that podcasting is just a bit too much work and not enough immediate financial payoff? Maybe it's the one too many times they're taken out of context by *Page Six*? Perhaps they've simply . . . *gasp* . . . run out of things to say. (These are often actors; they're used to being handed scripts!) As evidenced by these abandoned RSS feeds, the most popular category of celebrity podcast might actually be the dead one.

Let's plainly lay out reasons why a celebrity podcast might cease to exist.

1. Celebrity is bored.
2. The podcast is not making enough money. *Why?*
    a. Podcast ad rates are actually not so great when compared to other projects. Perhaps there are more lucrative ad deals to be had *outside* the sphere of podcasting.
    b. Celebrity does not want to read ads anymore. They are embarrassing.
3. Celebrity or their co-host (friend, sibling, or parent) is canceled.
4. Celebrity commits a crime and is sent to prison.
5. Celebrity dies. (Like, *actually* dies.)

The graveyard of podcasts started by celebs is as crowded as the field of active podcasters. Amy Schumer's *3 Girls 1 Keith* ran for thirty-five episodes; Brie Larson's *Learning Lots* ran for twenty; Demi Lovato's *4D* ran for twenty-five; Jamie Lee Curtis's *Good Friend* ran for thirty-three, maybe because she ran out of "good friends" to appear as guests. After comedian Gilbert Gottfried died in 2022, you might imagine that his long-running show, *Gilbert Gottfried's Amazing Colossal Podcast,* would die with him. But it keeps chugging, publishing reruns and encores as if nothing ever happened. (Obviously, the pod acknowledges Gottfried's death on its website, but it still finds a way to keep its RSS feed pumping, proving death does not have to end a successful podcasting career.) Todd and Julie Chrisley, both stars of the TLC reality series *Chrisley Knows Best,* had to put their 221-episode podcast *Chrisley Confessions* on pause when they were convicted of tax fraud. (Their daughter's podcast, *Unlocked with Savannah Chrisley,* kept up its weekly churn and often used the platform as a way to share updates about the famous incarcerated couple with fans.) But after a presidential pardon from Trump, the Chrisleys got back to work behind the mic: They erased all 221 episodes from their RSS feed and started fresh. Now with the creative moniker *Chrisley Confessions 2.0,* the two promise: "It's raw. It's real. It's Todd and Julie back and better than ever."

After teasing her new podcast for months leading up to its 2022 release, Lindsay Lohan's *The Lohdown* ran for a paltry thirteen episodes. Perhaps this is what happens when your host's heart isn't in the game, and the podcast's description reads like AI slop: "She's here to share with you the things, people, places, and ideas that she loves. From the greatest undiscovered music to the global causes that need your attention and support. She's like the big sister that you never had, or if you just need an extra sister who's ready to lend and [*sic*] ear to hear about your joys and your dilemmas." To Lohan's credit, we have found only a few other celebrity podcasts that ran for close to her low number of episodes—*Radical Musings with Rosanna Arquette* ran for twenty, *Meaningful Conversations with Maria Shriver* ran for twenty-two, and Joey McIntyre's *The Move* ran for thirteen. The winner? Jaleel White's 2020 podcast, *Ever After,* ran for nine. It ended on an episode where Jaleel interviews Brian Austin Green, "filmed just before the pandemic." Uh-oh.

It's funny to see a podcast described as "filmed," because although it was once a lack of a better term employed by Urkel (taped? recorded?), the audio-only standard of podcasting has now become very much video-only. When appearing on a podcast might once have been appealing to a celebrity because of the *lack* of prep required—by "prep" we mean the hair, makeup, and so on required to appear on camera when you're famous—the likes of *Call Her Daddy* and *New Heights with Jason & Travis Kelce* have pushed podcasting to become an on-camera medium.

Even Kelly Ripa, *who already hosts a daily television talk show* alongside her husband, isn't satisfied with the amount of celebrity-on-celebrity chatter afforded to her. So she launched *Let's Talk Off Camera.* Maybe celebrity podcasts have become so popular because you don't need a cable box or streaming service to access them. (Even the free promotional clips from those linear shows appear online at least twenty-four hours after they're aired.) On the celebrity's side of things, now they don't need to drive to a TV studio set or deal with a live audience—compared to the travel and long hours that come with shooting movies and TV shows. Especially when you're already rich enough to set up a home studio. In fact, it often adds to the charm of these interviews. (Maron famously taped nearly nine hundred episodes out of his garage.)

BEFORE SO MANY podcasts went on camera, the low lift of an audio-only podcast allowed celebrities to have much more intimate conversations without the stress of figuring out hair and makeup, or even the need for a publicist to get involved in the go-between. And before publications caught on to the gossip they could extract from these recorded convos, podcasts might allow a celeb to communicate with their fans *without* fear of making headlines. Tabloid writers wouldn't have time to scrub through hours-long audio, searching for something that might serve as a pull quote. As we once wrote on *Slate* in a piece called "The Safe Space of the Celebrity-on-Celebrity Podcast" in 2018, "You've got to hand it to famous people: They've found a way to make us work harder to boost their celebrity while putting in even less effort themselves. So far, we're entirely happy to oblige."

Alas, that was the golden era. The celebrities didn't know what was just around the corner: *transcription*. The proliferation of celebrity podcasting, which goes hand-in-hand with the decline of access to celebrities for traditional journalism, meant that these podcasts would become an abundant source of gossip for the remaining tabloids. They started tuning in, figuring out ways to read transcripts (or perhaps ask an intern to listen at two-times speed) and pick out the juiciest moments, where a celeb might slip up and reveal something relatively compelling. You'd think celebs would've learned by now that podcasts are not the "safe space" we once deemed them in 2018—but so many "exclusives" are pulled from audio these days that we've started a segment dedicated to them on our podcast (meta!) called "Podcast Mouth." Here's where actor Dean Cain claims his *Lois & Clark* co-star Teri Hatcher could be "difficult to work with" (on the *Inside of You* podcast) or where actor Sarah Paulson told the hosts of *SmartLess* that an actor named Tricia Hawkins once gave her six pages of notes on a theater performance she did in 2013: "It was really outrageous. Trish Hawkins, I have not forgotten it, and I hope to see you never." Calling out Hawkins on *SmartLess* was funny *in context*, but once pulled from the podcast episode it produced such damning headlines as "Sarah Paulson Eviscerates Actress Who Critiqued Her with 6 Pages of Notes," "Sarah Paulson Trounces Actor for 'Outrageous' 6-Page Email of Notes on Her Performance," and "'I hope to see you never': Sarah Paulson Shades Actor Who Criticised Her Performance."

Perhaps that's the price you pay for the platform to really show off your personality, something celebs are always craving more of—forever walking that tightrope between over- and under-exposed. This used to divide the Whos and Thems for us: Those seeking more attention were the Whos, while the Thems remained simply too famous to engage. *They didn't need to!* Now there are more forces at play, pulling Thems into the podcasting space, making it no longer just for Whos. (*Thanks, Obama!*) But both Whos and Thems are seeing podcasting as not only a personality play but the opportunity to better carve out a personality brand—lucrative for bigger synergistic opportunities with actual brands, but also with their own community of fandom. Now membership platforms like OnlyFans, Patreon, and Substack make it so anyone with an audience can go directly to them for financial support. Quite like how celebs once took their "exclusive" content away from the tabloids and placed it directly onto Instagram, generating followers and peppering in sponcon, the podcast is yet another piece of content for a celeb to offer up for sale.

Online video goes in and out of style (just ask those of us in the trenches during the ill-fated Facebook Live era in the mid-2010s), but somehow advertisers will always swing back to demanding video. It's more lucrative for a podcaster to film their show for a multitude of reasons: Advertising is one, but so is the ability to chop it up into bite-size pieces for visual social media like TikTok or Instagram Reels. We once relished how podcasts were decidedly *not* video—it was in fact one of the reasons *Who? Weekly* is able to thrive, stay topical, and not drive us absolutely insane. Now we're asked all the time why we don't do video. Well, we're a *podcast*! We shouldn't have to!

But that hasn't stopped the industry from moving swiftly in that direction. Where there's money, trends will follow. And celebrity-hosted podcasts were the first targets: If they're already used to being in front of cameras, why not just add a few more to the equation? For one, it removes the aspect of podcasting that had celebs casually spilling their guts without a second thought. Now that bright lights and foundation makeup have been added to the equation, it's not likely we're getting any more revealing long-form conversations like those that once aired on Marc Maron's *WTF*. There will likely be less and less of that as these podcasts get closer to actual TV shows—and then what use do we have for the actual linear broadcast shows that center on celebrity interviews? Not that a filmed podcast even comes close to the spectacle of a late-night show presentation; once again, these are celebrities, not journalists. What's at stake for them? Why make things purposefully uncomfortable for their guests in the name of truth? There exists no one less curious, less willing to ask the burning questions that make an interview potent than . . . someone who is also famous.

Chapter 12

On Rita Ora

Singer, Actor, Host, Spokesperson & Fashion Icon

THIS LOVELY RITA
HONORED HER HERITAGE
BY WEARING
AN ALBANIAN
FOLK COSTUME
IN THE VIDEO FOR
HER 2021 EP "BANG"

"Who is Dua Lipa?" answered *Jeopardy!* contestant Donna, bespectacled and wearing a smart beige cardigan. She ultimately won the 2023 episode, her victory notwithstanding that particular answer, to which the correct answer was not Dua Lipa. Should she have realized the question would include the name Rita due to its category being titled "LOVELY RITA"? Probably. But this was the $1,000 clue, the most challenging one. Despite knowing perhaps everything there is to know about the correct response, we completely understand her mistake. Donna was close—she popped off the name of a famous

Albanian pop star with brunette hair—but unfortunately not all Albanian brunette pop stars are the same. The correct "Lovely Rita" is the multitalented, deeply iconic, ravishingly beautiful, wholly inescapable patron saint of our podcast, Rita Ora.

Listeners of *Who? Weekly* would've smashed their buzzer multiple times well before the answer was finished being read (even if they hadn't yet heard her underrated aforementioned 2021 EP, *Bang*), so it's fair to assume no contestant on that day's episode was a listener of the podcast, as none of them got it correct. Their lack of knowledge in this specific niche meant no one—no, not even then-host Mayim Bialik—would utter the phrase "Who is Rita Ora?" Yet it's the question we have attempted to answer every week for over a decade.

This is because when we decided to start the podcast and take on a category we'd only just begun to define ("Whos"), one of the first ideas we had was to keep tabs on a celebrity we had deemed at the time to be the most exemplary and, in our estimation, easy-to-understand Who. "What's Rita Up To?" and its accompanying jingle (a catchy number by our friends Katie Notopoulos and Eric Topolsky of The Whos) would become a defining feature of the show, and act as the closing segment of one episode a week—*every single week*. When we chose her to follow with such a regular cadence, Rita's name had already become representative of the types of niche, hyperactive celebrities that U.S. tabloids just loved to cover, even despite their readership's less-than-robust understanding of their "whole deal."

Did it help that Rita was at that point better known abroad, especially in her native U.K., where her music had been much more successful? Surely. But it didn't stop the question from being asked. And asked again. Her music was part of a "bubbling under" class of pop, those sonically familiar but authorially opaque songs by artists who always seemed to be one meager hit away from utter superstardom. These tracks are a kind of ambient noise in public spaces, but not necessarily those you'd choose to listen to on your own. Occupying the space between Muzak and Top 40 pop, it's a category of song meant to accompany the aimless browsing of shelves in a store or nursing well vodka sodas at a bar where the music is loud but no one is actually dancing. If you happened to see Rita's face on the cover of a magazine, you might stop and feel a spark of faint recognition but struggle to connect it with a name. And if you were as clued-in to popular culture as the two of us are, perhaps your friends would ask, "Who is Rita Ora?" and you'd have to answer something like, "Well, hmmm, that's a complicated question, but, uhhh, I guess you could say she's a pop star," without actually being able to remember the names of her pop *songs*. "But I swear she has some good ones," you'd insist. "You've definitely heard them and thought, *This is fine! This is fun!*" You'd tell your friend that she also aligned herself with other, more famous musicians, but on songs that rarely made a cultural impact. Iggy Azalea, Chris Brown, and Charli XCX were some of her early collaborators . . . but don't you *dare* insist that "Black Widow," her track with Azalea, made any sort of cultural dent. (It's worth noting that if you happen to be a big crossword fan, you might recognize Rita by her last name, a favorite of puzzle writers for its short, vowel-heavy construction, much like "Yoko Ono" or "Brian Eno.")

Before we get into what made and continues to make Rita Ora so important to the fundamental question of Whodom, it would only be fair to give a brief rundown of how she made her way into our world as a person. Less "What's Rita Up To?" and more "Who the Hell Is Rita?" OK, fine, that probably doesn't have legs, but we'll only be doing it once.

Rita Sahatçiu Ora was born in Albania, making her one of the surprisingly large number of internationally famous pop stars to claim Albanian heritage, specifically—and from Whoiest to Themmiest—Ava Max (known for her asymmetrical bob haircut); Bebe Rexha (known for her "*crunch, crunch*" in an ad for Lay's potato chips); and Dua Lipa (confused for Rita by Donna on that iconic episode of *Jeopardy!*). Rita's grandfather, Besim Sahatçiu, was a prolific filmmaker and theater director whose favorite film star, Rita Hayworth, is his granddaughter's namesake. That *sahatçiu* means "watchmaker" in Albanian, and *ora* means "time," is pure poetry. (And chosen for that reason by her father, Besnik.) With a name like that, she was born to be watched like a clock.

In 1991, the year after her birth, the persecution of ethnic Albanians under the regime of Slobodan Milošević led Besnik and his wife, Vera, to move their family from Pristina, SFR Yugoslavia, to London. Rita was just a baby when her father opened up a pub called the Queens Arms in Kilburn. "I love eating at my dad's pub. It does a traditional Albanian spinach pie," she told the *Evening Standard* in 2012 in a piece where she spoke proudly of her heritage. She eventually started singing at the Queens Arms and other open-mic nights across the city, and word of her musical talents quickly spread far enough to reach English singer Craig David (of "7 Days" fame), who asked her to provide vocals for his song "Awkward" in 2007. In 2009 she auditioned for the Eurovision Song Contest in a televised special that aired on BBC One. Though she made it to the finals, Rita cannily decided the contest could potentially tank her career before it had a chance to start up, and she dropped out. Next came a stint in musical theater (including a part in *Chitty Chitty Bang Bang*) and, finally, a recording contract and production deal with Jay-Z's famed U.S.-based label, Roc Nation.

A BRIEF TANGENT about our beloved Eurovision: Rita would eventually make it to Eurovision in 2023, but not as a contestant. She was hired as an interval act—essentially meant to be a recognizable face among a sea of unknown artists vying for the continent's most famous song prize. She performed a triumphant medley of her hits that, if you knew her history, implied that she didn't need the international song contest to launch her career. "Imagine if I'd stayed!" she later said of the audition experience, a little rudely if you ask us (albeit correctly). "It would probably have been all over for me. At best, I'd be a contestant on that diving show? *Splash!*" In case you don't speak U.K. TV (it really is its own dialect of English), *Splash!* is a reality show where celebrities compete in diving, a pointed callout because not only did singer and Sugababes member Jade Ewen represent the U.K. in Eurovision the year Rita dropped out, she also competed on *Splash!* "Easy to mock when you are enjoying success. *Eurovision* and *Splash!*? Proud of both. Some manage to sleep their way to success, some have morals," Ewen tweeted in 2013. She came in fifth in Eurovision and appeared in just one episode of *Splash!*, the first contestant to be eliminated from the diving show.

Rita's Eurovision drags aside, her Roc Nation deal would ultimately prove problematic—arguably disastrous—and lead to a lawsuit, but not before a 2012 debut album that spawned a few genuine hits: "How We Do (Party)" (which debuted at #1 on the U.K. Singles chart, co-written by Katy Perry's once-secret weapon Bonnie McKee); "Radioactive" (which went Platinum in the U.K.); and "R.I.P." (which did not). That her debut album spawned so many successful singles should have been more than enough of a reason for Roc Nation to invest heavily in her next project, but to Rita's surprise, they didn't, and her rising star suddenly came diving down to earth. So, in 2015, she made international headlines by suing the label, claiming they trapped her in what the suit describes as "an oppressive recording agreement." It continued:

> When Rita signed, Roc Nation and its senior executives were very involved with her as an artist. As Roc Nation's interests diversified, there were fewer resources available and the company suffered a revolving door of executives. Rita's remaining supporters at the label left or moved on to other activities, to the point where she no longer had a relationship with anyone at the company.

In short, she claimed she was abandoned by Jay-Z and his partners, and was left to float in the murky, treacherous waters of pop music all alone. So she argued her case by citing the famed "seven-year rule," a section of the California Labor Code that says, in essence, if it's been seven years since they signed a contract, an artist is no longer beholden to it. In January 2016, Roc Nation sued Rita right back, and the two parties reached a settlement with undisclosed terms. She's currently signed with BMG.

On one hand, Rita's legal battle stalled her music career and caused her to lose momentum on the charts she had up to that point been dominating. On the other, it created fertile ground from which her Who-lebrity could sprout. Ever the workaholic—a hallmark of most Whos—Rita used her "time out" period to expand her career, taking a plethora of non-album, non–Roc Nation projects that kept her name in the press and her work in the public eye while she and her lawyers figured out the label battle. She became a judge on Britain's popular talent competition series *The X Factor* (replacing Australian pop-star Them, Kylie Minogue). She also recorded "Grateful," an original song for the criminally underrated Gina Prince-Bythewood film *Beyond the Lights.* After the song's writer, Diane Warren, received an Academy Award nomination for the track (one of her better late-career efforts), Rita even performed it at the Oscars. "Grateful" lost to "Glory," written for the film *Selma,* but Oscar audiences—not to mention stars in attendance like Julianne Moore, John Legend, and Ava DuVernay—heard Rita's name and watched her sing! She had also recently accepted her first major acting role in the highly anticipated film adaptation of *Fifty Shades of Grey*. She played the titular Christian Grey's sister, Mia. Was it a major part? *No.* Was she a standout? *Nope!* Was it well reviewed? *Also no.* But the movie and its two sequels, both of which Rita appeared in, made over a billion dollars at the box office worldwide. (Plus, the duet she contributed to the soundtrack, alongside One Direction's Liam Payne, "For You," became her twelfth top-ten hit in the U.K.) Not bad for someone just starting out in Hollywood!

One of the hallmarks of Who-lebrity is the constant grind—that deep-seated psychological need to create output for the public to consume—and Rita's drive during the era of her Roc Nation legal battle started a precedent for her cross-platform, seemingly indiscriminate workaholism that persists to this day. It's why we have something to say about her once a week: She's *always* up to something. And it's never a reach. By the time her sophomore album, the aptly named *Phoenix,* was released in 2018, Rita had, in addition to everything we've already explained, hosted a season of *America's Next Top Model* (replacing a Them, Tyra Banks), the 2017 MTV Europe Music Awards, and a competition series called *Boy Band;* she graced the covers of *Paper, Cosmopolitan* (U.K.), and *Cosmopolitan* (South Africa); she showed up as a featured vocalist for tracks by English DJs Sigma and American singer Chris Brown; she appeared in countless *Us Weekly* stories with headlines like "Rita Ora Flashes Her Butt in Revealing Dress at the Oscars 2015 Afterparty: See More Stars Go Without Underwear on the Red Carpet," and "Rita Ora Has a Blast at the Happiest Place on Earth While Her Ex-Boyfriend Calvin Harris Cuddles with Taylor Swift—All the Details." She was, as they say, booked and busy.

She's had a lot of jobs, but what about her love life? Going from a celebrity to one half of a celebrity *couple* always tends to make a person more famous, and Rita has defied the odds by remaining firmly in Who territory despite dating people whose fame levels run the full gamut. Her entry on WhosDatedWho.com (a somewhat unreliable database of rumors and confirmations) lists twenty-nine total "partners," including unverified pairings and, as they call them, mere "encounters," but up until she got married in 2022, her dating life reflected her professional one: unpredictable. For years we'd chronicle her latest rumored fling, be it with singer James Arthur, model Cara Delevingne, actors Andrew Garfield and Tessa Thompson, or nepo baby Raff (son of Jude) Law. Of the *confirmed* romances, she most notably dated sock entrepreneur and famous brother Rob Kardashian (who once claimed on Twitter she cheated on him "with 20 dudes"); DJ and producer Calvin Harris (who wrote one of the greatest pop songs of the twenty-first century, Rita's "I Will Never Let You Down," and then started dating Taylor Swift); Blink-182's Travis Barker (who went on to marry her ex Rob's sister Kourtney); and French film director Romain Gavras (who went on to date *Jeopardy!* Donna's favorite Albanian pop star, Dua Lipa). Do we actually believe she "dated" all the people on the Who's Dated Who list? Of course not. But we do understand all the rumors. One of the reasons Rita stays in the headlines is because she's a social animal, appearing out on the town, all over the world, seemingly every night of every week. So when we heard the rumor that she was dating Academy Award–winning writer/director Taika Waititi, a Who in a broad sense but a Them of the film world, we thought, *Well, that tracks.* Why? Because there was hardly a famous person who wouldn't. To us, Rita is a catch.

Her and Waititi's romance was (like a movie in which she once appeared in a cameo) fast and furious: The two married in 2022, just a year after meeting. For a brief, anxiety-inducing moment, we worried her relationship with someone as high-profile as Waititi would shoot both to Themdom. But even when their forces combined, the end result stayed decidedly Who-y. When Waititi, known for directing low-budget hits like his Oscar-winning *Jojo Rabbit* and studio blockbusters like Marvel's *Thor: Ragnarok,* directed videos for singles from Rita's marriage-inspired 2023 album *You + I,* they didn't really make any more of a splash than those that pre-dated him. After celebrating Waititi's fiftieth birthday in Ibiza, one of their favorite vacation spots, they were eclipsed by their more-famous guests (including Matt Damon, Cara Delevingne, and Kate Moss) in coverage of the affair.

RITA ORA IS among the rarefied group of British female solo artists with the most number ones in U.K. chart history. In the United States, she has far fewer chart appearances, and is perhaps best known for 2014's "I Will Never Let You Down," which isn't saying much, considering it is still a relatively underrated song. Since the release of *Phoenix,* Rita has continued her triple-threat mentality by accepting even more hosting gigs. She's done stints on *The Voice, New Year's Rockin' Eve with Ryan Seacrest,* and both the U.K. and U.S. versions of *The Masked Singer.* She's taken more acting gigs: starring in two installments of the popular *Descendants* franchise for Disney, having the co-lead in Carrie Fisher's final film *Wonderwell,* playing the Artful Dodger alongside Michael Caine in a contemporary adaptation of *Oliver Twist* called—what else?—*Twist,* and snagging a rumored role in an upcoming Marvel film (directed by her husband). And she's done all this while still putting out new music! She went on tour! She modeled for fashion campaigns! She released multiple lines of clothing with Primark *and* has her own tequila line!

So why is it that, despite her ubiquity, "Rita Ora" remains a two-word question? On *The Wendy Williams Show* in 2015, Williams was shown a picture of Rita gracing the cover of the U.K. edition of *Marie Claire* and spouted: "Who is this woman?" It was a sound bite that would end up haunting the culture for ages, thanks in part to it being used as the final line of our theme song. She added, in a charming third-person anecdote: "I surround myself with lots of young people, you know how Wendy likes to keep up with things. But you know what's really odd? Even my young people around here are like, 'We don't know.'" The audience agreed, rewarding Williams with typically rapturous applause.

The magic of Rita Ora is that she is a celebrity who is, thanks primarily to those years in creative limbo after suing Roc Nation, someone whose press attention always seems to be outsized compared to her level of fame. The coverage is constant, as our "What's Rita Up To?" segment proves, but the reporting and the tone rarely bring any clarity as to who Rita actually is. When she's covered by the press, it tends to be about what she's wearing, who she's been spotted with, or where she was spotted out and about. Whos can't sustain that spark without the help of tabloid mags to keep the fire going. *Us Weekly, People, Daily Mail,* and the like need the Whos like Rita just as much as the Whos need them—and that's the magic of *Who? Weekly,* as far as we're concerned. These middle-tier celebrities and the tabloid magazines that cover them create a perfect, symbiotic economy. They feed each other. Because the simple nature of a headline implies relevance, it suggests that somebody might just click and read—whether they know exactly who the person is or not, or whether there really must be *something* about them worth reading. But the celebrity ecosystem can only survive on eyeballs and the suggestion that someone is worth the attention. Here's just a selection of what it's like to catch up on what Rita Ora's up to on a weekly basis, courtesy of the rag that loves her the most, the *Daily Mail*:

"Rita Ora looks glum as she grabs a coffee before heading to £30k-a-year gym in London's Notting Hill" (July 2018)
The implication being that she's "glum" despite belonging to an overpriced gym?

"'New year, new beach!' Rita Ora shows off her gym-honed frame in a colourful bikini and semi-sheer pareo as she boasts about her jet-set lifestyle" (January 2023)
Gym-honed? A wordy way to say SEXY BIKINI PICS HERE.

"She doesn't travel light! Rita Ora causes a scene at Sydney Airport as she arrives with her entourage and 14 suitcases loaded on a trolley after wrapping up filming on *The Voice*" (June 2023)
FOURTEEN suitcases!?! That's surely enough to cause a scene.

"Rita Ora puts on a VERY leggy display as she flaunts her toned pins in a skimpy ensemble while kicking back on a chaise longue" (February 2025)
"Toned pins" is the King's English for sure.

"Rita Ora continues her desperate bid to crack the US by appearing on *The Masked Singer* after a bumpy road to make her mark on the States—with legal woes, a reality TV romance and FINALLY hitting the charts" (March 2024)

This last headline—a not-too-distant memory from Rita's current era—declares her "desperate" to break into the U.S. market (a struggle endured by Jess Glynne, Robbie Williams, the Sugababes, and countless other British artists), noting that a new job (*The Masked Singer*); songs that are actually charting (her cover/remix of Fatboy Slim's "Praise You" hit number one on the U.S. Dance/Mix *Billboard* chart); "legal woes" (the aforementioned Roc Nation suit); and "a reality TV romance" (her 2012 dalliance with Rob Kardashian) are proof that she'll do anything it takes to be recognized by the American public. But there's something interesting about how this *Daily Mail* headline implies some sort of pathetic grasping at fame when a list like this is usually the result of someone already glowing under the spotlight.

That Rita will often take whatever lucrative gig is thrown her way, be it a random hosting job, a random acting job, a random modeling job, or even a random performance at Wimbledon's "The Hill in New York" event presented by American Express (randomness the likes of which you simply couldn't imagine), is not pathetic or desperate, as the *Daily Mail* likes to imply; it's simply entertaining. More than that, it's *impressive.* In a world where pop stars have been conditioned to carve "eras" out of their career by siloing each individual music project and its accompanying promotional events as distinct and easily discernible periods of their lives (à la Beyoncé's *Renaissance* versus Beyoncé's *Cowboy Carter* / Taylor Swift's *The Tortured Poets Department* versus Taylor Swift's *The Life of a Showgirl*), Rita does whatever, whenever, and remains unmarried to any particular professional aesthetic or vibe. Her hairstyle has been known to defy the laws of Chris Appleton's salon by appearing long, buzzed, then long again in the span of a weekend. She's multifaceted in a way that used to get you praise but now tends to confuse people overwhelmed by not being able to place her neatly in the "pop star" bucket. And it's not as though she's bad at any of these things: Maybe her music doesn't live at the top of the *Billboard* charts, but she regularly takes fashion risks and designers love dressing her. Even her acting jobs are, at least to the people who hired her, wholly impressive. Few people who ask her to do something once fail to ask her back a second time. And just ask the nearest ten-year-old if they've seen the *Descendants* movies. *The Rise of Red* (which marked her debut in the Disney+ franchise) was the most-viewed premiere ever on the streaming service at the time of its release. Whether or not they can name the performer who played the Red Queen is a different story, but Rita's success proves that contemporary stardom is less about putting a name with a face than it is about seeing a face *everywhere.*

Rita Ora's ubiquity despite a clear category for what she does also extends to her brand deals. There's no doubt her image sells, or why would brands keep hiring her? Just look at her collaboration with fast-fashion brand Primark. Despite initial public ridicule, the collection was such a success that she made headlines in the non-tabloid press, with *The Guardian* writing, "Primark holds prices steady after Rita Ora helps lift sales." By their third collaboration together, Primark's head of fashion trends, John McCormack, said, "With each new collection we've been pushing ourselves with Rita and her team to create bolder, more daring looks." He's not totally wrong: the "Denim Split Maxi Skirt" from her Festival Collection (priced at a reasonable £20) is not to be missed.

If you're overwhelmed by all the Rita Ora we've thrown at you over the past few pages, well, good! That's the point! And if you're cynically thinking her career is merely a nonstop barrage of thoughtlessly-decided-upon gigs, then let us point you to a prescient interview with *Billboard* from 2017. When her first singles "underperformed" in the States, Rita says she "begged" her management to send her on a U.S. tour, noting, "I had an online 'cool' vibe going on, a presence." When they declined, she paid for the tour out of her own pocket. "I said to my team at the time, 'I really think I should go and do . . . not massive venues, but a few thousand people.' And they were like, 'Nah, what's the point? You're not releasing any music there.' I said, 'I'll show you the point—look at my followers. Look at how active my online presence is with my Instagram and Twitter. You guys are missing the point. This is the future! This is my age.'" The randomness of Rita's career is a feature, not a bug. It's also one she designed herself. "I think people . . . know that I work, a lot," she said of her reputation with American audiences. "The perception of me is different in different regions. I've released an album overseas, done festivals, played the Pyramid Stage at Glastonbury—which for me is an iconic stage to be on. And over here, I've kind of . . . dipped into the pies? As in like, features, TV. And I've only done that because those were the only pies that I could reach at that point."

The perception Rita speaks of is as such: In the U.K. she's a bona fide star who has performed for King Charles, while in the United States she inhabits what we call the dreaded "Khia asylum." If we were in charge, we might call her a "working pop star"—part of the plentiful sector of mid-tier musicians that make a living in pop music but don't quite achieve chart-topping pop hits. Which really shouldn't be a requirement for musicians, especially if they're able to produce with creative freedom within the confines of the music industry without having some sort of nepo-baby slush fund. (And often, they do.) Kim Petras, Carly Rae Jepsen, Tinashe, to name a few who might receive the Khia accusation, have all had brief flirtations with the charts. No matter their *Billboard* success, each is able (with the help of sponcon and the like) to continue to work in music. But that doesn't come without the internet's gentle ribbing. "Dropping my new song monday if this get 100,000 retweets," @RitaOra tweeted in 2014, a goal she *perhaps* thought she could achieve in three days' time. Alas, it wasn't happening, thus the next missive became legendary: "By the way my Twitter got hacked somebody is threatening to release new music I've worked really hard on. Nothing comes out until I'm ready." *Oh no.* She goes on: "Luckily I caught the hacker really quickly and deleted the post. Thank you!!" It was a quick and unbelievable pivot, indeed. Why would this "hacker" (if there, in fact, ever was one) choose to wield their access to her account *in this way*? It made no sense, and that's why we're able to easily source a screenshot of that original tweet. It now lives forever in the annals of pop history.

The "hacking" drama was more meme than genuine scandal, but even when Rita becomes embroiled in *actual* scandals, she manages to come out on the other side blemish-free, as famous (or non-famous) as ever. It can take a Them eons to outrun controversies, but as a Who, it's hard to fall from grace when you're not all that high off the ground to begin with. When it was reported that Rita had thrown a birthday bash in London during a pandemic lockdown—that a CCTV had been switched off at the request of the birthday girl—she and her team claimed to have voluntarily paid a £10,000 fine to the city. Later, the city claimed they never received any payment. Despite the conflicting reports, the story quickly fell out of the press. Well before Covid-19, Rita apologized (in an officially released statement—Notes app be damned!) for "Girls," an ill-advised collaboration with fellow Albanian pop star Bebe Rexha, Charli XCX, and Cardi B that received backlash for being a song about sapphic romance sung by women who weren't all of that . . . proclivity. (Cardi B hyped up the song in a pre-release tweet, the perhaps unintended subtext of which was that she was the only Them of the bunch. She wrote, "After i finish my album I'm collabing with 3 artist that I'm cool with. They not big but they soo talented 💪💪💪") But perhaps the most dangerous scandal Rita's been dragged into was when she became the main character in Beyoncé's *Lemonade*. The unidentified woman in "Sorry" suspected to have had an affair with Bey's husband, Jay-Z? Alongside Rachel Roy (and, again, somehow Rachael Ray) on the shortlist of suspects? *Rita*. "I wish I had good hair," Rita said of the incident years later to host Davina McCall on her podcast, *Begin Again*. "It was the first time I experienced what it means to be in a messy situation." (A patently untrue statement, if you've been paying attention.) The Beyhive masses eventually stopped coming for her, and she clearly didn't think her hair was *that* bad: In 2024 she came out with a haircare line, TYPEBEA. Not even the once-dangerous accusation of being associated with "good hair" could stop Rita from eventually making a buck.

Covid restrictions aside, getting in trouble for *partying too hard?* Only our girl Rita could rack up such an offense. Quickly forgotten, too, at least by most people, and her post-pandemic partying picked up as quickly as any bon vivant's might. Unlike so many celebrities who tend to go out on the town within promotional cycles, either Rita's always promoting something or she genuinely enjoys the glitz and glamour of a Hollywood event. In our minds (and go with this fan fiction for a minute), she's the celeb other celebs actually want to see on the guest list—someone who brings guaranteed fun, is easy to talk to, and is genuinely the life of the party. "I love hanging out with Rita," Charli XCX (a musician who's turned her love of parties into a critically acclaimed album, *Brat*) once told *People* about her friend. "She just feels like someone I grew up with—she's very down to earth and I love that. She knows how to party."

A YEAR AFTER her viral "Who is this woman?" sound bite, Wendy Williams invited Rita onto her show. Graciously, considering the things Williams had said about her over the years, she accepted, even exclaiming to the host, "I've been waiting to be on this show, on this couch. I am such a fan. And I love you so much."

Williams responded, "I know you from being the fashion girl. Every single magazine you open up, you always see Rita Ora, and I always say, Oh hey! But what else does she do, what else does she do—[now] I got it."

We get it. With over ten years of Rita Ora coverage under our belts, any criticism we've ever had has melted into genuine standom. By turning her status as a permanent Who into a seemingly endless series of professional and personal successes, she has proven that there is nothing wrong with the distinction. We take offense when listeners ask if we fear the day she "escapes Whodom," as it implies that Who-lebrity is a kind of prison. Rita Ora is one of our greatest celebrities, and she's confident in her Who-y behavior—she embodies all the values and opportunities that being a Who can give you! The monoculture is gone, and it can be utterly delightful when a celebrity leans into this nü fame of being everywhere and nowhere, all at once.

Acknowledgments

It would be so easy to just thank Rita Ora for giving us the inspiration to write this book (and to produce a podcast for over a decade), but we'd be lying if we said she acted alone. Thanks to our editor, Aubrey Martinson, for having faith in this book and making it better with every draft. Thanks to everyone at Crown, including Allyson Coy, Julie Cepler, Andrea Lau, Mary Moates, and Josie McRoberts. Thank you to Chris Allen for the beautiful cover! To our agents, Noah Ballard and Elise Bergerson; to our early readers, Max, Emily, and Jamie; and to our fact-checker, Julie Tate.

Big thank you to our podcast team at Audacy: Leah, Patrick, Peter, Eric. To Jenna Weiss-Berman, Bari Finkel, Caitlin Thompson, Aminatou Sow, and the team at Headgum for the early encouragement and unwavering support.

To the many group chats that keep us sane and are often breaking the news that ends up in the pod (and in this book!)—Trainoring Season, R3GAL, Todos—the logs and tapbacks mean everything to us.

To the always-editorializing Timmy Ngo, who has been such an essential addition to *Who? Weekly* that we can hardly remember how we functioned before he joined the team.

To the Wholigans, once again. Thanks for reading, thanks for listening, thanks for calling, and of course, thanks for crunching.

Lindsey: Thank you to my friends for being gracious enough to listen to me complain about "having to write a book during the summer." To the girlies, Andrew's Couch, The Law Firm, Sacred Group, Alien Aunts, my Rockaway fam—I am really lucky to have so many funny, weird, and loving friends in my life. To my family—the Webers: Mom, Dad, David, Jacquie, little baby Leon! Thank you to Bobby for being my business partner for ten years, and friend for more. I feel lucky every day that I get to do this.

Bobby: Thanks to my friends and family for listening (or pretending to listen) to our show for over a decade and providing endless encouragement to keep at our silly, silly full-time jobs of talking about celebrities no one's ever heard of for a living. This book—and *Who? Weekly* in general—wouldn't exist without all of y'all. And, of course, thanks to Lindsey for being the friend, co-host, and, now, co-author of my dreams.

Notes

Chapter 1: A Grand Theory of Whos and Thems

1 **"secretly dating a stunning US actress":** Camilla Tominey, "His Majesty's Pleasure: Prince Harry Secretly Dating US TV Star Meghan Markle," *Express,* October 31, 2016, https://www.express.co.uk/news/uk/726701/prince-harry-meghan-markle-suits-actress-girlfriend-royal-family-relationship-secret-lover.

1 **"[I] witnessed her and a [*Suits*] castmate":** Prince Harry, Duke of Sussex, *Spare* (Random House Publishing Group, 2024), 297.

2 **"everyone wants to be famous":** Jeff Guin and Douglas Perry, *The Sixteenth Minute: Life in the Aftermath of Fame* (Jeremy F. Tarcher/Penguin, 2005), 364–65.

4 **"EXCLUSIVE: My name is Meg":** Caroline Graham, *Daily Mail,* March 24, 2018, https://www.dailymail.co.uk/lifestyle/article-5539893/Meghan-Markle-video-1990-shows-dressed-Queen.html.

4 **"Meghan Markle's royal wedding":** Emily Smith and Oli Coleman, *Page Six,* April 26, 2018, https://www.pagesix.com/2018/04/26/meghan-markles-royal-wedding-overshadows-her-suits-nuptials.

4 **"Princess Diana 'will be there'":** Emmeline Saunders, *The Mirror,* March 29, 2018, https://www.mirror.co.uk/3am/celebrity-news/princess-diana-prince-harrys-royal-12257398.

4 **"Meghan Markle allegedly asked":** Jessica Sager, *Page Six,* August 15, 2018, https://www.pagesix.com/2018/08/15/meghan-markle-allegedly-asked-her-father-to-stop-speaking-to-her-sister/.

4 **"Meghan Markle Isn't Speaking to Her Dad":** Iliana Magra, *The New York Times,* December 17, 2018, https://www.nytimes.com/2018/12/17/world/europe/meghan-markle-father-interview.html.

5 **"an actress, a writer":** Meghan Markle, "Meghan Markle: I'm More Than an 'Other,'" *Elle*, December 22, 2016, https://www.elle.com/uk/life-and-culture/news/a26855/more-than-an-other.

5 **"What began as a passion project":** Madeleine Luckel, "Meghan Markle Just Shut Down Her Lifestyle Website," *Vogue*, April 7, 2017, https://www.vogue.com/article/meghan-markle-shuts-down-lifestyle-website.

5 **"Mushroom Pasta with Creamy Truffle Sauce":** Megan Markle, *The Tig*, February 28, 2017, https://www.web.archive.org/web/20170309153654/http://thetig.com/.

5 **"first holiday together":** Karren Mizoguch, "Prince Harry and Meghan Markle Spend First Holiday Together in Norway to See Northern Lights: Report," *People*, January 7, 2017, https://www.people.com/royals/prince-harry-meghan-markle-first-holiday-together-norway-northern-lights.

5 **"Awards Season Entertaining Tips":** Meghan Markle, *The Tig*, January 25, 2017, https://www.wattpad.com/708701372-the-tig-archives-awards-season-entertaining-tips.

6 **"After close to three beautiful years":** Meghan Markle, *The Tig*, https://www.thetig.com.

6 **"The Tig has been a labor of love":** Diana Pearl, "As Meghan Markle Shuts Down Her Lifestyle Site, Source Says Speculation It's Related to Prince Harry Is 'False,'" *People*, April 7, 2017, https://www.people.com/royals/meghan-markle-is-shutting-down-her-lifestyle-website-the-tig-its-time-to-say-goodbye.

6 **"If Markle and Prince Harry are indeed":** Sam Kashner, "Meghan Markle, Mad About Harry!," *Vanity Fair*, October 2017, https://www.archive.vanityfair.com/article/2017/10/wild-about-harry.

7 **"After many months of reflection":** The Duke and Duchess of Sussex (@sussexroyal), "After many months of reflection and internal discussions, we have chosen to make a transition this year in starting to carve out a progressive new role within this institution," Instagram, January 8, 2020, https://www.instagram.com/p/B7EaGS_Jpb9/.

7 **"concerns and conversations":** Meghan Markle, interview with Oprah Winfrey, *Oprah with Meghan and Harry*, CBS, March 7, 2021.

8 **"a deal in the neighborhood of $100 million":** Brooks Barnes, "Prince Harry and Meghan Sign Megawatt Netflix Deal," *The New York Times*, September 2, 2020, https://www.nytimes.com/2020/09/02/business/media/harry-meghan-netflix.html.

10 **"Stanny White was killed":** Frederick N. Rasmussen, "The Fatal Attraction of Evelyn Nesbit," *The Baltimore Sun*, June 8, 2008, https://www.baltimoresun.com/2008/06/08/the-fatal-attraction-of-evelyn-nesbit.

10 **"The trial, said one lawyer-spectator":** "The Law: Piloting Patty's Defense," *Time*, February 16, 1976, https://www.content.time.com/time/subscriber/article/0,33009,918025,00.html.

10 **"coercive persuasion and brainwashing":** Edgar H. Schein, Inge Schneier, and Curtis H. Barker, *Coercive Persuasion: A Socio-psychological Analysis of the "Brainwashing" of American Civilian Prisoners by the Chinese Communists* (W. W. Norton, 1961), 7, 18, 283, 284.

10 **"a kind of peculiarly":** "The Law: Piloting Patty's Defense."

10 **"If her acting is as good as her looks":** Hadley Hall Meares, "Blazing Blonde Bombshell: Barbara Payton's Boulevard of Broken Dreams," *Vanity Fair,* January 6, 2021, https://www.vanityfair.com/hollywood/2021/01/barbara-payton-autobiography-old-hollywood.

11 **"living in a falling-down, red brick apartment":** John O'Dowd, *Kiss Tomorrow Goodbye: The Barbara Payton Story* (BearManor Media, 2015), 609.

11 **"Even though the place":** O'Dowd, *Kiss Tomorrow Goodbye,* 613–14.

15 **"What's fortnight":** Colin Stevens, "Lady Gaga Replies to Ninja Perfectly," IGN, updated October 16, 2019, https://www.ign.com/articles/2019/10/16/lady-gaga-asked-what-fortnite-is-and-the-internet-answered-perfectly.

16 **"No one understands":** Delia Cai, "The Femininomenonal Ascent of Chappell Roan," *The Face,* September 16, 2024, https://www.theface.com/music/chappell-roan-pop-music-famous-interview-good-luck-babe.

16 **"Would you go up to a random lady":** Chappell Roan (@chappellroan), TikTok, August 19, 2024, https://www.tiktok.com/@chappellroan/video/7404955808980667690.

17 ***"You make me money":*** "Perfect Celebrity," by Lady Gaga, written by Lady Gaga, Andrew Watt, Henry Walter, and Mike Lévy, produced by Lady Gaga, Andrew Watt, and Cirkut, Interscope Records, 2025.

Chapter 2: The 2010s Killed the Cover Star

20 **"Such a tale":** Martin Loiperdinger, "Lumière's *Arrival of the Train:* Cinema's Founding Myth," *The Moving Image: The Journal of the Association of Moving Image Archivists* 4, no. 1 (Spring 2004): 91.

20 ***Motion Picture* was founded by J. Stuart Blackton:** M. P. Publishing Co., *The Motion Picture Story Magazine* (February–July 1911). With MBRS Library of Congress, 1911. Internet Archive, http://archive.org/details/motionpicturesto01moti.

20 ***Photoplay* was backed:** Sumiko Higashi, "Adapting Middlebrow Taste to Sell Stars, Romance, and Consumption," *Feminist Media Histories* 3, no. 4 (October 2017): 126–161, https://doi.org/10.1525/fmh.2017.3.4.126. https://online.ucpress.edu/fmh/article-abstract/3/4/126/91960/Adapting-Middlebrow-Taste-to-Sell-Stars-Romance?redirectedFrom=fulltext.

20 **"Despite the fact that statistical analyses":** Mary Ann Doane, *The Desire to Desire: The Woman's Film of the 1940s* (Indiana University Press, 1987), 4.

21 **"References to a female star":** Stephen Sharot, " 'Hollywood Is a Woman's Town': Masculinity and the Leading Man in American Fan Magazines of the 1930s," *Gender & History* 35, no. 2 (July 2023): 642–666, https://doi.org/10.1111/1468-0424.12597.

21 **Anne Helen Petersen attests:** Anne Helen Petersen, *Scandals of Classic Hollywood: Sex, Deviance, and Drama from the Golden Age of American Cinema* (Plume, 2014).

22 **"thick with incense":** Michael Mayo, "On Theda Bara and the Origins of the Vamp," *CrimeReads,* September 27, 2022, https://crimereads.com/theda-barra-origins-vamp/.

22 **"the reincarnation of a daughter":** Pam Keesey, *Vamps: An Illustrated History of the Female Fatale* (Cleis Press, 1997), 75.

22 **"the sort of figure":** Anne Helen Petersen, "Scandals of Classic Hollywood: The Most Wicked Face of Theda Bara," *The Hairpin,* January 8, 2013, https://medium.com/the-hairpin/scandals-of-classic-hollywood-the-most-wicked-face-of-theda-bara-2aa85ce1a79f.

22 **"In the old days":** Alex Belth, "The Art of Hanging Out: On the Golden Age of the Celebrity Profile," *Literary Hub,* June 14, 2024, https://lithub.com/the-art-of-hanging-out-on-the-golden-age-of-the-celebrity-profile/.

22 **"Fan magazine writers":** Anthony Slide, *Inside the Hollywood Fan Magazine: A History of Star Makers, Fabricators, and Gossip Mongers* (University Press of Mississippi, 2010), 75.

23 **caused the star to threaten:** Michael Schulman, "The Celebrity Profile, from Piaf to Kardashian," *The New Yorker,* August 21, 2022, https://www.newyorker.com/magazine/2022/08/29/the-celebrity-profile-from-piaf-to-kardashian.

23 **"Do you blame":** Hugo H. Smythe, "By Their Feet Shall Ye Know Them," *Photoplay.*

23 **"Umbrella Holders":** "Umbrella Holders: Handlers? Ha! Stars Provide Shelter from Storms," *Us Weekly,* March 4, 2013.

23 **"Celebs Earning Their Keep":** "Celebs Earning Their Keep! Soaking Up the Sun or Dancing in the Streets, These Stars Make Their Jobs Look like a Breeze," *Us Weekly,* February 4, 2013.

23 **"It's like the other day":** Truman Capote, "The Duke in His Domain," *The New Yorker,* November 2, 1957.

24 **"It is hard to explain":** Tom Wolfe, "The Birth of 'The New Journalism'; Eyewitness Report by Tom Wolfe," *New York,* September 15, 2023, https://nymag.com/article/tom-wolfe-birth-of-new-journalism-eyewitness-report.html.

24 **"It was obvious":** Gay Talese, "Frank Sinatra Has a Cold," *Esquire*, May 14, 2016, https://www.esquire.com/news-politics/a638/frank-sinatra-has-a-cold-gay-talese/.

25 **"She doesn't seem angry":** Nancy Collins, "Demi's Big Moment," *Vanity Fair,* August 1991, https://archive.vanityfair.com/article/1991/8/demis-big-moment.

26 **"Yo, Taylor":** MTV Video Music Awards, directed by Hamish Hamilton, aired September 13, 2009, on MTV.

27 **"I'M SOOOOO SORRY":** Simon Vozick-Levinson, "Kanye West Apologizes for Interrupting Taylor Swift at the VMAs: 'I'm Not Crazy . . . I'm Just Real,'" *Entertainment Weekly,* September 13, 2009, EW.com, https://ew.com/article/2009/09/13/kanye-taylor-swift-apology/.

27 **"I'm sorry Taylor":** "Kanye West Tweets Apology to Taylor Swift," *The Wall Street Journal,* September 4, 2010, https://www.wsj.com/articles/BL-SEB-46055.

27 **"I like [West] as a person":** Josh Duboff, "Taylor Swift: Apple Crusader, #GirlSquad Captain, and the Most Influential 25-Year-Old in America," *Vanity Fair,* August 4, 2015, https://www.vanityfair.com/style/2015/08/taylor-swift-cover-mario-testino-apple-music.

27 **"*I feel like me and Taylor*":** "Famous" by Kanye West, written by Kanye West, Kejuan Muchita, Patrick Reynolds, Enzo Vita, Ross Birchard,

Giampiero Scalamogna, Sergio Bardotti, Winston Riley, Jimmy Webb, Ernest Brown, Kasseem Dean, Mike Dean, Andrew Dawson, Noah Goldstein, Cydel Young, Chancelor Bennett, Nina Simone, Ophlin Russell, Luis Bacalov, GOOD Music / Def Jam Recordings, 2016.

28 **"I called Taylor":** Harriet Gibsone, "Kanye West Faces Backlash over Taylor Swift Lyric Attack," *The Guardian*, February 12, 2016, https://www.theguardian.com/music/2016/feb/12/kanye-west-claims-taylor-swift-came-up-with-famous-diss-lyric.

28 **"Kanye did not call":** Lars Brandle, "Taylor Swift Cautioned Kanye West About 'Famous' and Its 'Strong Misogynistic Message,'" *Billboard*, February 12, 2016, https://www.billboard.com/music/music-news/taylor-swift-cautioned-kanye-west-famous-misogynistic-6874870/.

28 **In the story, she referenced "video proof":** Caity Weaver, "Kim Kardashian West on Kanye and Taylor Swift, What's in O.J.'s Bag, and Understanding Caitlyn," *GQ*, June 16, 2016, https://www.gq.com/story/kim-kardashian-west-gq-cover-story.

28 **"That moment when Kanye":** Emily Yahr, "Read the Secret Kanye West/Taylor Swift Phone Call That Kim Kardashian Posted on Snapchat," *The Washington Post*, July 18, 2016, https://www.washingtonpost.com/news/arts-and-entertainment/wp/2016/07/18/read-the-secret-kanye-westtaylor-swift-phone-call-that-kim-kardashian-posted-on-snapchat/.

29 **"I cooked up one":** Danielle Jonas (@daniellejonas), "I cooked up one of @kevinjonas's favorite meals," Instagram, https://imgur.com/a/5hzs8Ho.

31 **Profiles such as Swift's from 2013:** Nancy Jo Sales, "Taylor Swift's Telltale Heart," *Vanity Fair*, April 2013, https://archive.vanityfair.com/article/2013/4/taylor-swifts-telltale-heart.

31 **"the past three years of her life":** Brian Hiatt, "Taylor Swift: The *Rolling Stone* Interview," *Rolling Stone*, September 18, 2019, https://www.rollingstone.com/music/music-features/taylor-swift-rolling-stone-interview-880794/.

31 **aforementioned "Frank Sinatra Has a Cold":** Gay Talese, "Frank Sinatra Has a Cold," *Esquire*, May 14, 2016, https://www.esquire.com/news-politics/a638/frank-sinatra-has-a-cold-gay-talese/.

31 ***Vanity Fair* profile of Julia Roberts:** Krista Smith and Jane Sarkin, "Mommy's Being Famous Right Now," *Vanity Fair*, February 10, 2007, https://www.vanityfair.com/news/2007/12/Mommys-Being-Famous-Right-Now.

31 **vague, lazy non-sentiments:** Lulu Garcia-Navarro, "How Reese Witherspoon Figured Out Who She Really Is," *The New York Times*, September 20, 2025, https://www.nytimes.com/2025/09/20/magazine/reese-witherspoon-interview.html.

32 **"Nowadays, there's an inescapable feeling":** Ian Hurley, "PS Picks: The Evolution of the Celebrity Profile," *The Pacific Standard*, August 23, 2018, https://psmag.com/ps-picks/ps-picks-the-evolution-of-the-celebrity-profile/.

32 **Beyoncé surprised fans:** Brooklyn White, "Beyoncé, The Boss," *Essence*, February 23, 2024, https://www.essence.com/beauty/beyonce-2024-essence-cover-cecred/.

32 **"Chris Evans Is Having Second Thoughts":** Zach Baron, *GQ*, September 19, 2023, https://www.gq.com/story/chris-evans-october-cover-profile-2023.

32 **"Greta Lee Is Getting Used to This":** Cat Zhang, *The Cut,* February 14, 2024, https://www.thecut.com/article/greta-lee-past-lives-interview.html.

32 **"Robert Downey Jr. Doesn't See Things the Way You Do":** Ryan D'Agostino, *Esquire,* April 8, 2024, https://www.esquire.com/entertainment/a60314472/robert-downey-jr-interview-2024/.

32 **"Keke Palmer Is in Control":** Ruhama Wolle, *Glamour,* July 13, 2022, https://www.glamour.com/story/keke-palmer-cover-story.

32 **"Madison Beer, Her Way":** Alaska Riley, *Paper,* January 16, 2026, https://www.papermag.com/madison-beer-cover-story-paper.

33 **"What do you think":** "Is This Why Beyoncé Stopped Doing Interviews?," ITN Archive, March 1, 2023, https://www.youtube.com/watch?v=lBsVxKPNeDU.

34 **"I'm a protector":** Haniyah Philogene, "Living Her 'Destiny': How Yvette Noel-Schure Parlayed Her Sony Success into an Entrepreneurial Dream," *Forbes,* August 5, 2022, https://www.forbes.com/sites/haniyahphilogene/2022/08/05/living-her-destiny-how-yvette-noel-schure-parlayed-her-sony-success-into-an-entrepreneurial-dream/.

34 **For *GQ*, she ate sushi:** Amy Wallace, "Beyoncé," *GQ,* January 10, 2013, https://www.gq.com/story/beyonce-cover-story-interview-gq-february-2013. https://archive.ph/61G01.

35 **"I think there's a decision":** Jason Gay, "Beyoncé Knowles: The Queen B," *Vogue,* February 11, 2013, https://www.vogue.com/article/beyonce-knowles-the-queen-b.

36 **"Why would [audiences] pay":** Zak Cheney-Rice, "Michael B. Jordan Did the Impossible," *Vulture,* June 2, 2025, https://www.vulture.com/article/michael-b-jordan-interview-sinners-thomas-crown-affair-ryan-coogler.html.

Chapter 3: Gossip: A Reckoning

37 **during his marriage to Maria Shriver:** Ann Louise Bardach, "The Hush-Hush Deal That Made Arnold Schwarzenegger Governor," *Los Angeles Magazine,* September 1, 2004, https://www.lamag.com/news/the-hush-hush-deal-that-made-arnold-schwarzenegger-governor.

38 **"The edict came down":** Bardach, "The Hush-Hush Deal."

38 **"That's what they do":** Peter Nicholas and Carla Hall, "Tabloid's Deal with Woman Shielded Schwarzenegger," *Los Angeles Times,* August 12, 2005, https://www.latimes.com/archives/la-xpm-2005-aug-12-me-arnold12-story.html.

39 **local crime blotters:** Toria Sheffield, "Pregnant 22-Year-Old Shot at Sports Bar. Her Unborn Baby Died, and 'Reckless Behavior' with a Gun May Be to Blame," *People,* June 15, 2025, https://people.com/pregnant-22-year-old-shot-at-alabama-sports-bar-her-unborn-baby-died-11754999.

39 **aggregating TikToks and Reddit threads:** Ashley Vega, "Widow Demands Her Kids Get a Share of Late Husband's Ashes Despite His Dying Wish Stating Otherwise," *People,* June 15, 2025, https://people.com/woman-faces-family-conflict-over-late-fathers-ashes-as-widow-demands-share-reddit-11742277.

39 **adding an affiliate link:** "Brittany Mahomes Just Proved a Black One-Piece Swimsuit Is Always in Style—Shop Inspired Looks from $21," *People,* February 15, 2026, https://people.com/brittany-mahomes-black-swimsuit-amazon-february-2026-11905186.

39 **a regular woman named Jennifer:** Virginia Chamlee, "Woman Tells Husband His Cooking Is 'Trash.' Now He's Thinking of Ending Their Marriage," *People,* April 1, 2025, https://people.com/man-says-he-wont-be-cooking-for-wife-after-she-literally-retched-from-a-meal-he-made-11687448.

40 **"All literature is gossip":** Truman Capote interview with Beverly Gary Kempton, "After Hours: Books," *Playboy,* December 1976.

40 **"chinless wonder":** Michael Riedel, "Why Sinatra Loved to Eat in His Car, and More on His Secret NYC Life," *New York Post,* March 6, 2015, https://nypost.com/2015/03/07/why-frank-sinatra-loved-to-eat-in-his-car-and-more-on-his-secret-nyc-life/.

40 **"How good a fuck are you?":** Ann Helen Petersen, "How Rona Barrett Became the Gossip Industry's Forgotten Trailblazer," *BuzzFeed,* May 15, 2016, https://www.buzzfeed.com/annehelenpetersen/all-the-dirt-on-rona-barrett-the-forgotten-gossip-girl.

41 **"Photographers have agreed":** Philip French, "A Woman of Consequence," *The Guardian,* July 6, 2003, https://www.theguardian.com/film/2003/jul/06/artsfeatures.

41 **"They liked each other a lot":** Amy Fine Collins, "The Powerful Rivalry of Hedda Hopper and Louella Parsons," *Vanity Fair,* April 1, 1997, https://www.vanityfair.com/hollywood/2016/02/rivalry-hedda-hopper-louella-parsons-gossip-columnists.

41 **"Louella Parsons is a reporter":** Collins, "The Powerful Rivalry."

41 **"L.A. is now a town with no gossip column":** Collins, "The Powerful Rivalry."

41 **"an insider, not a tattle":** Ben Widdicombe, "Liz Smith's Final Triumph," *Vanity Fair,* November 13, 2017, https://www.vanityfair.com/style/2017/11/liz-smith-remembered.

42 **"I don't pay attention":** Philip Gaines, "Oh, How They Like to Dish," *The New York Times,* April 25, 2014, https://www.nytimes.com/2014/04/27/fashion/a-conversation-with-liz-smith-gossip-columnist-and-jess-cagle-editorial-director-of-people-magazine.html.

42 **"She was confounded":** Widdicombe, "Liz Smith's Final Triumph."

42 **"I'm more trustworthy than *Page Six*":** Tyler Gray, "Pop Goes Perez: How a Pudgy Miami Poseur Became Gossip's New Queen," *Radar,* September 28, 2006, https://www.web.archive.org/web/20070209022056/http://www.radaronline.com/features/2006/09/perez_hilton_blogger_baron.php.

43 **"I don't want to be that person":** Oprah Winfrey, "How Perez Hilton Changed the Negative Energy in His Life," *Oprah's Lifeclass,* April 23, 2012, https://www.oprah.com/oprahs-lifeclass/how-perez-hilton-changed-the-negative-energy-in-his-life-video.

43 **"I am feeling numb":** Perez Hilton, "I'm Going to Be Doing Things Differently," YouTube, October 13, 2010, https://www.youtube.com/watch?v=glRZpHuGj6Q.

43 **"We completely acknowledge":** Erin Carlson, "Celebrity 'Stalker' Web Site Launched," Associated Press, March 22, 2006.

44 **"Spotted outside the Carroll St. stop":** Jessica Coen, "Gawker Stalker: Sienna Miller Speaks Out," *Gawker,* October 17, 2005, https://www.gawkerarchives.com/131455/gawker-stalker-sienna-miller-speaks-out.

44 **"You're throwing rocks at people":** *Larry King Live,* "Paparazzi: Do They Go Too Far?," CNN, 2007.

44 **"Our posts are written by ordinary people":** Emily Gould, "Coordinates of the Rich and Famous," *The New York Times,* May 4, 2007, https://www.nytimes.com/2007/05/04/opinion/04gould.html.

45 **"I've always stayed true":** Allie Jones, "Deuxmoi, Instagram's Biggest Gossip," *The New York Times,* November 17, 2020, https://www.nytimes.com/2020/11/17/style/deuxmoi-gossip.html.

45 **"I don't want to be Perez Hilton":** Maureen O'Connor, "The Joy and Agony of Being @deuxmoi, Instagram's Accidental Gossip Queen," *Vanity Fair,* February 4, 2021, https://www.vanityfair.com/style/2021/02/deuxmoi-instagrams-accidental-celebrity-gossip-queen.

45 **"Believe what you want":** O'Connor, "The Joy and Agony of Being @deuxmoi."

45 **"I don't work with any publicists":** Sara Belcher, "Anon Please! Deux Moi Creator Reveals She Has Received Tips From Celebs (EXCLUSIVE)," *Distractify*, October 6, 2021, https://www.distractify.com/p/is-deux-moi-accurate.

45 **"I'm not afraid to say":** Belcher, "Anon Please!"

46 **"Which superstar's daughter":** Michael Musto, *Village Voice,* October 13, 2010, https://web.archive.org/web/20101015060821/http://www.villagevoice.com/2010-10-13/columns/blind-items-about-abortions-and-trannie-chasers/.

46 **"This A-list mostly movie actress":** Enty Lawyer, "Blind Item #3," *Crazy Days and Nights,* January 19, 2022, https://www.crazydaysandnights.net/2022/01/blind-item-3_19.html.

46 **"PSST! I can't name names now":** *National Examiner,* March 23, 1999, http://www.agcwebpages.com/BLINDITEMS/OLDER/1999/MARAPRIL.html.

46 **"Years ago, this A+ diva":** "Blind Item: Which Diva Was Lost in NYC?," *Gawker,* August 30, 2022, https://www.gawkerarchives.com/celebrity/blind-item-no-address-found.

46 **"This lovable funny boy":** curators of pop culture (@deuxmoi), Instagram, November 2021.

48 **In her paper:** Deborah Schaffer, "SHOCKING SECRETS REVEALED! The Language of Tabloid Headlines," *ETC: A Review of General Semantics* 52, no. 1 (1995): 27–46, http://www.jstor.org/stable/42577612.

49 **"I don't go to the gym":** "Winslet Sues Newspaper for Libel," BBC News, May 8, 2009, http://news.bbc.co.uk/2/hi/entertainment/8040190.stm.

49 **"She might say it is down":** *Winslet v Associated Newspapers Ltd.* (June 19, 2019), https://vlex.co.uk/vid/winslet-v-associated-newspapers-793901921.

50 **Rooney posted that she'd blocked:** Coleen Rooney (@coleen_rooney), "This has been a burden in my life for a few years now and finally I have got to the

bottom of it," Instagram, October 9, 2019, https://www.instagram.com/p/B3ZHjyjBhSV/.

50 **"substantially true":** "Wagatha Christie: Rebekah Vardy Loses Libel Case Against Coleen Rooney," BBC News, July 29, 2022, https://www.bbc.com/news/entertainment-arts-61719250.

50 **"[It was] most unfortunate":** "Vardy's 'Nasty' Text Not About Rooney, Court Told," BBC News, February 9, 2022, https://www.bbc.com/news/newsbeat-60323900.

50 **"Lindsay Lohan's mom":** Eugene Volokh, "Lindsay Lohan's and Her Mother's Libel Lawsuit Against Fox News and Michelle Fields," *The Washington Post,* February 5, 2015, https://www.washingtonpost.com/news/volokh-conspiracy/wp/2015/02/04/lindsay-lohans-and-her-mothers-libel-lawsuit-against-fox-news-and-michelle-fields.

50 **"Truth is a defense":** Joyce Chen, "Judge Throws Out Lindsay Lohan's Defamation Case Against Fox News," *Us Weekly,* September 19, 2015, https://www.usmagazine.com/celebrity-news/news/judge-throws-out-lindsay-lohans-defamation-case-against-fox-news-2015199/.

50 **"Dad, [Mom's] on cocaine":** "Lindsay Lohan—'Dad, [Mom's] On Cocaine!' " *TMZ,* October 11, 2012, https://www.tmz.com/watch/0-5ypcl2dq/.

51 **with a little twist:** "Tyra Banks Is Embarrassed by Old Throwback Photos Just Like the Rest of Us," *BuzzFeed,* March 11, 2016, https://www.buzzfeed.com/michaelblackmon/ty-ty-was-not-feelin-the-tbt.

51 **"13 TV Stars":** Angelo Spagnolo, "13 TV Stars from the '90s You Probably Had a Crush On," *BuzzFeed,* March 11, 2016, https://www.buzzfeed.com/angelospagnolo/tv-boners-r-serious.

51 **"I scroll around":** Chris Smith, "In Conversation: Jon Stewart," *New York,* November 2, 2014, https://nymag.com/intelligencer/2014/10/jon-stewart-rosewater-in-conversation.html.

52 **"stopped working around 2009":** Ben Smith, "Why *BuzzFeed* Doesn't Do Clickbait," *BuzzFeed,* November 6, 2014, https://www.buzzfeed.com/bensmith/why-buzzfeed-doesnt-do-clickbait.

52 **"There's no 'off' button":** Emma Madden and Ollie Millington, "Inside Pop Crave, the Disruptive Media Brand That Called the Election," *Business Insider,* November 11, 2020, https://www.businessinsider.com/pop-crave-the-viral-twitter-account-disrupting-music-media-election-2020-11.

52 **"Rachel spills the tea":** Rachel Zegler Source (@ZeglerSource), "Rachel spills the tea on playing Fiona, Juliet and Evita for British Vogue," X, June 25, 2025, https://x.com/ZeglerSource/status/1937892552486576492.

52 **"New look at Joseph Quinn":** Joseph Quinn HQ (@JoeQuinnHQ), "New look at Joseph Quinn as Johnny Storm in 'THE FANTASTIC FOUR: FIRST STEPS,' " X, August 6, 2025, https://x.com/joequinnhq/status/1953214952744825058.

53 **"Lola Young stuns in new photo":** Pop Crave (@PopCrave), "Lola Young stuns in new photo," X, March 20, 2025, https://x.com/PopCrave/status/1902785836883517465.

53 **"Andrew Cuomo concedes":** Pop Crave (@PopCrave), "Andrew Cuomo concedes New York City Democratic mayoral primary to Zohran Mamdani," X, June 24, 2025, https://x.com/PopCrave/status/1937704403231809768.

53 **"well before it was shared":** Henry Chandonnet, "How Pop Crave and Pop Base Became Major News Sources in the 2024 Presidential Election," *Fast Company,* November 5, 2024, https://www.fastcompany.com/91222753/pop-crave-pop-base-election-news.

53 **"CHARLIE SHEEN'S AIDS":** Michelangelo Signorile, "Charlie Sheen, HIV Stigma and Why the Media Panic Is Ugly," *HuffPost,* updated November 20, 2016, https://www.huffpost.com/entry/charlie-sheen-hiv-stigma_b_8582436.

53 **"LISA MARIE AND EX-HUBBY":** *National Enquirer,* July 25, 1995.

53 **"IT'S NOT BRAD'S BABY":** "Pictures!," *Chicago Tribune,* June 14, 2006, https://www.chicagotribune.com/2006/06/14/pictures-1861/.

53 **"TOMKAT KAPUT!":** *New York Post,* June 30, 2012.

53 **"HUMA CUTS OFF WEINER":** *New York Post,* August 30, 2016.

53 **Just as pop star:** Pop Crave (@PopCrave), "Sabrina Carpenter stuns at Dior's Men fashion show in Paris," X, June 27, 2025, https://x.com/PopCrave/status/1938659195022447024.

53 **actual celestial object:** Pop Crave (@PopCrave), "Strawberry Moon stuns in the UK," X, June 10, 2025, https://x.com/PopCrave/status/1932602948346851593.

53 **"Malia and Sasha Obama":** Pop Crave (@PopCrave), "Malia and Sasha Obama stun with Destin Conrad at his album listening party," X, April 29, 2025, https://x.com/PopCrave/status/1917319019796848889.

53 **"Chappell Roan stuns in elevator":** Pop Crave (@PopCrave), "Chappell Roan stuns in elevator & car," X, May 16, 2025, https://x.com/PopCrave/status/1923460752100208793.

53 **"In the *Pop Crave* journalistic universe":** Tobias Hess, "A Literary Guide to Pop Crave," *Paper,* November 15, 2023, https://www.papermag.com/pop-crave-literary-guide.

54 **"i can't believe":** bald ann dowd (@ali_sivi), "'i can't believe i found out from popcrave," X, August 6, 2024, https://x.com/ali_sivi/status/1820809125082665105.

Chapter 4: When Thems Act Like Whos (and Vice Versa)

55 **"reflects a new smoochiness in [her] life":** MTV Video Music Awards, aired September 7, 1995, on MTV, https://www.youtube.com/watch?v=FEdm_U8-Sdg.

59 **"pretty overwhelmed by the world":** Mona Thomas, "Shawn Mendes Finally Explains *That* Painfully Slow Walk with Camila Cabello," *E! Online,* October 2, 2020, https://www.eonline.com/news/1194300/shawn-mendes-finally-explains-that-painfully-slow-walk-with-camila-cabello.

60 **"Its editor and publisher":** Dierdre Carmody, "THE MEDIA BUSINESS; Politics as Entertainment, Politics Even as Play," *The New York Times,* February 20, 1995, https://www.nytimes.com/1995/02/20/business/the-media-business-politics-as-entertainment-politics-even-as-play.html.

61 ***The Hollywood Reporter* published:** Lisa DePaulo, "John F. Kennedy Jr. and *George* Magazine: A Story of Politics, Love and Loss, 20 Years Later," *The Hollywood Reporter,* April 9, 2019, https://www.hollywoodreporter.com/

movies/movie-features/john-f-kennedy-jr-george-magazine-stars-share-stories-project-1200375/.

63 **"That can't be right":** Eric Todisco, "Gwyneth Paltrow Forgot That She Was in 7 Marvel Movies," *New York Post,* March 20, 2025, https://nypost.com/2025/03/20/entertainment/gwyneth-paltrow-forgot-that-she-was-in-7-marvel-movies/.

63 **"all big internet companies":** Russ Martin, "Cannes 2016: Gwyneth Paltrow Preps Goop for Growth," *Marketing,* June 24, 2016, http://marketingmag.ca/cannes/cannes-2016-gwyneth-paltrow-talks-goop-in-cannes-177724.

63 **painfully basic newsletter:** Elaine Lui, "Gwyneth Paltrow's Second GOOP Newsletter Sent Out," *LaineyGossip,* October 4, 2008, https://www.laineygossip.com/gwyneth-paltrow-s-second-goop-newsletter-sent-out/.

65 **"a Tuscan inspired":** Gwyneth Paltrow (@gwynethpaltrow), "This was a Tuscan inspired high protein #boyfriendbreakfast skillet with sausage from the local butcher," Instagram, June 14, 2025, https://www.instagram.com/reels/DK4totXu9Fl/.

66 **"I got tired":** Marc Malkin, "Eva Mendes on Quitting Acting: 'I Don't Really Miss It,'" *Variety,* September 7, 2022, https://variety.com/2022/film/news/why-eva-mendes-quit-acting-1235351470/.

66 **"Like so many people":** Malkin, "Eva Mendes on Quitting Acting."

68 **among the first high-profile celebrity:** Sarah Anne Hughes, "Tyra Banks Graduates from Harvard's Executive Education Program," *The Washington Post,* February 24, 2012, https://www.washingtonpost.com/blogs/celebritology/post/tyra-banks-graduates-from-harvards-executive-education-program/2012/02/24/gIQASv0vXR_blog.html.

68 **"Do you know how good":** Kara Brown, "Tyra Banks Launches Cosmetics Line, Still Insists She Went to Harvard," *Jezebel,* October 3, 2014, https://www.jezebel.com/tyra-banks-launches-cosmetics-line-still-insists-she-w-1642150472.

69 **including the cover of *Elle*:** Sylvia Obell, "Blue Origin's All-Female Flight Crew Isn't Afraid to Take Up Space," *Elle,* April 2, 2025, https://www.elle.com/culture/celebrities/a64341516/blue-origin-female-flight-crew-space-interview-2025/.

72 **"oh SHIT":** Cher (@cher), "Oh SHIT / GUMMY BEARS fk," Twitter (now X), July 26, 2012, https://x.com/cher/status/228738869632319488.

72 **"@cher hi":** Cher (@cher), "@cher hi," Twitter (now X), September 12, 2013, https://x.com/cher/status/378311589276831744.

72 **"I'm dyslexic":** Cher (@cher), "I'm dyslexic & #'s Are hard 4 me," Twitter (now X), May 20, 2023, https://x.com/cher/status/1659977398371364865.

72 **"I have a theory":** Viola Davis (@violadavis), "Does this speak to you? 💫❤️," Instagram, November 3, 2025, https://www.instagram.com/p/DQn_b0zDNzt/?img_index=1.

72 **"Courage is being yourself":** Viola Davis (@violadavis), "❤️❤️❤️," Instagram, September 2, 2025, https://www.instagram.com/p/DOH55_sDOvl/.

73 **"Why you keep bringing up my album??":** Cardi B (@iamcardib), "Why you keep bringing up my album??," X, September 29, 2025, https://x.com/iamcardib/status/1972869116378624053.

73 **"Fans alarmed":** Caroline Blair, "Fans Alarmed by Madonna's 'Disturbing' New TikTok: 'What Happened to Her?,'" *Page Six,* November 4, 2022, https://pagesix.com/2022/11/04/fans-alarmed-by-madonnas-disturbing-new-tiktok/.

73 **"Madonna's 'unsettling'":** Samantha Ibrahim, "Madonna's 'Unsettling' Pre-Grammys TikTok Video Sparks Fan Concern," *New York Post,* April 4, 2022, https://nypost.com/2022/04/04/madonnas-unsettling-pre-grammy-tiktok-sparks-fan-concern/.

73 **"*Have you ever been punched*":** "vent," by Baby Keem, written and produced by Hykeem Carter, Columbia Records, 2021.

74 **"I have a confession":** Caroline Blair, "Madonna Makes Bizarre Circumcision Confession on Instagram," *Page Six,* October 21, 2022, https://pagesix.com/2022/10/21/madonna-makes-bizarre-circumcision-confession-on-instagram/.

74 ***Page Six* called the confession "bizarre":** Blair, "Madonna Makes Bizzare Circumcision Confession on Instagram."

74 **"The art of shame":** Ellen Gamerman, "Behind Jacob Elordi's Dramatic Transformation into Frankenstein's Monster," *The Wall Street Journal,* September 30, 2025, https://www.wsj.com/arts-culture/film/jacob-elordi-interview-frankenstein-71a05c6b?reflink=desktopwebshare_permalink.

Chapter 5: How Reality TV Changed the Reality of Celebrity

75 **"If I were ever to pass you":** Russell Steinberg, "How Sue Hawk's 'Snakes and Rats' Speech at the 1st 'Survivor' Finale Still Hits Hard 25 Years Later (Exclusive)," *Us Weekly*, August 8, 2025, https://www.usmagazine.com/entertainment/news/how-sue-hawks-snakes-and-rats-speech-helped-make-survivor/.

77 **"I guess there really is someone":** Luke Greenfield, dir., *The Animal*, Columbia Pictures, 2001.

78 **"Can't have this living":** Tina Wesson (@wesson3411), "Can't have this living by the house!" Instagram, June 14, 2025, https://www.instagram.com/p/DK5FeNwR0tA/.

78 **"helped viewers find designer styles":** "Watch *The View* TV Show—ABC.com," ABC, https://web.archive.org/web/20091001070444/http://theview.abc.go.com/staff/Elisabeth-Hasselbeck/bio.

78 **"four or five women":** Ramin Setoodeh, *Ladies Who Punch: The Explosive Inside Story of "The View"* (Thomas Dunne Books, 2019).

79 **married her college sweetheart:** Associated Press, "PLUS: PRO FOOTBALL; Hasselbeck Leads Eagles Past Packers," *The New York Times,* August 11, 2002, https://www.nytimes.com/2002/08/11/sports/plus-pro-football-hasselbeck-leads-eagles-past-packers.html.

79 **"In the US, we were not used to":** Setoodeh, *Ladies Who Punch.*

79 **the two exchanged heated words:** Sheldon Drobny, "Did Rosie Call Our Troops Terrorists?," *HuffPost,* May 23, 2007, https://www.huffpost.com/entry/did-rosie-call-our-troops_b_49186.

80 **"When painting there is a point":** "'Scarborough Country' for May 24," NBC News, May 30, 2007, https://www.nbcnews.com/id/wbna18940560.

80 **she was fired from the show:** Joyce Chen, "Elisabeth Hasselbeck Leaving *The View* After Nine Years, Viewers Found Her 'Too Extreme and Right Wing,'" *Us Weekly,* March 8, 2013, https://www.usmagazine.com/celebrity-news/news/elisabeth-hasselbeck-leaving-the-view-after-nine-years-viewers-found-her-too-extreme-and-right-wing-201383/.

81 **"voyage of discovery":** N. R. Kleinfeld, "Barefoot in the Loft: A Real New York Story," *The New York Times,* March 22, 1992, https://www.nytimes.com/1992/03/22/arts/television-barefoot-in-the-loft-a-real-new-york-story.html.

85 **"found resonance by delivering":** Chuck Klosterman, "THE YEAR in IDEAS; Celebrities Are Just Like You and Me," *The New York Times,* December 15, 2002, https://www.nytimes.com/2002/12/15/magazine/the-year-in-ideas-celebrities-are-just-like-you-and-me.html.

85 **"I loved watching *The Osbournes*":** Rachel Levy, "'They Throw Each Other in the Pool!': Ryan Seacrest Talks on the Audition Tape That Won the Kardashians Their First Reality Show," *Daily Mail,* January 18, 2015, https://www.dailymail.co.uk/tvshowbiz/article-2915784/Ryan-Seacrest-says-winning-audition-tape-won-Kardashians-reality-show.html.

86 **"There's not much of a show here:** Brian Lowry, "Keeping Up with the Kardashians," *Variety,* October 10, 2007, variety.com/2007/scene/markets-festivals/keeping-up-with-the-kardashians-1117935063.

86 **they wrote with obvious disdain:** Ginia Bellafante, "The All-Too-Easy Route to Stardom," *The New York Times*, October 13, 2007, https://www.nytimes.com/2007/10/13/arts/television/13bell.html.

87 **"I was thinking [the series]":** Ramin Setoodeh, "Kim Kardashian West on Her Empire and Bruce Jenner's Transition," *Variety,* April 24, 2015, https://variety.com/2015/tv/news/kim-kardashian-west-bruce-jenner-transgender-empire-brand-1201479125/.

88 **"[She] has created her own brand":** Julie Naughton, "Kim Kardashian Discusses First Scent," *WWD,* October 2, 2009, https://wwd.com/beauty-industry-news/beauty-features/feature/kim-kardashian-discusses-first-scent-2324791-1427736/.

88 **"mobile moguls":** Natalie Robehmed, "Kim Kardashian West, Mobile Mogul: The *Forbes* Cover Story," *Forbes,* July 11, 2016, https://www.forbes.com/sites/natalierobehmed/2016/07/11/kim-kardashian-mobile-mogul-the-forbes-cover-story/.

89 **5 'Achievements' You Could Potentially Earn**: "Kim Kardashian: Hollywood Wiki," Fandom, https://kimkardashianhollywood.fandom.com/wiki/Achievements.

Chapter 6: What's Love Got to Do with It?

94 **Studies have shown:** Tobias Greitemeyer, "Unattractive People Are Unaware of Their (Un)Attractiveness," *Scandinavian Journal of Psychology* 61, no. 4 (2020): 471–83, doi:10.1111/sjop.12631.

95 **"Welcome to the O.C.":** Josh Schwartz, dir., "Pilot," *The O.C.*, season 1, episode 1, Hypnotic, 2003.

96 **"Do you think either of us":** Heidi Montag and Spencer Pratt, *How to Be*

Famous: Our Guide to Looking the Part, Playing the Press, and Becoming a Tabloid Fixture (Grand Central Publishing, 2009), 95.

96 **"She was running the media game":** Morgan Baila, "How Spencer Pratt Manipulated the Media & Why He Had That Flesh-Colored Beard," *Refinery29,* June 2, 2016, https://www.refinery29.com/en-us/2016/06/112649/spencer-pratt-pop-culture-died-2009-interview.

99 **"It was serving them":** Emma Paige, "Know Your Worth & Onto the Next: Gigi Paris Breaks Her Silence," *Too Much,* June 10, 2025, https://www.youtube.com/watch?v=g9BwKR51_Q0.

101 **"Mr. and Mrs. Ross Vegas":** Max Hardy, "Angelina Jolie, Brad Pitt and Others Use Fake Names," news.com.au, October 24, 2008, https://www.news.com.au/travel/travel-updates/angelina-jolie-brad-pitt-and-others-use-fake-names/news-story/c8da0fa989bacdf43b96d171b0e3480.

101 **"uncoupling":** Giles Hattersley and Chioma Nnadi, "Gwyneth's Second Coming: 'I'm Much Easier on Myself, I Would Say,'" *British Vogue,* October 15, 2025, https://www.vogue.co.uk/article/gwyneth-paltrow-british-vogue-interview.

102 **"I used to think":** Deb Baer, "Katie Holmes: I'm Definitely Not a Goody-Goody," *Seventeen,* October 2004.

102 **"I learned real fast":** Marisa Laudadio, "Kevin Federline: My Side of the Story," *People,* December 3, 2008, https://people.com/celebrity/kevin-federline-my-side-of-the-story/.

103 **"By all accounts":** "K-Fed: Father of the Year?," ABC News, October 3, 2007, https://abcnews.go.com/GMA/story?id=3682555&page=1.

103 **"Kevin Federline won't win":** Michael Erman, "Is K-Fed Better Than Spears?," *The Sydney Morning Herald,* October 4, 2007, https://www.news.com.au/entertainment/is-kfed-better-than-spears/news-story/8f471664cea11eb20d54d600b3b050c3.

104 ***Bossip* was the first publication:** Janeé Bolden, "Did Ariana Grande Dump Mac Miller to Let THIS *SNL* Actor Chop Her 4 Octave Cakes to Smithereens?," *Bossip,* May 18, 2018, https://bossip.com/1641939/did-ariana-grande-dump-mac-miller-to-let-this-snl-actor-chop-her-4-octave-cakes-to-smithereens/.

104 **"just started":** "Ariana Grande and Pete Davidson Are Seeing Each Other: 'It's Very Casual,' Says Source," *People,* May 21, 2018, https://www.people.com/music/ariana-grande-pete-davidson-dating-casually/.

104 **"Kondomless Klown":** Janeé Bolden, "Kondomless Klown King Tristan Thompson Kries Krocodile Tears to Khloé over Infant Indiscretion, Apologizes for Rampant Raw Doggery," *Bossip,* January 4, 2022, https://bossip.com/2115496/tristan-thompson-apologizes-khloe-kardashian-baby-paternity/.

104 **"Bae of the Day":** Aiesha Letman, "Bae of the Day: 'WAGS Miami' Star Darnell Nicole Is Beautifully Stacked Like a Dolphin," *Bossip,* October 14, 2017, https://bossip.com/1592667/bae-of-the-day-wags-miami-star-darnell-nicole-is-beautifully-stacked-like-a-dolphin/.

104 **"Caucasity Audacity":** Jason Lee, "Caucasity Audacity: Soft-Boiled Ostrich Egg Taylor Swift Gets Buried, Burned and Blown Away for Earth, Wind and Fire Cover," *Bossip,* April 13, 2018, https://bossip.com/1634604/caucacity

-audacity-soft-boiled-ostrich-egg-taylor-swift-gets-buried-burned-and-blown-away-for-earth-wind-and-fire-cover-43081/.

104 **"Poon-Sizzling Villain Bae":** Alex Ford, "Poon-Sizzling Villain Bae Michael B. Jordan Is Destroying Dashiki Drawls Across Wakanda," *Bossip,* October 16, 2017, https://bossip.com/1592953/poon-sizzling-villain-bae-michael-b-jordan-is-destroying-dashiki-drawls-everywhere/.

104 **"In White Folks News":** Rebecah Jacobs, "In White Folks News: Bradley Cooper and Irina Shayk Have Reportedly Called It Quits," *Bossip,* June 7, 2019, https://bossip.com/1737829/in-white-folks-news-bradley-cooper-and-irina-shayk-have-reportedly-called-it-quits/.

105 **popularized in part:** Allison P. Davis, "Do You Have Big Dick Energy?," *The Cut,* June 26, 2018, https://www.thecut.com/2018/06/pete-davidson-ariana-grande-big-dick-energy.html.

106 **"*I'm so fuckin' grateful*":** "Thank U, Next" by Ariana Grande, written by Ariana Grande, Tayla Parx, and Victoria Monét, produced by Tommy Brown, Charles Anderson, and Michael Foster, Republic Records, 2018.

106 **"The twinkling chorus":** Hanif Abdurraqib, "The 200 Best Songs of the 2010s," *Pitchfork,* October 7, 2019, https://pitchfork.com/features/lists-and-guides/the-200-best-songs-of-the-2010s/.

106 **"It's really annoying":** "Pete Davidson Says Ariana Grande Made Him Famous: 'She Made Me and Created Me,'" WFAA, March 5, 2020, https://www.wfaa.com/article/entertainment/entertainment-tonight/pete-davidson-says-ariana-grande-made-him-famous-she-made-me-and-created-me/603-4b94f10b-3986-4ab6-9dd9-b762569ad7a5.

107 **"This isn't the first time":** Alejandra Gularte, "Kim Kardashian West and Pete Davidson Smooch as Jasmine and Aladdin on *SNL,*" *Vulture,* October 10, 2021, https://www.vulture.com/2021/10/watch-kim-kardashian-west-and-pete-davidson-kiss-on-snl.html.

108 **"appeared to be":** Desiree Murphy, "Kanye West Spotted on a Date with Actress Julia Fox in Miami," *Page Six,* January 2, 2022, https://pagesix.com/2022/01/02/kanye-west-spotted-on-a-date-with-actress-julia-fox-in-miami/.

108 **"After dinner Ye had a surprise":** Julia Fox, "Date Night," *Interview,* January 6, 2022, https://www.interviewmagazine.com/culture/date-night.

108 **Fox published her bestselling memoir:** Julia Fox, *Down the Drain* (Simon & Schuster, 2023).

Chapter 7: Fame Means Always Having to Say You're Sorry

111 **"There's no such thing":** Elizabeth Kolbert, "What P. T. Barnum Understood About America," *The New Yorker,* July 29, 2019, https://www.newyorker.com/magazine/2019/08/05/what-p-t-barnum-understood-about-america.

111 **"In showbiz":** Chris Gardner, "RuPaul Joins Drag Queens' Fight Against Facebook," *The Hollywood Reporter,* September 24, 2014, https://www.hollywoodreporter.com/news/general-news/rupaul-joins-drag-queens-fight-735369/.

113 **"The Pennsylvania Railroad Company":** "STATEMENT FROM THE ROAD. It Declares the Rails on the Bridge Must Have Fitted Exactly," *The*

New York Times, October 30, 1906, https://www.nytimes.com/1906/10/30/archives/statement-from-the-road-it-declares-the-rails-on-the-bridge-must.html.

113 **"openness and honesty":** "The First Press Release," NewsMuseum, https://www.newsmuseum.pt/en/spin-wall/first-press-release.

113 **"This is not a secret press bureau":** K. Miller Russell and C. Bishop, "Understanding Ivy Lee's Declaration of Principles: W.S. Newspaper and Magazine Coverage of Publicity and Press Agentry, 1865–1904," *Public Relations Review* 35, no. 2 (2009): 91–101.

114 **"Let me start":** Public Apology Central, "Hugh Grant Apologizes for Sleeping with Prostitute," YouTube, August 11, 2017, https://www.youtube.com/watch?v=LtItMwwoiVY.

115 **"All the fault":** "Lance Armstrong & Oprah Winfrey: Interview Transcript," BBC, January 18, 2013, https://www.bbc.com/sport/cycling/21065539.

116 **"Is it okay to call":** Natalie Michie, "Chrissy Teigen Apologizes Amid Bullying Controversy: 'I Was a Troll, Full Stop,'" *Fashion,* June 15, 2021, https://fashionmagazine.com/flare/celebrity/chrissy-teigen-old-tweets-apology/.

116 **"I'm going to keep working":** Chrissy Teigen, "Hi Again. Hi All . . . ," *Medium,* June 14, 2021, https://chrissyteigen.medium.com/hi-again-3bb3faffa76d.

116 **"I hate Americans":** *TMZ,* "Ariana Grande: 'I Hate Americans. I Hate America,'" YouTube, July 8, 2015, https://www.youtube.com/watch?v=cb3i1dejBsI.

116 **"Not here to make any excuses":** Wilfred Chan, "Ariana Grande Apologizes and Explains Doughnut Licking," CNN, July 10, 2015, https://edition.cnn.com/2015/07/09/entertainment/ariana-grande-donut-licking-america.

117 **"I truly apologize":** Jazz Monroe, "Ja Rule Apologizes for Fyre Festival Disaster, Says It Was 'NOT A SCAM,'" *Pitchfork,* April 28, 2017, https://pitchfork.com/news/73166-ja-rule-apologizes-for-fyre-festival-disaster-says-it-was-not-a-scam/.

117 **"I would like to publicly apologize":** Jake Coyle, "Will Smith Apologizes to Chris Rock, Says He Was 'Out of Line,'" *PBS NewsHour,* March 29, 2022, https://www.pbs.org/newshour/arts/will-smith-apologizes-to-chris-rock-says-he-was-out-of-line.

117 **"I've seen the messages":** Madeleine Aggeler, "Sure, Justin," *The Cut,* February 12, 2021, https://www.thecut.com/2021/02/justin-timberlake-apologizes-to-britney-spears-janet-jackson.html.

117 **"every bad decision":** Mark Savage, "Justin Bieber Opens Up About Fame, Drug Use and Depression," BBC News, September 3, 2019, https://www.bbc.com/news/entertainment-arts-49562637.

118 **"I was attempting to explain":** Jen Juneau, "Tati Westbrook Is Striving to Put Feud with James Charles 'To a Rest' After 'Toxicity and Chaos,'" *People,* March 20, 2019, https://people.com/style/tati-westbrook-james-charles-feud-ceasefire-twitter/.

118 **"While attempting to provide":** Emily Yahr, "As Armie Hammer Becomes More Famous, Can He Still Get Away with Saying Whatever He Wants?," *The Washington Post,* December 27, 2018, https://www.washingtonpost.com/entertainment/as-armie-hammer-becomes-more-famous-can-he-still-get

-away-with-saying-whatever-he-wants/2018/12/24/cc6ebd56-fff3-11e8-83c0-b06139e540e5_story.html.

118 **"I'm often reminded":** Caitlin Doughty and Logan Paul, "YouTube Star Logan Paul Apologizes for Video of Apparent Suicide Victim Amid Severe Backlash," ABC News, January 2, 2018, https://abcnews.go.com/Entertainment/youtube-star-logan-paul-apologizes-video-apparent-suicide/story?id=52095528.

118 **"His Holiness often teases people":** Cherylann Mollan, "Dalai Lama Defended over Tongue-Sucking Remark," BBC News, April 13, 2023, https://www.bbc.com/news/world-asia-india-65272213.

118 **"Well now since you lil nosey fucks":** Laura Snapes, "Cardi B and Offset Announce Birth of Baby Girl," *The Guardian,* July 11, 2018, https://www.theguardian.com/music/2018/jul/11/cardi-b-and-offset-announce-birth-of-baby-girl.

119 **Joey Graziadei mixes up:** Samantha Whidden, "'The Bachelor's' Joey Graziadei Apologizes for Gypsy Rose Blanchard, Ruth Bader Ginsburg Mix-Up," *Suggest,* February 20, 2024, https://www.suggest.com/the-bachelor-joey-graziadei-apologizes-for-gypsy-rose-blanchard-ruth-bader-ginsburg-mix-up/2793991/.

119 **Tyler Posey pretends:** Bruna Nessif and McKenna Aiello, "*Teen Wolf*'s Tyler Posey Apologizes for Offending LGBT Community Amidst Fake Coming Out," *E News,* July 30, 2016, https://www.eonline.com/news/783905/teen-wolf-s-tyler-posey-apologizes-for-offending-lgbt-community-amidst-fake-coming-out.

119 **Angela Simmons carries a handgun:** Randi Richardson, "Angela Simmons Apologizes for Bringing Gun-Shaped Purse to BET Awards," *Today,* July 2, 2024, https://www.today.com/popculture/awards/angela-simmons-bet-awards-apology-purse-rcna159920.

119 **Pierce Brosnan walks in:** Carson Blackwelder, "Pierce Brosnan Apologizes for Walking in 'Thermal Area' at Yellowstone National Park," ABC News, March 15, 2024, https://abcnews.com/GMA/Culture/pierce-brosnan-apologizes-walking-thermal-area-yellowstone-national-park/story?id=108152493.

119 **Lorde apologizes for posting:** Abid Rahman, "Lorde Apologizes for Bathtub Post with Whitney Houston Lyric on Instagram," *The Hollywood Reporter,* April 5, 2018, https://www.hollywoodreporter.com/news/general-news/lorde-apologizes-bathtub-instagram-whitney-houston-lyrics-1100298/.

120 **"bleakosity":** Mariah Carey (@MariahCarey), "@lindseyweber define 'bleakosity'?," Twitter (now X), March 5, 2009, https://x.com/MariahCarey/status/1286940557.

120 **"These videos appear off the cuff":** Ronda Kaysen, "The Celebrity Apology Video Aesthetic," *The New York Times,* September 22, 2023, https://www.nytimes.com/2023/09/22/realestate/celebrity-apology-videos-drew-barrymore.html.

121 **"sprawling French Neoclassical mansion":** Mayer Rus, "Step Inside Ashton Kutcher and Mila Kunis's Sustainable L.A. Farmhouse," *Architectural Digest,* August 3, 2021, https://www.architecturaldigest.com/story/step-inside-ashton-kutcher-and-mila-kuniss-sustainable-la-farmhouse.

121 **"I know there is just nothing":** Alex Abad-Santos, "Drew Barrymore Tried to Live, Laugh, Scab Her Way Across the Picket Line. It Didn't Work," *Vox*, September 19, 2023, https://www.vox.com/culture/2023/9/19/23880858/drew-barrymore-show-writers-strike-backlash-apology.

121 **"surprisingly normal":** Stephanie Soteriou, "Two Months After Drew Barrymore's Living Room and Tiny TV Went Viral, She Has Shown Off Even More of Her Surprisingly Normal Home," *BuzzFeed*, March 19, 2024, https://www.buzzfeednews.com/article/stephaniesoteriou/drew-barrymore-surprisingly-normal-home-kitchen-bathroom.

121 **"Why is drew barrymore's tv so small":** Bec Shaw (@Brocklesnitch), "Why is drew barrymore's tv so small and bad," X, January 10, 2024, https://x.com/Brocklesnitch/status/1745191933151170607.

121 **"exclusive video for JustJared.com":** David Niederhoffer, "Jason Momoa Apologizes to Fans Offended by His Sistine Chapel Visit (Exclusive Video)," Just Jared, May 14, 2022, https://www.justjared.com/2022/05/14/jason-momoa-apologizes-to-fans-offended-by-his-sistine-chapel-visit-exclusive-video/.

121 **"The only comment left":** Niederhoffer, "Jason Momoa Apologizes."

123 **"James Kennedy Apologizes":** Miranda Siwak, "James Kennedy Apologizes for Posting Photo with the Tate Brothers: I 'Condemn Their Beliefs,'" *Us Weekly*, March 9, 2025, https://www.usmagazine.com/celebrity-news/news/james-kennedy-apologizes-for-posting-pic-with-andrew-and-tristan-tate/.

123 **"Pitch Perfect's Ester Dean Apologizes":** Johnni Macke, "Pitch Perfect's Ester Dean Apologizes for Writing Beyonce Diss on Keri Hilson Remix: 'It Was Childish,'" *Us Weekly*, April 9, 2025, https://www.usmagazine.com/entertainment/news/ester-dean-apologizes-for-writing-beyonce-diss-on-keri-hilson-remix/.

123 **"Benson Boone apologizes":** Emlyn Travis, "Benson Boone Apologizes for 'Aggressively' Grabbing Crotch After Grammys Performance," *Entertainment Weekly*, February 3, 2025, https://ew.com/benson-boone-apologizes-grabbing-crotch-after-2025-grammys-performance-8784751.

123 **"become the father of a new baby":** Eileen Reslen, "Dave Grohl's Relationship with 'Alt Porn Goddess' Revealed After He Welcomes Baby Outside of Marriage," *Page Six*, September 13, 2024, https://pagesix.com/2024/09/13/celebrity-news/dave-grohls-relationship-with-alt-porn-goddess-revealed-after-he-welcomes-baby-outside-of-marriage/.

Chapter 8: From Selling Out to Selling Crap

126 **"*concrete jungle where dreams are made*":** "Empire State of Mind" by Jay-Z and Alicia Keys, written by Shawn Carter, Alexander Shuckburgh, Janet Sewell-Ulepic, Angela Hunte, Alicia Keys, Sylvia Robinson, and Bert Keyes, produced by Al Shux, Janet Sewell-Ulepic, and Angela Hunte, Roc Nation / Roc-A-Fella Records, 2009.

126 **And this grand achievement:** "The Corruption of the Press," op-ed, *The New York Times*, December 5, 1870, via TimesMachine, https://timesmachine.nytimes.com/timesmachine/1870/12/05/93250569.html.

127 **In a piece for *The Guardian*:** Alexis Petridis, "The Who Sell Out: Still a Searing Satire on Pop's Commercial Breakdown," *The Guardian,* April 26, 2021, https://www.theguardian.com/music/2021/apr/26/the-who-sell-out-reissue.

127 **"groups not afraid":** Petridis, "The Who Sell Out."

127 **"The Who may run into legal problems":** "B.O., Baked Beans, Buns and The Who," *Rolling Stone,* December 14, 1967, https://www.rollingstone.com/music/music-news/b-o-baked-beans-buns-and-the-who-188382/.

127 **"We have a song about a girl":** "B.O., Baked Beans, Buns and The Who."

128 **"Jewel, what the hell":** Tom Key, "Jewel—Intuition/ Leave the Lights On—Carson Daly (7/2/2003) 4K HD," YouTube, December 14, 2024, https://www.youtube.com/watch?v=zD6uBNeNkY0.

129 **"This seems so blatantly contradictory":** Rob Walker, "Shilling for Schick," *Slate,* July 7, 2003, https://slate.com/business/2003/07/jewel-shills-for-schick.html.

129 **"Selling out is compromising":** Kirk Baird, "'Warning'—Don't Call Green Day a Sellout," *Las Vegas Sun,* July 20, 2001, https://lasvegassun.com/news/2001/jul/20/warning----dont-call-green-day-a-sellout/.

129 **"OUT OF STOCK":** Keurig, "Keurig® x Green Day 'American Idiot' Anniversary Edition Brewer Bundle, https://www.keurig.com/Keurig%C2%AE-x-Green-Day-%27American-Idiot%27-Anniversary-Edition-Brewer-Bundle/p/Keurig-Green-Day-American-Idiot-Anniversary-Edition-Brewer-Bundle#Black_color.

130 **"For relaxing times":** Sophia Coppola, dir., *Lost in Translation,* Focus Features, 2003.

131 **"When you hear Nespresso":** Nespresso, "Reviving Origins by Nespresso—It's About the People 30" | USA," August 26, 2019, YouTube, https://www.youtube.com/watch?v=rVpMeJ6nVr0.

131 **"High-priced, superstar actors":** Associated Press, "Catch the Hidden Stars: Actors Endorse Products in Voice Only," *Deseret News,* March 25, 1994, https://www.deseret.com/1994/3/25/19099038/catch-the-hidden-stars-actors-endorse-products-in-voice-only-br/.

134 **"I don't think so":** Amanda Fortini, "Break the Internet: Kim Kardashian," *Paper,* November 12, 2014, https://www.papermag.com/break-the-internet-kim-kardashian-cover.

135 **One of her most notorious:** Molly Mulshine, "The FDA Just Made Kim Kardashian Delete One of Her Selfies on Instagram," *Business Insider,* August 11, 2015, https://www.businessinsider.com/kim-kardashian-morning-sickness-drug-post-deleted-2015-8.

136 **The press release declared:** Frito-Lay North America, "Lay's Partners with Bebe Rexha to Create Perfect Harmonies with First-Ever Music-Inspired Chip Flavors That Unlock New Custom Songs," press release, February 28, 2019, https://www.prnewswire.com/news-releases/lays-partners-with-bebe-rexha-to-create-perfect-harmonies-with-first-ever-music-inspired-chip-flavors-that-unlock-new-custom-songs-300803797.html.

136 **"Flavor and music can trigger":** Lay's, "Lay's Turn Up the Flavor with Bebe Rexha," February 27, 2019, YouTube, https://www.youtube.com/watch?v=DdHmLCDFbcQ.

137 **Vanessa Hudgens:** Vanessa Hudgens (@vanessahudgens), "#ad Tomorrow is @MyLittlePony Friendship Day!," Instagram, July 29, 2016, https://www.instagram.com/p/BIdKwYYhEIL/.

137 **Danielle Brooks:** Danielle Brooks (@daniebb3), "So elated to finally share this news with you all," Instagram, July 2, 2019, https://web.archive.org/web/20191008071249/https://www.instagram.com/p/Bza5rF0jkhx/.

137 **Antoni Porowski:** Antoni Porowski (@antoni), "Happy #NationalGuacamoleDay!," Instagram, September 16, 2018, https://www.instagram.com/p/Bny3eO5FbvB/.

137 **Paula Abdul:** Paula Abdul (@paulaabdul), "#ad I'm ecstatic to announce my newest partnership with @psychics1on1," X, February 24, 2023, https://x.com/PaulaAbdul/status/1629221500598505472.

137 **Kristen Chenoweth:** Kristen Chenoweth with Town House Crackers, "#ad Making my #DipForDinner dreams a reality tonight with NEW Town House Crackers Dippers," Facebook, June 24, 2020, https://www.facebook.com/kristinchenoweth/videos/kristin-chenoweth-town-house-crackers-making-dip-for-dinner-dreams-a-reality/2861145404010892/.

139 **"And now we're Instagram FRIENDS":** Jennifer Aniston (@jenniferaniston), "And now we're Instagram FRIENDS too. HI INSTAGRAM 👋," Instagram, October 15, 2019, https://www.instagram.com/p/B3o8vWDhlOh/.

140 **"play an active role":** Sarah Hearon, "Ryan Reynolds Is the New Owner of Aviation American Gin," *Us Weekly*, February 21, 2018, https://www.usmagazine.com/celebrity-news/news/ryan-reynolds-is-the-new-owner-of-aviation-american-gin/.

140 **"Started from the bottom":** Will Oremus, "BlackBerry Spokeswoman Alicia Keys Blames iPhone Tweet on Drake-Obsessed Hacker," *Slate,* February 12, 2013, https://slate.com/technology/2013/02/alicia-keys-hacked-blackberry-creative-director-blames-hacker-for-iphone-tweet.html.

140 **"pretty broad":** Chuck Salter, "What Justin Timberlake Does at Myspace, Beyond a SXSW Secret Show," *Fast Company,* March 22, 2013, https://www.fastcompany.com/3007378/what-justin-timberlake-does-myspace-beyond-sxsw-secret-show.

141 **"I feel like there's no reason":** J. Clara Chan, "Ryan Reynolds' Viral Ad Agency Gears Up to Make 'Super Bowl-Level' Ads Year-Round," *The Hollywood Reporter*, February 21, 2022, https://www.hollywoodreporter.com/business/digital/ryan-reynolds-super-bowl-ads-mntn-maximum-effort-1235096328/.

Chapter 9: The Plight of the Nepo Baby

143 **"Daniel Day-Lewis will no longer":** Brent Lang, "Shocker! Daniel Day-Lewis Quits Acting (EXCLUSIVE)," *Variety,* June 20, 2017, https://variety.com/2017/film/news/daniel-day-lewis-quits-acting-oscar-winner-1202472766/.

143 **"Daniel Day-Lewis Comes Out of Retirement":** Andrew McGowan, "'Anemone' Trailer: Daniel Day-Lewis Comes Out of Retirement After 8 Years in Family Drama Directed by His Son," *Variety,* August 21, 2025,

https://variety.com/2025/film/news/daniel-day-lewis-ends-retirement-anemone-trailer-1236494359/.

145 **Jane Fonda gets her first-ever mention:** Army Archerd, "Just for *Variety,*" *Variety,* January 9, 1958, https://read-archive.variety.com/html5/reader/production/default.aspx?pubname=&edid=f237f318-016d-462c-9f7f-ddceb07bc8f4&pnum=2&search=%22jane+fonda%22.

145 **two brand-new one-act plays:** Brooks Atkinson, " 'GARDEN DISTRICT'; Short Plays by Tennessee Williams Put On in an Off-Broadway House," *The New York Times,* January 19, 1958, https://www.nytimes.com/1958/01/19/archives/garden-district-short-plays-by-tennessee-williams-put-on-in-an.html.

145 **Eugenia, the stepdaughter of Mervyn LeRoy:** Peter B. Flint, "Mervyn LeRoy, 86, Dies; Director and Producer," *The New York Times,* September 14, 1987, https://web.archive.org/web/20230412044018/https://www.nytimes.com/1987/09/14/obituaries/mervyn-leroy-86-dies-director-and-producer.html.

148 **"She Has Her Mother's Eyes":** Nate Jones, "She Has Her Mother's Eyes. And Agent. Extremely Overanalyzing Hollywood's Nepo-Baby Boom," *New York,* December 19, 2022, https://nymag.com/magazine/toc/2022-12-19.html.

148 **"Wait I just found out":** girl idk . . . (@MeriemIsTired), "Wait I just found out that the actress that plays Lexie is a nepotism baby omg," Twitter (now X), February 20, 2022, https://x.com/meriemistired/status/1495548990926041094.

149 **"Actually, no":** Nick M, "Ellen vs Dakota Johnson," YouTube, August 1, 2020, https://www.youtube.com/watch?v=jnL96RajmzY.

149 **"secret" nepo baby:** Miranda Knox, "Meet the New Wave of Secret 'Nepo Babies'—Do You Know Their VERY Famous Parents Who They've Distanced Themselves From?," *The Sun,* July 7, 2024, https://www.thesun.co.uk/fabulous/28923867/secret-nepo-babies-famous-parents-nico-parker-margaret-qualley/.

149 ***Cosmopolitan* published a piece:** Janaya Wecker, "I Present: All the Celebs You Didn't Know Were Nepo Babies," *Cosmopolitan,* February 16, 2023, https://www.cosmopolitan.com/entertainment/celebs/g42757376/nepo-babies-in-hollywood-list/.

149 ***People* first published their running list:** Alex Apatoff, "See Hollywood's 'Nepotism Babies' Side-by-Side with Their A-List Parents in Their Breakout Roles," *People,* August 1, 2022, https://web.archive.org/web/20220803041339/https://people.com/celebrity/nepotism-babies/.

150 ***Business Insider* publishing a list of nepo babies:** Jyoti Mann, "Meet 12 'Nepo Babies' of Big Business Whose Family Connections Helped Them Get to the Top," *Business Insider,* https://www.businessinsider.com/nepo-babies-big-business-family-connections-helped-reach-top-2023-1.

150 ***The Takeout* publishing a list:** Marnie Shure, "The Nepo Babies of the Food World," *The Takeout,* December 21, 2022, https://www.thetakeout.com/the-nepo-babies-of-the-food-world-1849914783/.

150 **"53 Celebrities You Forgot Were Nepo Babies":** Kristyn Burtt and Delilah

Gray, "53 Celebrities You Forgot Were 'Nepo Babies' from Famous Families," Yahoo!, September 2, 2024, https://www.yahoo.com/entertainment/celebrities-forgot-famous-families-174100722.html.

150 **"undeniably fortunate":** Carly Thomas, "Lewis Pullman Is Blazing His Own Trail," *The Hollywood Reporter,* May 2, 2025, https://www.hollywoodreporter.com/movies/movie-features/lewis-pullman-marvel-thunderbolts-career-nepotism-interview-1236204517/.

151 **"I think it's incredibly important":** Kim Renfro, "Nico Parker Says 'The Last of Us' Creator Messaged Her Father Before She Was Cast and That Famous Parents Make It 'Way Easier to Get in the Room,'" *Business Insider,* February 2, 2023, https://www.businessinsider.com/nico-parker-says-famous-parents-make-it-easier-to-get-in-the-room-2023-2.

151 **"It's completely normal":** Gabriella Paiella, "Zoë Kravitz on Playing Catwoman and Falling in Love with Channing Tatum," *GQ,* November 15, 2022, https://www.gq.com/story/zoe-kravitz-men-of-the-year-cover-2022.

152 **"Other than my genes":** Ethan Shanfeld, "Sam Nivola Breaks Out: 'The White Lotus' Favorite on Getting 'Lost' in Character, Why Hollywood Must 'Create New Stars' and Getting 'Cut Out' of 'Maestro,'" *Variety,* August 7, 2025, https://variety.com/2025/tv/features/sam-nivola-white-lotus-incest-hollywood-fears-maestro-1236478577/.

152 **"I never really turned to my dad":** Lindsey Kupfer, "Why Dan Levy Never Asked Dad Eugene for Acting Help," *Page Six,* March 21, 2018, https://pagesix.com/2018/03/21/why-dan-levy-never-asked-dad-eugene-for-acting-help/.

152 **"People can argue nepotism":** Nicholas Rice, "Steven Spielberg's Daughter Destry Responds to Claims of Nepotism After Ben Stiller Sparks Debate," July 30, 2021, https://people.com/movies/steven-spielbergs-daughter-destry-on-claims-of-nepotism/.

152 **EJ Dickson asked how it felt:** EJ Dickson, "Don't Ask Ben Platt This One Question," *Rolling Stone,* July 14, 2023, https://www.rollingstone.com/tv-movies/tv-movie-features/ben-platt-theater-camp-nepo-baby-new-york-magazine-molly-gordon-1234786447/.

153 **"Of course, I acknowledge":** Samuel Maude, "Ben Platt Shares How the Cast of *Parade* Came Together After a Traumatizing Moment," *Elle,* May 28, 2024, https://www.elle.com/culture/theater/a60924282/ben-platt-interview-palace-residency/.

153 **"As the child of somebody":** Hailey Rhode Bieber, "Smoothie Queens Gwyneth Paltrow & Hailey Chat Skincare & Play Game of Smells | WHO'S IN MY BATHROOM?," YouTube, July 27, 2022, https://www.youtube.com/watch?v=Y6Snp_DXeHU.

155 **"I can definitely say":** Véronique Hyland, "Lily-Rose Depp Is an Idol Rising," *Elle,* November 16, 2022, https://www.elle.com/culture/celebrities/a41894075/0125-0141-an-idol-rising-december-2022/.

156 **"Yes, I get the whole":** YeEun Kim, "Model Vittora Ceretti Responds to Lily-Rose Depp's Thoughts on Being Called a 'Nepo Baby,'" *Hypebae,* November 17, 2022, https://hypebae.com/2022/11/lily-rose-depp-nepo-baby-interview-vittoria-ceretti-model-response.

156 **Depp did buy:** Meredith Galante, "HOUSE OF THE DAY: Johnny Depp Just

Bought a $4.4 Million Hollywood Home for His Ex," *Business Insider,* September 12, 2012, https://www.businessinsider.com/johnny-depp-buys-44-million-home-for-ex-2012-9.

156 **"I will speak":** Janelle Sessoms, "12 Stars Chiming in on the Nepo Baby Discourse—Nepo Baby Responses to Nepotism," *L'Officiel,* March 28, 2023, https://www.lofficielibiza.com/culture/nepo-baby-celebrity-response-nepotism.

157 **She attended preschool:** Liana Satenstein, "There's Something About Gigi! The Model Talks Guess Kids, Sweatsuits, and Candice Swanepoel," *Vogue,* December 16, 2014, https://www.vogue.com/article/gigi-hadid-model-guess-baby.

157 **"Technically I'm a nepotism baby":** Ellie Austin, "Gigi Hadid: 'I Don't Think I'm the Prettiest Person in the World," *The Times,* March 5, 2023, https://www.thetimes.com/life-style/article/gigi-hadid-i-dont-think-im-the-prettiest-person-in-the-world-38tkdgt27.

158 **"There's not a day":** Kimberly Nordyke, "Jamie Lee Curtis Says 'Nepo Baby' Debate Is 'Designed to Try to Diminish and Denigrate and Hurt,'" *The Hollywood Reporter,* December 23, 2022, https://www.hollywoodreporter.com/movies/movie-news/jamie-lee-curtis-nepo-baby-debate-advantages-1235287111/.

158 **"[My parents] found their way":** David Canfield, "Jamie Lee Curtis Is 'Both Weepy and Giddy' About Her First Oscar Nomination," *Vanity Fair,* February 7, 2023, https://www.vanityfair.com/hollywood/2023/02/jamie-lee-curtis-little-gold-men-oscar-nominee-awards-insider.

158 **"I know you look at me":** Jen Juneau, "Jamie Lee Curtis Praises Her Late Parents, Declares 'I'm 64' and Gets Standing Ovation at SAG Awards 2023," *People,* February 26, 2023, https://people.com/movies/sag-awards-2023-jamie-lee-curtis-wins-supporting-actress/.

158 **"And my mother and father":** Scarlett O'Toole, "Jamie Lee Curtis Sobs as She Wins First Oscar and Pays Tribute to Parents," *The Mirror,* March 13, 2023, https://www.mirror.co.uk/3am/us-celebrity-news/breaking-jamie-lee-curtis-sobs-29439046.

Chapter 10: Fandom Isn't Enough, It's Time to Stan

161 **"*You a fan, a phony*":** "Ether" by Nas, written by Nasir Jones and Rondell Turner, produced by Ron Browz, Ill Will Records / Columbia Records, 2001.

161 **"*Hey, man*":** "The Night I Fell in Love" by Pet Shop Boys, written by Neil Tennant and Chris Lowe, produced by Pet Shop Boys, Parlophone/EMI, 2002.

162 **"an extremely or excessively":** *Merriam-Webster Dictionary,* "stan," https://www.merriam-webster.com/dictionary/stan.

162 **"The culture industries":** Henry Jenkins, *Convergence Culture: Where Old and New Media Collide* (New York University Press, 2006), 136.

162 **"A man with one machine":** Marshall Sella, "The Remote Controllers," *New York Times Magazine,* October 20, 2002, https://www.nytimes.com/2002/10/20/magazine/the-remote-controllers.html.

162 **"Could it be that stan culture":** Nicole Karlis, "How the Loneliness Crisis Is Fueling 'Stan Culture,'" *Salon,* February 19, 2024, https://www.salon.com/2024/02/19/how-the-loneliness-is-fueling-stan-culture/.

163 **The first recorded use of "stan":** *Oxford English Dictionary,* "stan," https://www.oed.com/dictionary/stan_v.

163 **"I stan for Santogold":** Sarah Berman, "We Asked 'Stan' Actor Devon Sawa Who He Stans," *Vice,* December 12, 2018, https://www.vice.com/en/article/we-asked-stan-actor-devon-sawa-who-he-stans/.

163 **"And what tremendous rejoicing":** Heinrich Heine, "Lisztomania," *Lapham's Quarterly* (1844), https://www.laphamsquarterly.org/celebrity/lisztomania.

163 **"They stamp unceasingly":** Dorian Lynskey, "Beatlemania: 'The Screamers' and Other Tales of Fandom," *The Guardian,* September 28, 2013, https://www.theguardian.com/music/2013/sep/29/beatlemania-screamers-fandom-teenagers-hysteria.

163 **"A physician whose specialty":** Heine, "Lisztomania."

165 **"My cousin in Trinidad":** Nicki Minaj (@NICKIMINAJ), "My cousin in Trinidad won't get the vaccine cuz his friend got it & became impotent," Twitter (now X), September 13, 2021, https://x.com/NICKIMINAJ/status/1437532566945341441.

165 **"BITCH YOUR DAYS":** Brad Callas, "Nicki Minaj Calls Out Reporters for Allegedly Harassing Her Family Amid Vaccine Comments Criticism," *Complex*, September 17, 2021, https://www.complex.com/music/a/brad-callas/nicki-minaj-calls-out-reporter-for-allegedly-harassing-her-family-amid-vaccine-comments-criticism.

165 **"Dear Barbz":** Nardine Saad, "Nicki Minaj Tells Long-Combative Barbz 'to Never Threaten Anyone on My Behalf,'" *Los Angeles Times*, November 7, 2023, https://www.latimes.com/entertainment-arts/music/story/2023-11-07/nicki-minaj-tells-long-combative-barbz-to-never-threaten-anyone-on-my-behalf.

165 **"Becky with the good hair":** "Sorry" by Beyoncé, written by Beyoncé, Diana Gordon, and Sean Rhoden, produced by Beyoncé, MeLo-X, and Diana Gordon, Parkwood Entertainment / Columbia Records, 2016.

166 **"I'm sorry there's a Judas":** kelly (@kellwhyyy), "I'm sorry there's a Judas x Jesus fancam set to My Tears Ricochet??," X, March 30, 2024, https://x.com/kellwhyyy/status/1774275776000508358.

166 **"It was easier to get noticed":** @rint4991, "Popheads that have stan Twitter accounts, why did you decide to make your account?," r/popheads, Reddit, 2020, https://www.reddit.com/r/popheads/comments/ea9i1p/popheads_that_have_stan_twitter_accounts_why_did/.

167 **"a very large fan base":** Ikran Dahir, "All Rise, the TikTok Courtroom of Amber Heard and Johnny Depp Is Now in Session," *BuzzFeed,* April 28, 2022, https://www.buzzfeednews.com/article/ikrd/milani-cosmetics-tiktok-about-johnny-depp-and-amber-heard.

167 **"The reviling of Ms. Heard":** Jessica Bennett, "Why We Love to Watch a Woman Brought Low," *The New York Times,* May 20, 2022, https://www.nytimes.com/2022/05/20/opinion/johnny-depp-amber-heard-social-media-sexism.html.

168 **"Looks like our guy":** Ewan McGregor Daily (@EwanDaily), "Looks like our

guy was hanging out at some boat show in Southampton," Instagram, September 24, 2025, https://www.instagram.com/p/DO-3xb0kbDf/.

168 **"Updates & media content":** best of hailey bieber (@ArchivesHailey), X, https://x.com/archiveshailey.

168 **"Bebe Rexha is performing":** Nolan Feeney, "Slay, Flop, Iconic: What It's Like to Be a Pop Music Stan," *Entertainment Weekly,* November 1, 2017, https://ew.com/music/2017/11/01/stans-pop-music-kesha-beyonce-beyhive-lady-gaga-monsters.

168 **"i love it this way":** RAYE (@Raye), "i go on to twitter to check Raye updates to see how where is my husband is doing," X, September 27, 2025, https://x.com/raye/status/1972035286302707897.

168 **"madelaine petsch is so stunning":** best of madelaine petsch (@madelainefiles), "madelaine petsch is so stunning," X, September 28, 2025, https://x.com/madelainefiles/status/1972280400807641388.

168 **"This man right here":** best of paul mescal (@paulmescalfiles), X, September 22, 2025, https://x.com/paulmescalfiles/status/1970195372502094161.

169 **"Happy 20th anniversary":** Anne Hathalegend (@AnneHathabae), "Some things never change," Twitter (now X), July 31, 2021, https://x.com/AnneHathabae/status/1421511196352598018.

169 **"Happy Pride month":** Ryan Gosling Source (@GoslingSource), "Happy Pride Month #RyanGosling #RusselCrowe," Twitter (now X), June 6, 2022, https://x.com/GoslingSource/status/1533870741287993344.

169 **"First Monday of may":** Dianna Agron Updates (@Agron_Updates), X, May 6, 2024, https://x.com/agron_updates.

169 **"During these eight years":** Evan Ross Katz, "Dianna Agron Updates: Musings from a Retired Fan Account," *Shut Up Evan: The Newsletter,* Substack, January 7, 2025, https://evanrosskatz.substack.com/p/dianna-agron-updates-musings-from.

169 **"It's a nice environment":** Interview with the authors.

170 **"Sike. We condemn the actions":** Ansel Elgort Updates (@ElgortUpdate), "Sike. We condemn the actions that pig has made towards every single victim," Twitter (now X), June 19, 2020, https://x.com/ElgortUpdate/status/1274160408249733120.

170 **"why we decided to unstan":** Kendall Updates (@knjdaily), "why we decided to unstan: a thread," Twitter (now X), July 1, 2017, https://x.com/knjdaily/status/881218912523874305.

170 **"[Kendall] has young fans":** Ann-Derrick Gaillot, "Stan Down: When Super Fans Move On," *The Outline,* July 24, 2017, https://theoutline.com/post/1955/kendall-jenner-stans-unstan-problematic-faves.

170 **"I will always respect her":** Shaad D'Souza, "This Sky Ferreira Stan Account Is Losing Hope," *Paper,* July 7, 2020, https://www.papermag.com/sky-ferreira-updates-stan-stories-masochism.

171 **"This account was initially to help":** Katz, "Dianna Agron Updates."

171 **"SORRY I HAVEN'T BEEN POSTING":** reactions (@reactjpg), "bts army stan account instagram post sorry," Twitter (now X), March 24, 2021, https://x.com/reactjpg/status/1374942762655653893.

171 **"I don't believe in blind stanning":** Joseph Longo, "Stan Accounts Are

Holding Their Celebrity Faves Accountable," *MEL,* June 30, 2020, https://melmagazine.com/en-us/story/ana-de-armas-updates-accountable-stan-twitter.

171 **at the peak of the pandemic:** Ana de Armas Updates (@ArmasUpdates), "Ana de Armas & Ben Affleck get early morning coffee and walk their dogs together," Twitter (now X), April 10, 2020, https://x.com/ArmasUpdates/status/1248648432924983297.

171 **tweeted in the spring:** Ana de Armas Updates (@ArmasUpdates), "Ana de Armas & Ben Affleck walk their dogs outside instead of praying for the pandemic to go away on Easter Sunday," Twitter (now X), April 12, 2020, https://x.com/ArmasUpdates/status/1249456348250718216.

171 **"BREAKING":** Ana de Armas Updates (@ArmasUpdates), "BREAKING: Golden Globe nominee and movie star Ana de Armas has recently blocked us!," X (now Twitter), April 14, 2020, https://x.com/ArmasUpdates/status/1250246558169403393.

172 **"It's definitely a persona":** Joan Summers, "A Chat with @ArmasUpdates, the Ana de Armas Stan Account That Deserves to Be Unblocked," *Jezebel,* May 19, 2020, https://www.jezebel.com/a-chat-with-armasupdates-the-ana-de-armas-stan-accoun-1843527798.

172 **"THIS IS HER LOOKING AT ME":** Alejandra Gularte, "Ana de Armas Updates Met Ana de Armas," *Vulture,* September 9, 2022, https://www.vulture.com/2022/09/ana-de-armas-updates-twitter-blonde-venice-film.html.

172 **"I feel like not posting it":** Sydney Sweeney Fans (@SweeneyDailyX), "Hi, I know some people might get upset with me," X, September 26, 2025, https://x.com/sweeneydailyx/status/1971612479412224289.

173 **"Meet the 30-Year-Old+ Super Fans":** Ella Kemp and Tabby Kibugi, "Club Chalamet: Meet the 30-Year-Old+ Super Fans of Timothée," *Refinery29,* January 18, 2019, https://www.refinery29.com/en-gb/timothee-chalamet-fan-pages.

173 **which began with the release:** Adrian Horton, "Timothée Chalamet's Unhinged *Marty Supreme* Promo Tour Is Fun—but What Really Sells a Film in 2025?," *The Guardian,* December 23, 2025, https://www.theguardian.com/film/2025/dec/23/supreme-publicity-timothee-chalamet.

174 **"If you're feeling distressed":** Angela Yang, "A Timothée Chalamet Fan Account Blasted Kylie Jenner. But Even Some Fellow Stans Think the Posts May Have Gone Too Far," NBC News, September 7, 2023, https://www.nbcnews.com/pop-culture/viral/timothee-chalamet-fan-account-kylie-jenner-backlash-rcna103731.

174 **"We've never even seen them":** CT Jones, "The Club Chalamet Blow-Up Proves There's Something Deeply Wrong with Stan Culture," *Rolling Stone,* September 8, 2023, https://www.rollingstone.com/culture/culture-commentary/timothee-chalamet-kylie-jenner-club-chalamet-stan-culture-controversy-1234820673/.

174 **"The most generous interpretations":** Jodi Walker and Julianna Ress, "The Biggest Oscars 2025 Story Lines, Told Only Through the Lens of Timothée Chalamet's Biggest Fan," *The Ringer,* February 28, 2025, https://www

.theringer.com/2025/02/28/oscars/oscars-story-lines-timothee-chalamet-fan-club-chalamet.

174 **"Timothée should attend events":** Claire Guinan, "Diving into Club Chalamet's Unhinged Manifesto on How Timmy Can Finally Win an Oscar," *Jezebel,* August 15, 2025, https://www.jezebel.com/diving-into-club-chalamets-unhinged-manifesto-on-how-timmy-can-finally-win-an-oscar.

Chapter 11: Stop Giving Celebrities Podcasts!!!

177 **"Steve Austin to real housewife Heather DuBrow":** Madeline Berg, "Streaming the Stars: The Rise of the Celebrity Podcast," *Forbes,* April 14, 2016, https://www.forbes.com/sites/maddieberg/2016/04/14/streaming-the-stars-the-rise-of-the-celebrity-podcast/.

178 **"not-great relationship advice":** iHeartMedia, "iHeartMedia Brings 'Anna Faris Is Unqualified' Podcast Series to Top 40 Broadcast Radio in a Groundbreaking Deal—Faris' Series Also Provides iHeartRadio Podcast Network with Exclusive Content Just for iHeartRadio Listeners," press release, June 26, 2018, https://www.iheartmedia.com/press/iheartmedia-brings-anna-faris-unqualified-podcast-series-top-40-broadcast-radio.

178 **"I'm in love with you Anna":** @dbjsoxsinanfnfdslsfdnf, Podbay, https://podbay.fm/p/anna-faris-is-unqualified/reviews.

179 **"I'm not a journalist":** Sam Wolfson, "Bill Gates, Dua Lipa, Meghan, Hillary: How Interview Podcasts Became a Must-Have for Celebrities," *The Guardian,* March 16, 2024, https://www.theguardian.com/tv-and-radio/2024/mar/16/longform-interview-podcasts-joe-rogan-marc-maron-keke-palmer.

179 **"What qualifies me":** Dax Shepard, *Armchair Expert with Dax Shepard,* "Introducing: Armchair Expert with Dax Shepard," February 6, 2018, https://armchairexpertpod.com/pods/introducing-armchair-expert.

179 **"Interviewees frequently take them up on this":** Eliza Brooke, "Dax Shepard Is Listening," *The New York Times,* December 30, 2019, https://www.nytimes.com/2019/12/30/style/dax-shepard-armchair-expert.html.

180 **"The podcast might be called *SmartLess*":** Sridhar Pappu, "With 'SmartLess,' Jason Bateman, Will Arnett and Sean Hayes Are Building a Media Empire," *The New York Times,* October 5, 2024, https://www.nytimes.com/2024/10/05/business/smartless-podcast.html.

181 **"Someone said":** Jason Lynch, "Conan O'Brien Is *Adweek*'s 2022 Media Visionary," *Adweek,* October 9, 2022, https://www.adweek.com/convergent-tv/adweek-media-visionary-conan-obrien-gets-sirius-about-his-audio-empire-and-a-tv-return/.

181 **"His weirdness translates well":** Nicholas Quah, "Conan O'Brien Is the Perfect Podcast Host," *Vulture,* January 10, 2019, https://www.vulture.com/2019/01/conan-obrien-needs-a-friend-comedy-podcast-review.html.

182 **"I'm Justin Long":** Justin Long, host, *Life Is Short with Justin Long,* podcast, Wondery.

182 **"joined by old friends":** Rachel Bilson and Olivia Allen, hosts, *Broad Ideas with Rachel Bilson & Olivia Allen,* podcast, Headgum.

185 **"I wanted two volumes":** Wesley Morris, "Barbra Streisand Is Ready to Tell

All. Pull Up a Seat," *The New York Times,* November 7, 2023, https://www.nytimes.com/2023/11/07/movies/barbra-streisand-memoir-book.html.

187 **"It's raw":** *Chrisley Confessions 2.0,* July 16, 2025, https://podcasts.apple.com/us/podcast/were-back-baby-the-debut-of-chrisley-confessions-2-0/id1430295246?i=1000717555677.

187 **"She's here to share":** *The Lohdown with Lindsay Lohan,* April 11, 2022, https://podcasts.apple.com/ca/podcast/the-lohdown-with-lindsay-lohan/id1618992662.

188 **"You've got to hand it":** Bobby Finger and Lindsey Weber, "The Safe Space of the Celebrity-on-Celebrity Podcast," *Slate,* November 12, 2018, https://slate.com/human-interest/2018/11/celebrity-podcast-gwyneth-paltrow-julia-roberts-goop.html.

189 **"difficult to work with":** Stephanie Wenger, "Dean Cain Addresses Rumors That Teri Hatcher Was Difficult to Work with on *Lois & Clark*: 'I Just Wanted to Finish and Go Home,'" *People,* May 7, 2025, https://people.com/dean-cain-addresses-rumors-that-teri-hatcher-was-difficult-to-work-with-on-lois-and-clark-11730153.

189 **"It was really outrageous":** Jen Juneau, "Sarah Paulson Reveals Actor Who Sent Her 6 Pages of Notes on Broadway Show: 'I Hope to See You Never,'" *People,* May 14, 2024, https://people.com/sarah-paulson-reveals-actor-who-sent-6-pages-of-notes-broadway-show-trish-hawkins-8648139.

189 **"Sarah Paulson Eviscerates Actress":** Jacob Bryant, "Sarah Paulson Eviscerates Actress Who Critiqued Her with 6 Pages of Notes: 'I Have Not Forgotten It and I Hope I See You Never,'" Yahoo Entertainment, May 13 2024, https://www.yahoo.com/entertainment/sarah-paulson-eviscerates-actress-critiqued-213904009.html.

189 **"Sarah Paulson Trounces Actor":** Marco Margaritoff, "Sarah Paulson Trounces Actor for 'Outrageous' 6-Page Email of Notes on Her Performance," Yahoo Entertainment, May 14 2024, https://www.yahoo.com/entertainment/sarah-paulson-trounces-actor-outrageous-174333320.html.

189 **"Sarah Paulson Shades Actor":** Sam Damshenas, "'I Hope to See You Never': Sarah Paulson Shades Actor Who Criticised Her Performance," *Gay Times,* May 15 2024, https://www.gaytimes.com/sarah-paulson-shades-actor-who-criticised-her-performance/.

Chapter 12: On Rita Ora

191 **"Who is Dua Lipa?":** Darian Lusk, "Ora You Serious? *Jeopardy!* Fans 'Scream' After Contestants Mix Up Their Pop Stars in 'Painful' Moment," *The U.S. Sun,* June 28, 2023, https://www.the-sun.com/entertainment/8482492/jeopardy-rita-ora-donna-painful-moment/.

194 **"I love eating at my dad's pub":** "Rita Ora's My London," *The Standard,* August 31, 2012, https://www.standard.co.uk/lifestyle/rita-oras-my-london-8095827.html.

194 **"Imagine if I'd stayed!":** "Remember When Rita Ora Auditioned for Eurovision?," *Cosmopolitan,* May 9, 2018, https://www.cosmopolitan.com/uk/entertainment/news/a39698/rita-ora-eurovision-audition-video/.

194 **"Easy to mock":** Zara Kenyon, "Remember When Rita Ora Auditioned for Eurovision?," *Cosmopolitan,* May 9, 2018, https://www.cosmopolitan.com/uk/entertainment/news/a39698/rita-ora-eurovision-audition-video/.

195 **"an oppressive recording agreement":** Eriq Gardner, "Rita Ora, Pointing in Lawsuit to Roc Nation's New Interests, Demands Freedom," *The Hollywood Reporter,* December 17, 2015, https://www.hollywoodreporter.com/business/business-news/rita-ora-pointing-lawsuit-roc-849559/.

197 **"Rita Ora Flashes Her Butt":** Candace Amos, "Rita Ora Flashes Her Butt in Revealing Dress at the Oscars 2015 Afterparty: See More Stars Go Without Underwear on the Red Carpet," *Us Weekly,* February 23, 2015, https://www.usmagazine.com/stylish/news/rita-ora-gigi-hadid-more-stars-go-without-underwear-oscars-2015-2015232/.

197 **"Rita Ora Has a Blast":** Sierra Marquina, "Rita Ora Has a Blast at the Happiest Place on Earth While Her Ex-Boyfriend Calvin Harris Cuddles with Taylor Swift—All the Details," *Us Weekly,* April 3, 2015, https://www.usmagazine.com/celebrity-news/news/rita-ora-goes-to-disneyland-while-calvin-harris-gets-cozy-with-taylor-201534/.

197 **"with 20 dudes":** Staff, "Rob Kardashian Claims Rita Ora Cheated on Him with '20 Dudes,'" *Us Weekly,* December 4, 2012, https://www.usmagazine.com/celebrity-news/news/rob-kardashian-claims-rita-ora-cheated-on-him-with-20-dudes-2012412/.

199 **"Who is this woman?":** Reaction Encyclopedia (@gay_reactions), "Wendy Williams dragging D-list celebrity, Rita Ora, for 1 minute and 8 seconds," X, February 3, 2026, https://x.com/gay_reactions/status/2018813588480332040.

199 **"Rita Ora looks glum":** Andrew Bullock, *Daily Mail,* July 30, 2018, http://www.dailymail.co.uk/tvshowbiz/article-6006549/Rita-Ora-looks-glum-grabs-coffee-heading-30k-year-gym-Londons-Notting-Hill.html.

200 **"'New year, new beach!'":** Ellie Phillips, *Daily Mail,* January 2, 2023, https://www.dailymail.co.uk/tvshowbiz/article-11592349/Rita-Ora-poses-colourful-bikini-boasts-jet-set-lifestyle.html.

200 **"She doesn't travel light":** Kinta Walsh-Cotton, *Daily Mail,* June 23, 2023, https://www.dailymail.co.uk/tvshowbiz/article-12225741/Rita-Ora-causes-scene-Sydney-Airport-arrives-14-suitcases.html.

200 **"Rita Ora puts on a VERY leggy display":** Niomi Harris, *Daily Mail,* updated February 19, 2025, https://www.dailymail.co.uk/tvshowbiz/article-14368595/Rita-Ora-leggy-display-toned-pins.html.

200 **"Rita Ora continues":** Laura Fox, *Daily Mail,* March 28, 2024, https://www.dailymail.co.uk/tvshowbiz/article-13248505/Rita-Ora-continues-desperate-bid-crack-energetic-appearance-Masked-Singer-turbulent-journey-make-mark-States.html.

201 **"Primark holds prices steady":** Sarah Butler, "Primark Holds Prices Steady After Rita Ora Helps Lift Sales," *The Guardian,* January 23, 2024, https://www.theguardian.com/business/2024/jan/23/primark-prices-rita-ora-sales-boohoo.

202 **"With each new collection":** Nigel Taylor, "Primark Launches Third Rita Ora Collab Collection," *Fashion Network,* March 21, 2024, https://kr.fashionnetwork.com/news/Primark-launches-third-rita-ora-collab-collection.1617338.html.

202 **a prescient interview with *Billboard*:** Jason Lipshutz, "What's Rita Ora Up To?," *Billboard,* July 13, 2017, https://www.billboard.com/music/pop/rita-ora-interview-7865871/.

203 **"Dropping my new song monday":** "Rita Ora Denies Twitter Promo Fail Saying She Was Hacked," BBC News, November 3, 2014, https://www.bbc.com/news/newsbeat-29876844.

203 **When it was reported:** "Rita Ora: Venue Was Paid to Breach Covid Rules, Police Tell Committee," BBC News, January 28, 2021, https://www.bbc.com/news/uk-england-london-55840764.

203 **The city claimed they never received:** "Rita Ora: Venue to Keep Licence After Admitting Lockdown Breach," BBC News, February 4, 2021, https://www.bbc.com/news/uk-england-london-55933374.

203 **"After i finish my album":** Cardi B (@IamCardiB), "After i finish my album I'm collabing with 3 artist that I'm cool with," Twitter (now X), January 13, 2018, https://x.com/iamcardib/status/952313872307732481.

204 **"I wish I had good hair":** Tionah Lee, "Rita Ora Reveals Beyoncé's Reaction to Rumors She Was 'Becky with the Good Hair,'" *E! Online*, July 3, 2025, https://www.eonline.com/news/1419419/rita-ora-says-beyonce-defended-her-amid-jay-z-affair-rumors.

204 **"It was the first time I experienced":** Lee, "Rita Ora Reveals Beyoncé's Reaction to Rumors She Was 'Becky with the Good Hair.'"

204 **"I love hanging out with Rita":** George Stark, "Charli XCX on Wild Nights Out with Rita Ora, Writing 'Fancy' in 30 Minutes," *People*, September 4, 2016, https://people.com/celebrity/charli-xcx-on-wild-nights-out-with-rita-ora-writing-fancy-in-30-minutes.

205 **"I've been waiting":** Kate Dries, "Rita Ora Joins Wendy Williams on Her Show a Year and a Half After Wendy Wondered Who She Was," *Jezebel,* December 9, 2016, https://www.jezebel.com/rita-ora-joins-wendy-williams-on-her-show-a-year-and-a-1789937340.

About the Authors

Bobby Finger and **Lindsey Weber** are the hosts of *Who? Weekly*, the podcast that tells you everything you need to know about the celebrities you don't. Finger is the author of *Four Squares, The Old Place,* and *We Are Gathered Here Today*. Weber is a freelance writer and editor who spends the majority of her free time in the Rockaways. They both live in Brooklyn, New York.